JAGUAR

JAGUAR

*One man's struggle to save
Jaguars in the wild*

ALAN RABINOWITZ

COLLINS
8 Grafton Street, London W1 · 1987

William Collins Sons & Co Ltd
London · Glasgow · Sydney · Auckland
Toronto · Johannesburg

BRITISH LIBRARY CATALOGUING IN PUBLICATION DATA

Rabinowitz, Alan
  Jaguar: one man's struggle to save
  jaguars in the wild.
  1. Jaguars   2. Mammals—Central America
  I. Title
  599.74'428   QL737.C23

  ISBN 0-00-217827 3

First published in the U.S. in 1986
First published in Great Britain by William Collins 1987

Made and printed in Great Britain by
William Collins Sons and Co. Ltd., Glasgow

CONTENTS

Existence is beyond the power of words
To define:
Terms may be used
But are none of them absolute.
In the beginning of heaven and earth there were
        no words,
Words came out of the womb of matter;
And whether a man dispassionately
Sees to the core of life
Or passionately
Sees the surface,
The core and the surface
Are essentially the same,
Words making them seem different
Only to express appearance.
If name be needed, wonder names them both:
From wonder into wonder
Existence opens.

—Lao Tzu, *The Way of Life*

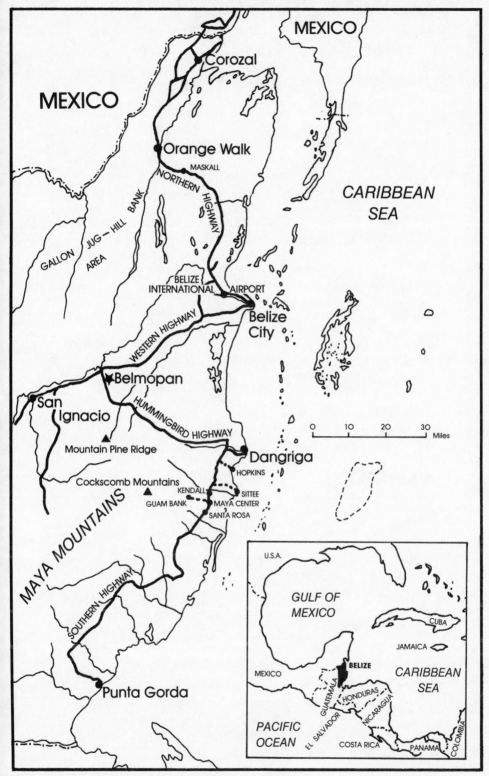

Map of Belize showing the major towns and villages visited by the author

GOD, JAGUAR, AND MAN

God decided to make man because the jaguar already existed. He took some mud and started to fashion man, but the jaguar was watching him, and God didn't want him to see how man was made. So he sent the jaguar to the river to fetch some water, giving him a jar and a calabash with holes in it to scoop the water out of the river. This way he hoped he'd have time to make man, while the jaguar was vainly trying to fill the jar with the leaking calabash. The jaguar tried and tried to fill the jar, but didn't succeed. Then the frog called out to him, *"Chohac, Chohac, Chohac!* Put mud over the holes."

The jaguar did, but by the time he had filled the jar and had taken it back, God had already made thirteen men of mud and twelve guns to go with them. As the jaguar came up, he saw that God was also making a dog out of mud.

"That animal is going to be for me to eat," the jaguar said.

"No," said God. "The dog is to be the servant of man and these guns, further, will teach you to respect him."

"I am not afraid of the gun," replied the jaguar. "I'll catch the shots that are fired at me."

"All right, let's see," said God, and he made the jaguar stand some way away. Then one of the newly created men fired at the jaguar, wounding him in the paw. The man bandaged up the wound. Again the jaguar said, "The dog is for me to eat."

But the man said, "No," and sent the dog after the jaguar and drove it up into a tree, and again shot him in the paw.

"Now you have learned your lesson that you must not eat man or dog. The other animals you can eat. Go away and live in the bush."*

*Story told to J. Eric S. Thompson by Maya Indians from Southern Belize. From J. Eric S. Thompson, *Ethnology of the Mayas of Southern and Central British Honduras.* Field Museum of Natural History, Chicago, Anthropological Series, vol. 17, no. 2, 1930.

1 BELIZE

I could tell it was midday as I maneuvered my truck off the two-lane dirt road called the Southern Highway onto the narrow dirt track that led into the jungle. My stomach was growling as dust swirled into the truck, stinging my eyes and penetrating every pore in my body. Seminaked Maya Indians were sitting at the junction of the two roads.

The sun had been blazing since 6 A.M. that morning. My throat felt parched, and the dry tropical heat threatened to cook my brain. But I was finally at the entrance to Cockscomb Basin in Belize, Central America, nearing the end of the journey I had started in New York City two weeks before.

I turned to look at the Maya Indians, and when I looked back, another truck was coming straight at me. I slammed on the brakes and pulled to the side of the road to avoid a head-on collision. I had just driven five thousand miles. I didn't want to wreck my truck six miles from the place that was to be my research station for the next two years.

The driver of the other truck pulled alongside me. I yelled through the dust at him, "Where can I find Mr. Don Smith, who runs the timber operation in Cockscomb Basin?"

"That's me," he replied. "You must be that Rabinowitz fella. Well, I can't talk with you now; a man of mine just got killed. A tree fell on his head. I have to go and see the family. Go on in and wait for me and we can talk when I get back."

He was off before I could reply. I started up the truck and looked again at the Indians who had gathered to watch us. I smiled and waved. A small Maya boy whispered to his friend, pointed at me, and laughed. He spoke to the men behind him, and they joined in the laughter. I turned and abruptly sped off down the rutted jungle road.

As I drove deeper into the forest, I felt I was sinking into the depths of a green sea. The heat, the silence, the thickness of the vegetation, created a feeling of fear and excitement that made my body tingle. Old questions without answers loomed in my mind. Could I make this project work? Was I running away, leaving behind a relatively safe way of life and the woman I thought I could love if I gave it a chance? For the hundredth time I pushed the thoughts from my mind. I had made my choice. I was more excited about this project than I'd been about anything in my life. It might be difficult and dangerous, but it was untouched scientific territory. I stuck my head out the window, let the breeze sweep through my hair, and yelled at the jungle, "I'm here!"

The timber camp, called Guam Bank, looked more run-down and abandoned than I'd remembered it from my trip there several months earlier. Yet it still seemed an oasis, surrounded by a seemingly impenetrable forest extending in all directions as far as the eye could see.

Within a cleared circular area, a quarter mile across, there were fifteen small wooden shacks for the timber workers, two larger wooden houses for the owners of the concession, a saw-mill, two small concrete buildings that served as a stockroom and an office building, and an open wooden shed that was a maintenance garage. East of the camp was a small airstrip that was starting to get overgrown. No planes had landed there for months. Only about a third of the shacks at the timber camp seemed occupied, while the others were in an advanced state of disrepair. Two hundred yards south of the camp, hidden from view but accessible by a well-traveled path, was a small Maya settlement. It consisted of nine thatched huts occupied by Indian families and a central hut, nicer than the rest, that served as a church.

I looked beyond the camp to the mountains in the distance. It was a clear, sunny day and to the north loomed the Cockscomb Range, a chain of mountains containing the tallest peaks in the country. These mountains served as a landmark for sailors over two hundred years ago. The highest summit, Victoria Peak, rose a little over thirty-six hundred feet and was the subject of much superstition among the locals.

I parked the truck and looked around. Two Maya women were walking nearby holding machetes and carrying large bundles of sticks held against their backs by straps around their foreheads. A scrawny little white dog that appeared on the verge of starvation came to beg at my feet. A Creole woman walked out the front door of one of the shacks, threw some dirty water in the grass, glanced at me, then went back inside. My arrival in Cockscomb was considered no great event.

Selecting one of the nicer and more accessible shacks, I brought some of my equipment in, hoping I could acquire the house by squatter's rights. I was torn between looking for a stream to bathe in and taking a nap, but a glance at the wooden cot in the back of the shack made my mind up for me. It was even hotter inside the shack than in the sun, but my body didn't care. Fatigue and excitement had taken their toll. I stretched out on the wooden planks of the bed and quickly drifted into oblivion.

▲ ▲ ▲

Eight months ago I had received my Ph.D. degree in wildlife ecology from the University of Tennessee. I had worked with bats, raccoons, and black bears and I wanted to continue field research, but it looked as if my career was becoming more and more academic. I wasn't about to give up on my dreams. Having survived growing up on the streets of New York City, I knew I could get what I wanted out of life, but I wasn't sure how.

A quirk of fate threw me into contact with Dr. George Schaller, the world-renowned zoologist and author of numerous books on wildlife. As the director of Wildlife Conservation International (WCI) of the New York Zoological Society (NYZS), Schaller became associated with the University of Tennessee when a friend of mine, Howard Quigley, assisted him on a project in Brazil. When Schaller came to Tennessee to confer with one of my former professors, Dr. Michael Pelton, an expert on black bears, I was invited to accompany him for a hike in the Smoky Mountains.

I was somewhat awed by Schaller, whom I found to be rather stern, quiet, and strongly opinionated. I quickly learned that he had an amazingly analytical mind, and that what I took to be rigid views came from an understanding of nature and wildlife that few humans ever attain. My awe quickly turned to fascination and then to pleasure as we talked through the day. When we parted company, I never expected to see him again.

A week later I was at a party when Mike Pelton arrived with a mysterious grin on his face and gently pulled me away from a group of people I had been talking with. There were no preliminaries.

"Schaller called and wants to know if you're interested in going to Belize to survey the country for jaguars." I stared at him without answering. I was trying to shake off the effects of several glasses of wine while searching his expression for any hint of a bad joke.

"I'm serious," he said.

"Tell him yes." I tried to remember exactly where Belize was.

"He wants you to think about it and call him within a week."

Pelton was smiling, knowing he had just changed the direction of my life.

The rest of the party went by in a blur. I was high, and not just from the wine. I sat up late that night looking at the tiny country of Belize on a world map. Situated on the Caribbean Sea, east of Guatemala and south of the Yucatán in Mexico, Belize is the smallest country in Central America except for El Salvador. But that night it filled the map. The next morning I called Schaller and told him I would go.

Within a week, I was in New York City explaining the decision to my family and finalizing plans with Schaller and Dr. Archie Carr III, assistant director of WCI and a person with whom I would establish a close friendship. In the following weeks I learned the details and scope of my assignment. It was more intriguing than I ever could have imagined.

Naturalists in Belize had been reporting a relatively dense jaguar population throughout the country. Carr felt the situation warranted further investigation, and Schaller agreed. Schaller had already begun some jaguar research in the Pantanal in the southern part of the state of Mato Grosso in Brazil, and his research was being continued by Howard Quigley. That vast swampy area is the historic home of the largest jaguars on record, but hunting and habitat destruction had drastically reduced their numbers there.

Belize was different. If the reports were accurate, here was an opportunity to examine one of the few remaining areas in the world where jaguars were still abundant and roamed tropical rain forests relatively unmolested. My task was to go to Belize for two months and determine the relative densities of jaguars throughout the country. Then we could see if more detailed research was feasible and select key areas where a jaguar preserve or park might be established.

I stared at the map of Belize as Carr explained different aspects of the study. There was only one major road along the coast, known as the Northern Highway in the north and the Southern Highway in the south; a second road, the Western

Highway, bisected the country in the middle. Every year there were at least two reported incidents of jaguars being hit by cars on these roads. The larger towns and cities were near the coast or on it. I read off some of the names—Corozal, Orange Walk, Monkey River, Dangriga, Punta Gorda. What are these places like? I wondered. Broken lines indicated timber roads through part of the interior. The majority of the map, however, was simply shades of green showing different elevations of uninhabited jungle and swamp. These were the areas I knew I'd have to penetrate to find the animal I would be searching for.

The first stop on my journey was not Belize but Brazil, where I spent six weeks with Quigley in that incredible desolate area of the world known as the Pantanal. It was my introduction to the rigors and hardships of tropical scientific fieldwork. Day after day we followed jaguars and checked traps, tromping through black murky waters, riding horses through vast wet grassy plains, and boating down narrow rivers that snaked deep into the jungle.

I quickly learned to identify tracks, scrapes, feces, and other jaguar "sign" while realizing how much time and labor went into just following these animals. At the end of six weeks, I was confident and eager to get on to Belize. But the experience of the Pantanal, especially the frequent sightings of wildlife, which included imperial macaws, jabiru storks, rheas, capybaras, caimans, peccaries, and ocelots, was imprinted vividly in my memory, and I appreciated it all the more when I realized how little one can actually see in a rain forest.

I tried to prepare myself for the jungle by reading everything I could about Belize and studying maps until I knew the country better than most natives, but I was still awed by the place when I stepped into it. "If the world had any ends, British Honduras would surely be one of them." Aldous Huxley said that in 1939, and it was almost as true in 1983.

Belize, called officially British Honduras until its independence in 1981, occupies an area of nearly nine thousand square miles and has a population of a hundred and fifty seven thousand. One third of the population resides in Belize City. The rest of the country consists of sparsely populated swamp and forest. While war, economic instability, and starvation rage throughout Central and South America, Belize sits peaceably, unaffected and all but oblivious to what is going on around it.

The only thing that mars this tranquil scene, but is the primary factor in maintaining it, is the very obvious British military presence. Visitors see it upon landing at the small airport, where the camouflaged Harrier jets and antiaircraft guns are all too obvious. Guatemala still does not officially recognize Belize's right to exist, so Britain maintains a close watch over its former colony.

Belize was founded in 1638 by shipwrecked British seamen, but the present population of Belize consists of Maya Indians, Creoles, Black Caribs, East Indians, Lebanese, Chinese, North Americans, and Europeans. The bulk of the population is Maya, Creole, or Black Carib. The Maya are the only truly indigenous people and account for about 13 percent of the total population.

You have to spend quite a bit of time in Belize City before discovering its distinctive personality and hidden charms. On the surface, the city appears shabby, with large decaying British colonial houses and foul smells from the open sewage canals built to accommodate far fewer people. Eventually I came to like Belize City, but when I first arrived there, I wanted nothing more than to get out of it as soon as possible. It didn't help that I was harassed continually by street urchins, who pictured me as another gringo tourist.

My first night in Belize I checked into a hotel that had been recommended as inexpensive, colorful, and friendly, the Posada Tropical. Run by two gay American men, John and Roger, it served as a hostel for travelers on tight budgets. Within a few days I met a Czechoslovakian sailor who had jumped ship, a former European actress, and two young American men later arrested for trying to smuggle sixty pounds of marijuana out of the country.

But all the while my mind was on the dark green forests I had flown over before landing, expanses of jungle with no obvious human dwelling from horizon to horizon. This was where I needed to go, deep into the areas that held the secrets and mysteries of the country, the places that were once the sites of the ancient Maya civilization and where the jaguar, one of the greatest and most elusive predators on earth, was still thought to roam wild and free.

There exists very little documented research on these animals. Before Schaller captured and radio-tagged two jaguars in the Mato Grosso in 1978, virtually all that had been written about these cats was undocumented or was based on captive or killed specimens. No one before Schaller and Quigley had investigated their behavior in the wild using scientific methodology, and no one had yet studied them in their tropical forest habitat. This was surprising, considering that it is the third largest cat in the world and the largest and most powerful land predator in Central and South America. In the highly competitive world of science, in the battle for funding and world acclaim, scientists dream of having the chance to study such an animal. I felt incredibly lucky that I had the opportunity to realize my dream.

When I arrived in Belize that first time, my immediate problem was how to get around the country. Public transportation and hitchhiking were unreliable. I bought a Honda 100-cc motorcycle to go up the many little dirt trails leading off into various parts of the forest. Any place this bike couldn't go, I could continue on foot. I divided the country into six geographic regions, tied a pack onto the bike's backrest, and took off.

I spent one to two weeks in each region, hiring Maya or Creole hunters to lead me into the forest. We'd drive as far as possible with the motorcycle along old logging roads or hunting trails, then hike in the rest of the way. Or we'd move slowly along the banks of rivers and streams in a dugout canoe, known locally as a dory, looking for cat sign.

Tracks are often the most definitive sign of an animal's presence, but scientists record any evidence of their movements and behavior: feces, scrapes (areas where a cat has clawed the ground), kills, and beds (areas where they have rested). If you measure tracks, particularly the pad, you can often distinguish between individual animals and estimate relative density in a given area. I learned from Belizean hunters and from my time with Quigley in Brazil that jaguars frequently travel on roads, on trails, and along waterways in their area, so most of my efforts were concentrated in those places.

The forest is teeming with wildlife, but you see and hear very little just by walking through it. It often seems simply a quiet, green darkness, but that appearance is deceiving. When you learn to read the signs of an animal's passing, it's like watching the wildlife. A nibbled twig tells you a red brocket deer has been feeding; a muddy wallow says a tapir has been by; chewed nuts from the cohune palm tree indicate that a paca has fed the night before; and a musky smell warns you that a group of peccaries may be closer than you'd like.

Within a few days I found abundant sign of jaguars and four other cat species: puma, ocelot, margay, and jaguarundi. So little was known about any of these cats in tropical areas that I knew any data I could collect would be valuable. There was also a plethora of sign from other species as well, particularly in areas where there were few hunters. These included pacas, tapirs, anteaters, armadillos, coatis, brocket and white-tailed deers, foxes, and peccaries. In areas frequented by hunters, signs of anything edible were rare. In many parts of Belize money is a sparse commodity, so wildlife often constituted the major source of meat.

Those ten weeks in Belize passed quickly. I learned to use a machete in thick brush without chopping off my foot, drank rum and swapped lies with Creole hunters, and had Maya women slam doors in my face, fearing my evil green eyes. In the three hundred miles that I drove and the nearly two hundred miles that I walked, I found plenty of evidence that there were indeed abundant jaguars throughout Belize. The primary reason was that Belize still had large areas of true unspoiled wilderness. The potential for conservation was tremendous, and the time to act was now.

The east-central part of Belize, known as the Stann Creek District, was the area with the best potential for jaguar research and preservation, and the ideal place within this district was a tract of government land called the Cockscomb Basin. It was surrounded on three sides by mountains, and the only easy access into it was a six-mile dirt road leading into a timber camp. The mountains to the west were part of the rugged Maya Mountain divide, which, with its deep canyons and intractable forest, was virtually impossible to cross. Beyond this divide stretched only more jungle, extending into the Petén lowland of Guatemala.

I returned with my data to the United States, knowing I had done all that was possible in the time I had. The results were clear. My feelings about the future were also clear. The country and its people intrigued me and I wanted to go back. I wanted to be the first person to unlock some of the mysteries surrounding the behavior of jaguars in the tropical forest.

Schaller and Carr reviewed my findings. They were impressed with the estimates of jaguar numbers and could see the conservation potential in this country. They asked me if I'd return to Belize and set up a long-term research project on jaguars.

I spent a week hidden in the mountains of Tennessee, weighing the options of staying in a world I knew so well and returning to a place that I had only barely become acquainted with. In truth, I had known my decision all along but wanted to make sure it was thought out carefully. When the week ended, I was on the phone to Carr.

"When can I start ordering equipment?" I asked.

2 COCKSCOMB

I awoke and wondered where I was. The soreness in my back and the dust on my clothes quickly reminded me. I looked outside and saw that Don Smith had returned sometime during my nap. He was sitting quietly in a rocking chair on the porch in front of his house. An American, in his early forties, he was a large man, nearly six and a half feet tall, and sturdily built. I got the impression he had fought many battles in his life, and was tired.

As I approached, he seemed surprised to see me still around. When I tried talking to him, he just put another plug of Red Man chewing tobacco in his mouth and looked toward Victoria Peak.

"You know why I'm here, Mr. Smith?" I asked.

"Yeah," he said, looking hard at me for the first time. "I heard you're gonna try to catch jaguars. Lord only knows why." He looked off into the distance again.

"To study them," I said. "I want to see how far they travel, what they eat, find out all I can about them. I'll put radios on them so I can follow them around." He wasn't listening, so I stopped. "I'll try not to be in your way," I said. "I wondered if I could use that little house that my truck's parked in front of?"

"You can have it. Welcome to it. Fact is, you can have any house in this place. They're nearly all empty now. What the hell you want here anyway?" He sounded almost angry.

I turned to go, but his voice stopped me. "You watch yourself now. This here's a rough place."

I went off to inspect my new field station and home.

The shack was palatial by field standards. It measured fifteen by twenty-five feet, and had some screening on all four windows and fewer than ten holes in the walls and roof. There were three rooms. The front room, the largest, took up most of the shack and had a water spigot rising up through a hole in the floor. This was my living and dining area. In the left rear corner of the house was my bedroom, with a large wooden cot below a window. The right corner of the shack was the bathroom, with a hole in the floor and a new toilet sitting unattached next to it. I had to hook that up or squat over the hole for the next two years.

It wasn't the house of my dreams, but it was a vast improvement over the tent I had with me. I walked around the shack twice, thinking of all the handyman skills I was about to learn and how the place would look once I fixed it up. It was March 28, 1983, and I felt like this moment was the official start of my jaguar project.

I spent two weeks making my new home comfortable. First I had to evict the hordes of large cockroaches that had made this shack their home for so long. I visited the nearest town, Dangriga, twenty miles and a one-hour trip from Cockscomb. I learned quickly that you don't go shopping in Dangriga for what you need or you'll be very disappointed. You either shop for what will work in place of what you need, or you readjust your needs. Then shopping becomes an exciting challenge, and indeed I was challenged in those first weeks.

I looked for roach traps, cans of insecticide, and mosquito coils, which, when burned, gave off acrid fumes that kept away the bugs. Then I purchased nails, hooks, pipes, screening, and a kerosene stove. Using extra timber from the camp, I built furniture that didn't slant too badly, attached a screen door on the front of the house, which only scraped the floor a little, and constructed an outdoor shower stall, serviced by a water hose connected to the indoor spigot. The timber camp still had a large diesel generator for operating the sawmill, so I had electricity for several hours each evening. This also powered an electric pump that brought water up from a deep well into an above-ground water tank that fed the camp. Once I hooked into the system, I had a single light bulb in the front room and running water for my spigot.

Then there was the hole in the bathroom floor and the unat-tached toilet. This sort of plumbing job fell completely outside my range of skills, so I ran thirty feet to the nearest patch of jungle and tried to time my urges so that they would occur during the daylight hours. I soon gave up trying to fight the bugs, and after a week my buttocks were like a landing strip for insects.

During the day, the mosquitoes weren't as bad as the insect known as the bottlas (or bottle-ass) fly, a tiny black gnat that leaves a small blood blister on the victim's flesh. They attacked me in swarms, seeming to prefer the buttocks to any other part of the body. After feasting, their abdomens swell, giving them the appearance of little bottles—hence the name. I had to get that toilet installed.

At night the mosquitoes took over. Their buzzing around my head nearly drove me crazy. Until I became used to it, I sur-rounded myself with mosquito coils and kept my head engulfed in smoke. The possibility of choking or shortening my life from the toxic fumes was preferable to these bugs.

▲ ▲ ▲

One afternoon three weeks after my arrival, Don Smith finally stopped by my shack. After our first meeting, I had found Don to be an extremely likable man who was lonely and disheartened. He and his brother had put everything they had into this timber concession, but because of the characteristics of Cockscomb itself, it had not proved to be a profitable enterprise. He hated the place now and wanted only to return to his family in the United States. Most of the time he'd just sit in his house and look out over the camp. Today, however, he was in a good mood and wanted to talk.

"Just got a good load of timber out," he said, stepping inside my house. "Think I'll be leaving for a few days next week, goin' home to see my family. My boy made honor roll in school. See you got this place fixed up pretty nice."

"It didn't take much," I replied, thinking I must have lost ten pounds in blood and sweat over the last few weeks.

"Yeah, can't wait to see my family again," he said, as if I hadn't spoken. "Seems harder and harder being apart from them. Got the toilet hooked up yet?" I knew Don could see me from his house whenever I ran into the jungle.

"Nope, I just haven't gotten around to it," I lied. It was time to ask him for some help, I decided.

"Well, the men say the skidder blew a piston," he said. "Need to keep it in the shop for a few days. I'll send Jorge over to help you put in a system for that toilet. Take some of the load off you; you look like you're losing weight." He smiled.

Jorge was one of the few workers remaining in camp. His job was to drive the skidder, a monster of a machine, built to eat through jungle and drag out large trees. He was amused by my predicament, but, like the others in camp, had not even introduced himself.

We dug a rectangular hole six feet long, three feet wide, and six feet deep. In the hole we connected two old empty oil drums with five-inch-diameter PVC pipe to make a two-phase septic system. We placed the toilet over the hole in the shack and used pipes and fittings of all the wrong sizes to connect the toilet to the drums. The hole was too close to the wall, so there was no space for the tank. A bucket of water had to be poured into the bowl to flush it. There were a few small leaks that I plugged up with dirt, but the toilet was a success and made my life in Cockscomb that much easier. It took us two days to do it. I never would have figured it out on my own.

Rumors soon started circulating as to why I was really in Cockscomb. There were ten people still working in camp and most of them thought my jaguar story was a cover for growing marijuana and shipping it to the United States. A few thought I was there to dig up Maya artifacts. When they realized that I actually was trying to catch jaguars—and what's more, not to sell them but to study them—they found it almost impossible to understand. In my spare time, I watched these people, and noted down some first impressions:

John, Nari, and *Tino*—Guatemalans. Father and two sons. Hard workers; drive logging trucks; always out to make a buck—legal or illegal. Trust them only if they benefit.

Jorge—Salvadoran. Sad, lonely, strong man. Hard drinker but I think might be a friend. Would like to get to know him better.

Boogle and *Irma*—Jamaican man and Creole woman. Out for themselves. Will take advantage of any situation; watch out. Irma a great cook; Boogle mean and tough, especially when drinking.

Leo and *Alphonsa*—Maya man and Coolie (East Indian) woman. He seems a hard worker. Doesn't associate with the other Maya. She is beautiful but can be nasty, very tempting; stay away.

Oral and *Viola*—Creoles. Great couple, hard workers, potential friends.

Theo—old Coolie man; claims he is seventy-eight. Tough, kind, gentle. Feel sorry for him. No family, no place to go when the timber operation closes. He sometimes steals small things and gives them away to other people.

Porfilio—Maya man. Sharp, intelligent, hard worker. Not typical Indian. Seems sad and lonely. Watches me strangely sometimes.

Beemer—black Spanish man. Tough, young, and strong. Has to prove himself. I think he likes me but stays away from me, like everyone else. I see him watching me sometimes. I wonder what he thinks?

In the ensuing months, I'd come to realize how accurate these initial impressions were.

The fifty-eight Maya Indians—nine families—living in Cockscomb at the time of my arrival stayed apart from the rest of the camp. They were considered lazy and simpleminded by the timber workers. When hired to work, they apparently worked only as long as it suited their own needs. Then they'd just walk away without a word, returning a week or even a month later expecting to pick up where they had left off.

My initial feelings about the Indians were biased by such stories. Yet it was these people I'd grow closest to. It was they who would help me adjust to the ever-increasing hardships of Cockscomb. In their cases my later impressions were radically different from my first ones.

Soon after I installed my toilet and was giving it one of its early tests, I heard giggling outside my front door. Four little Maya girls were sitting on my front steps. This was my first contact with the Indians in Cockscomb. The oldest, ten years old, was Juana. She looked very serious and cradled a frowning little two-year-old, Formenta. By her side sat five-year-old Agapita, with a huge toothless grin spread across her face, and four-year-old Prudencia, who didn't know whether to smile or cry. After telling me their names, they seemed content to sit and stare at me while drinking the warm Coca-Cola I gave them. Occasionally they'd gab away in Maya to each other and laugh, glancing at me to see if I understood. Juana knew some English but would speak it only in response to my questions. The encounter lasted thirty minutes and my heart had never been so quickly won over before.

My next visitor was a young Maya boy of fifteen, Julian, who seemed determined to try all his English on me in one sitting.

"Where your wife?" were his first words. He had walked in and sat down.

"I have no wife."

"How old you?"

"Twenty-nine."

He went into a fit of laughter. "You so old and no wife!"

I soon learned that Maya men usually marry before the age of twenty-one, and Maya women, before sixteen. A Maya girl of sixteen might already have one or two children.

I changed my shirt and Julian started laughing again. "Why you got hair all over?"

"That's how I was born, Julian."

"Why you no got hair all over face?"

"I cut hair on face off." I had fallen into the broken English or Creole being used all around me.

"So why you no cut hair off all over? It ugly." He was laughing.

"I need hair to study tiger. I need to feel and look like tiger."

Jaguars are commonly called tigers, or *tigres* in Spanish, throughout much of Central America. I later learned that my answer circulated among the Maya and was taken quite seriously.

Soon Indians came to my house regularly—first just the children, then the men. Often there was a language problem, particularly with the youngest and oldest of my visitors. Although English is the official language of Belize, the younger children didn't speak it because there was no school in Cockscomb. Only the Maya between ten and thirty years of age had some schooling and spoke English. But the language barrier never deterred anyone from coming to my house to sit and watch me. I decided it was up to me to learn some Maya.

The Indians in Cockscomb were part of a cultural subgroup known as the Mopan Maya. Their language seemed difficult, and my initial attempts met with a great deal of laughter, but I persisted. I tried to write down some of my first few words and phrases, spelling them the way they sounded:

Maka Kabah—What is your name?
Bikilets—How are you?
Top kitch panitch—You are pretty.
Inkatatch—I like you.
Balum—Jaguar.
Cho!—Damn!

My attitude of friendliness and curiosity was interpreted by the Maya as an open invitation, and soon I had no privacy. Every morning at 8 A.M., Juana, Formenta, Agapita, and Prudencia wandered over to play in my house or just sit and watch me. Often they'd be joined by their mother, Adriana, a heavyset, jolly woman who was twenty-nine years old and had already had ten children, three of whom had died.

Adriana became my closest friend among the Maya women. She never seemed to tire of coming to my house and making herself at home, whether I was there or not. She'd tell me all the gossip of Cockscomb, often laughing like a little girl. Yet when I would catch her unaware, washing clothes in the river or squatting over the fire making tortillas in her hut, the lines on her face and the heaviness of her movements revealed a life of hardship that could easily crush a human spirit. Then she'd see me watching her and the smile that would crease her face was almost beatific.

In the afternoons, the two teenage boys Julian and Pedro would stop by. Though considered men among their own people, they felt free in my house to act like boys again, laughing, rummaging through all my belongings, trying on my clothes. It soon got out of hand.

I'd often return home from the jungle to at least several Indians waiting or playing in my house. I tried ignoring them, going about my business as if they didn't exist, cooking, exercising, reading, or even going to sleep. That had no effect. They sat in my house even while I slept.

I tried other methods of getting rid of them. One day when Julian and Pedro were at the house, I started cleaning the tranquilizer gun I had brought to immobilize jaguars. When I had their full attention, I started shooting blank darts into the wall all around them. Sure enough, they left very quickly.

But they were back the next day with many more people to have the demonstration repeated.

I eventually learned that my ideas of politeness and hospitality had no meaning in Cockscomb. I could simply tell the Indians to leave and they were not offended. It took a while before I stopped worrying about losing their friendship. I realized that they'd laugh and go home, then return the next day until I'd throw them out again.

Soon I started spending more time at the Maya settlement and visiting some of the families that were coming to see me so often. In some huts, my presence was accepted readily, while in others, it made them uncomfortable, unsure of how to act.

At first the Maya did not easily volunteer family names and relationships, but as my presence became more accepted, they spoke freely. I found that this Maya community was, for the most part, an extended family unit, one in which all the members are related by birth or marriage. The only unrelated family, the Pops, had their relatives in Maya Center, the village at the entrance to Cockscomb. The families in Cockscomb were:

Emano Bolong—patriarch and headman of the community.
Eliana Bolong—his wife.

Margarito Bolong—son of Emano; preacher.
Florentina Bolong—his wife.
Children—Clara, Teresita, Mario, Antonio, Aratilda.

Prudencio Bolong—son of Emano.
Donata Bolong—his wife.
Children—Eladora, Antonia, Brehelio, Rosita, Philberto, Andrea.

Gregorio Sho—son-in-law of Emano.
Liberata Sho—his wife.
Children—Emiliana, Victoriano, Francisco, Damiana, Pastoriano.

Juan Tyul—son-in-law of Emano.
Iansenta Tyul—his wife.
Children—Katarino, Primativo, Genos, Louisa, Liberato, Thomas, Cindo.

Martin Chun—son-in-law of Emano.
Juana Chun—his wife.
Children—Julian, Gregorio, Telesporo, Oscar, Suzanna, Florencia, Alberta.

Cirillo Chun—brother of Martin Chun.
Florencia Chun—his wife.
Children—Christina, Petrona.

Ignacio Pop—no relations in Cockscomb.
Adriana Pop—his wife.
Children—Pedro, Bibiana, Juana, Agapita, Prudencia, Formenta, Sylvino.

As Don Smith spent more and more time away from camp, the morale of the workers declined, and the operation of the timber concession slid steadily downhill. Soon, several of them were spending their time helping me. Nari and Tino kept my truck running, Leo and Oral helped me clear some trails, and Theo ran errands for me. And when Jorge was sober, he was a man of many skills and a great help.

Once my shack was livable, I spent virtually all my waking hours driving my motorcycle and truck along the old logging roads and hiking through the jungle looking for jaguar tracks. There were about twenty miles of drivable logging roads and about six miles of trails opened by skidders to haul out logs. Jorge knew where all the roads and trails went and saved me considerable time and effort in mapping the area. He would never accept monetary payment from me—only bottles of rum. He lived by the Creole saying, "Rum done, fun over."

At first I often went alone into the jungle. Once I had overcome my initial fears of this dense, dark green world, I started to enjoy it. Sometimes I'd go into the forest just to watch and feel the life around me.

At almost any time I could find the leaf-cutting ants, called wee-wee ants by Belizeans, carrying leaf fragments many times their size and weight in their seemingly unending columns. Each colony of these ants may contain over a million workers, comprising one of the most complex societies of living things on earth. Size differences among the ants help specialize them for various functions. The ultimate purpose of the colony is to bring leaves and other vegetable matter underground, where, in a dark moist environment, they cultivate it into fungal gardens. The fungi grown on the masticated leaf fragments produce fruiting bodies, which the ants use for food.

Nearby, a spectacular iridescent blue morpho butterfly drinks from a little pool of water in the bananalike leaves of the colorful heliconia plant. A fluttering across my face turns out to be a rhinoceros beetle about six inches long. The bright red spots on another branch are the eyes of the gaudy leaf frog. A harsh scream that suddenly breaks the silence and causes me to tense up proves to be a large white hawk, watching me from high above in the treetops.

It didn't take me long to learn one elementary lesson: allowing your mind to drift in the jungle can be hazardous. Walking into old clearings or along trails, you're suddenly grabbed by a thin leafed grass that slices your skin like a razor; the wound immediately becomes red and swollen from perspiration. Grab the wrong tree for balance and large barbed spikes are embedded in your hand, or Azteca ants come rushing out angrily to defend their home. Rest in one place too long and you soon feel the bites of any number of insects on your legs. A sudden rustling at your feet may mean you haven't been watching the undergrowth for a deadly enemy, the venomous fer-de-lance snake, called yellow-jawed tommy-goff or plain tommy-goff in Belize.

If your field clothes consist of long Khaki pants, a long-sleeved cotton shirt, and a baseball cap, as mine did, nothing can stop the omnipresent mosquitoes, bottlas, and sand flies from feasting on any inch of your flesh that is left available. If it's been an unlucky day, you may have been bitten by a mosquito carrying the malaria protozoan or yellow fever virus, or by a sand fly carrying *Leishmania*, a parasitic protozoan. Or a mosquito may have deposited a botfly larva, which will burrow beneath your skin. You won't know it until weeks later, when it starts to eat its way out.

These botfly larvae gave me nightmares for the first few months. They get into humans by a strange route. The female botfly (not the same as the bottlas fly) lays her eggs on a mosquito, usually of the genus *Psorophora*. As it feeds, the mosquito leaves the eggs on its victim's skin. The body heat causes the eggs to hatch, and the resulting larvae burrow in. They can grow to be nearly two inches long while inside their host. When they decide it's time to feed, it feels like you're being stabbed with an ice pick. The larvae secrete antibiotic into their burrow to prevent bacteria and fungus from spoiling their living food. Thus the wounds they make are never infected while they're alive. Eventually the larvae leave their burrows, drop out, and pupate on the ground.

You have to come to terms with the bad as well as the beautiful in the jungle. You never get used to the hardships and dangers; you only become more aware of them. It is all part of the ongoing struggle for survival.

Every so often in those first weeks, my eyes would notice an indentation in the leaf litter or an area of matted grass by the side of the trail. My heart would beat faster as I'd bend to examine the sign. There it would be, about four inches long and three and a half inches wide, the track of *el tigre,* showing where he had passed the night before. Or the matted grass was clearly a "bed" where he had rested, perhaps after killing and eating his evening's meal. Sometimes when I stooped to examine the matted grass I could still smell the musky odor of the jaguar. A tingling sensation would pass through me and I would look into the dense jungle around me wondering how close he was.

I stayed in the forest from sunrise till late afternoon, when I returned to bathe in a creek by the Indian village or shower in my little stall. Then I wandered over to Irma's house, where she'd have a hot dinner waiting for me. Irma cooked for the workers who had no women in camp, and I thought this a good opportunity to get to know them.

Dinner usually consisted of rice and kidney beans cooked in coconut milk; chicken pieces; large flour tortillas measuring ten inches in diameter and about half an inch thick; and a side dish of whatever was in season, such as plantain, avocado, breadfruit, or cassava. We washed it down with numerous cups of lukewarm coffee mixed with sweet milk. There were only three dishes that, to the great amusement of the others, I preferred not to eat. These were cow's-foot soup (usually with the foot in the soup), pig tails, and chicken feet.

Part of the dinner ritual consisted of everyone taking a turn advising me how to capture jaguars. It usually turned into storytelling. I'd always listen patiently, trying to pick out relevant pieces of information among the exaggerations and lies. They kept repeating stories of old jaguar hunters who built traps baited with pigs. The problem was that no one could remember how the traps were built and what the triggering mechanisms were. But I knew the stories were true, for I had seen similar traps built with poles and vines by the Amazon Indians, who baited them with monkey, sloth, or agouti carcasses. These traps were usually built to capture ocelots, but occasionally they'd catch a jaguar. I started to design a jaguar trap in my mind.

3 PORFILIO

I tried several different materials and designs for a trap and finally settled on thick hardwood beams donated by Don Smith. The first trap I built was a little over six feet long, three feet wide, and three and a half feet high. The door was held open by a rope running over a pulley attached to a crossbeam above the trap. The other end of the rope was attached to a thick branch within the trap, held down by nails extending out of two poles staked into the ground. The heads of the nails were filed off so that the branch could slide easily from beneath them. The pig would be tied behind the poles. To get at the pig, the jaguar had to bump the horizontal pole from under the nails and—bang—the front door would slide down.

I built the trap during the day, and drove the roads at night, watching for jaguars and hoping to find a good site for the trap. I worked nineteen-hour days, partly because there was much to be done and partly to take my mind off the loneliness. Usually at night I saw nothing. However, one night, while returning to camp at about 9 P.M., I noticed the tracks of a jaguar who had trailed behind the truck for almost two miles before veering off into the jungle.

The next day I went back and followed the tracks into the forest. After several hours of chopping through the under-growth, I lost all sign of the animal and turned back. A hundred yards back along the trail I had cut, I glanced down and froze. There were fresh jaguar tracks inside of my own tracks!

The cat had intercepted my trail, followed me, and had gone back into the forest when I turned and headed back. I knelt down and looked more closely at the track. It was so fresh that a piece of dirt tottering on the edge of one of the toes fell into the depression as I watched. I had been told by hunters that a jaguar could follow you in the bush and you'd never see or hear it. I hadn't believed it until now.

He was still close, so close I imagined I could feel the heat of his body in back of me. I spun around. Nothing was there but dense, silent jungle. I knew he was not far away, watching.

That night I sat engrossed in thoughts about jaguars, the forest, and the Maya Indians. I almost didn't hear the tapping at the door.

"Alan, Alan, you dere?" an Indian's voice whispered. It was 10 P.M., late for an Indian to be about. I went to the door and found Porfilio waiting on the steps. He wore his beat-up black cotton fishing hat, which always enabled me to recognize him from a distance. I nearly dragged him inside, anxious to tell him of the day's events.

"I almost saw a tiger, Porfilio," I said excitedly. "He followed me as I walked in the forest. The track's big, almost as big as my hand, probably a large male tiger. You think so?"

Porfilio smiled at my outburst. "Dat what I want talk about," he said softly. "I work for you, Alan. I want help trap tiger."

I was curious. "What about the timber crew and your job? Why do you want to help me, Porfilio?"

"I help you trap tiger," he repeated. "I quit Mr. Smith." I knew that was all I'd get out of him. I had watched Porfilio over the last few weeks and knew his skills could help me in the jungle.

"If Mr. Smith no get mad, you can start work for me tomorrow," I told him. "We put out the trap."

"Okay, tomorrow." He turned and went to the door. He hesitated before leaving and turned back toward me. I knew something else was bothering him.

"Alan," he spoke abruptly, "no make master tiger mad." I started to feel uneasy.

"What master tiger, Porfilio?"

"Each animal have master who watch over he. Old people see it sometime in de bush. De master tiger, he white. You no can hurt master tiger, but he can hurt you. No make master tiger mad. Be careful." Porfilio turned and left.

The next day, Porfilio started working with me and immediately I wondered how I'd ever gotten along without him. We set the trap along the road where tracks showed the male jaguar to be walking regularly. I decided that, before we set it, we'd let it sit for a week with the door tied open. The dry season was ending and I could count on at least several hard rains within a week to wash away the human smells associated with the trap.

In the meantime, Porfilio and I visited a nearby Maya village, Santa Rosa, to buy a small pig for the trap. The villagers had already heard about the crazy white man in Cockscomb trying to catch live jaguars, so most of the inhabitants came out to look at me. Porfilio interpreted and answered their questions about how we planned to catch the jaguars. He told them that I wrestled with the jaguars and that was why I had such big muscles. They looked at me in awe and came over to squeeze my arms. I glowered at Porfilio. He smiled.

He convinced them to sell us a pig for 1 Belizean dollar (50 U.S. cents) per pound. We settled on a fifteen-pound pig, which fought like a hundred-pound pig when we tried to catch and hold it. I came to believe that Indian pigs are about as close to wild boars as any domestic pig can be. Handling them never became any easier, and I still bear the battle scars.

Several hours had already passed, and I knew that the best part of the day would be over by the time we got back to Cockscomb. This was something to which I had constantly to accustom myself. Whenever I wished to get something done that involved people other than myself, I would estimate the time it should take and multiply it by four. I would often become annoyed, but somebody would be quick to chastise me in Creole. "It no big ting man," they'd say, "saafly, saafly, tiger ketch monkey" (meaning I'd get what I wanted eventually).

The next day we tied the pig into the trap and gave it food and water. I invited Porfilio over to my shack that evening and we sat late into the night, talking and drinking coffee. For the first time in my life, I felt a growing need for close human contact. As a child, I had wrestled with a severe stuttering problem, and I had become a loner because of it. Now here I was wanting to get closer to other people, and the feeling took me by surprise.

I could feel a similar need in Porfilio. A little over five feet tall, he was twenty years old and led a different life from the other Indians. During the day he worked with the timber crew, and in the evenings he returned to the Maya settlement, where he lived in the hut of his brother-in-law, Prudencio Bolong.

I came to understand that Porfilio was considered a social outcast among the Indians. At an age when he should already be settled down, with a family and a little patch of land, he wished to better himself, which he could accomplish only by breaking with the traditional way of life of his people. But the timber crew didn't accept him either, because to them he was still an Indian.

I learned later that the reason he had wanted to work with me was because he had watched the way I interacted with his people. He could see I wanted to learn from, and be accepted by,

them. He knew I'd treat him as an equal, not as an Indian.
Porfilio never spoke of any of this at the beginning and I often
wondered why he wore such a sad, sullen expression on some
days.

We fell into a routine. Every morning Porfilio would be at my
door at 5:30 A.M.; I'd gulp down two cups of black coffee; and off
we'd drive four miles farther into the basin to check the trap.
Regardless of how sleepy I was when we started out, I'd be wide
awake by the time we made that final curve in the road that
brought us within sight of the trap. My heart would speed up
and my eyes would fasten on the spot where I knew the trap
door would first enter my field of vision. Seeing the door still
open was always a disappointment, but as long as there were no
tracks near the trap, I knew that the jaguar just hadn't come
around yet. We'd return to camp, eat breakfast, and be back out
exploring the jungle before 9 A.M.

Planning ahead, I looked for relatively high and accessible
patches of ground, where I could eventually mount antennas to
follow the radio-collared cats. Jaguars live solitary lives in deep
forest, so attaching small radios and following them at a distance
is virtually the only way to learn about their behavior. I had
captured no animals yet, but I needed to know just how well
these collars functioned in the dense jungle and where the best
locations were to pick up the radio signals. So Porfilio ran
around hiding the collars in different places in the forest, and
I'd try to find them. In the thick vegetation it was difficult to
hear the radio signals, and I realized that tracking the cats would
not be easy.

As Porfilio cleared our way up and down hills, he'd pass on
to me his knowledge about the forest. He showed me how to
hold and swing a machete, keeping my free arm behind my back,
so that I could almost run and chop at the same time without
missing a step. He taught me to watch for certain thick hanging
vines that would yield abundant cool fresh water at times when

there were no other water sources available. I learned the different fruits and nuts that could be eaten and how to spot a mountain cabbage palm through the thick greenery of the forest. Whenever Porfilio suddenly veered off the path, I knew it was usually because he had seen one of these palms. Called cabbage by the locals, it's a small tree with a narrow straight trunk and the head of a royal palm. He'd split the head open and peel the outer leaves to obtain the soft central core, the heart. It could be eaten raw or cooked, and either way it was delicious.

Sometimes he'd pick different plants and describe how to prepare them to treat coughs and fevers. I learned about a thin vine called tie-tie, strong enough to be used as rope, and a shrub with large leaves and a long thin white flower that I could eat if I needed a little boost while hiking. I watched as he imitated the sounds of birds, such as the tinamou, chachalaca, and curassow, calling them in to shoot them for food, or as he tracked pacas and armadillos to their dens.

I tried to tell Porfilio what I had learned about the jaguar. I explained that it was thought the animal's name was derived from *"yaguara"*, a word in a South American language meaning "the wild beast that can kill it's prey in a single bound." I told him that though coat patterns all look the same, no two are exactly alike. Some people believe that because of differences in size and skull structure, there are no less than sixteen kinds (subspecies or races) of jaguars throughout their range.

We'd look at maps and I'd show Porfilio how the jaguar once inhabited the southern United States also and is now distributed from Mexico through Central America and down into an area of South America bordered on the west by the Andes Mountains and on the south by Paraguay, Uruguay, and northern Argentina. I tried to explain to him that many years ago the jaguar was much larger than the biggest jaguar now. He listened with avid interest, occasionally asking questions, hungry to learn.

When I told Porfilio about black jaguars in the Amazon area, he nodded knowingly, though I knew of no confirmed reports of black jaguars this far north. When I told him that albino, or white, jaguars had been seen in Paraguay, he looked at me with surprise.

"So you know dis white tiger, master tiger?" he asked. "You know people who see dis ting?"

"No, it's not the white jaguar you were telling—" I stopped in mid-sentence. Who was I to say? Maybe the sighting of an albino or partial albino jaguar was responsible for some of the myths perpetuated here in Belize over the years.

Those first few months of sweat and toil hardened my body and calmed my spirit. I felt good and tried sharing my feelings with Porfilio because he was partly responsible. We grew closer and more dependent on each other by the day, and every evening he came by to drink coffee and talk or just sit in silence. One night, as I was recording birdcalls, I inadvertently recorded one of our conversations:

ALAN: You no like mango?

PORFILIO *(laughing):* If you want catch possum, put mango in trap.

ALAN: Possum like mango?

PORFILIO: Yes, man, possum love mango. Gibnut [paca] too.

ALAN: You know water fix now [*The water line had been broken*].

PORFILIO: Yes?

ALAN: Yeah. Donny come back and fix pump. *(Picks up Porfilio's cigarettes.)* These things kill you.

PORFILIO *(laughing):* Dey no kill me.

ALAN: They kill you faster than swallow rope *(referring to an Indian's chicken that had swallowed a rope and died the previous day).*

PORFILIO: Only if I sleep in wee-wee [leaf-cutting ant] nest.

ALAN: *(Holds up a small mango.)* This is your brain. *(Holds up a large mango.)* This is my brain.

PORFILIO *(laughing):* You got big brain and still stupid!

Porfilio came by one morning to tell me that he couldn't come with me into the bush. His sister was very sick with fever and chills. I knew it was malaria. I had seen it come and go several times already within the few months I'd been in Cockscomb. Most of the Maya refused to go to Dangriga for treatment. So far they were lucky—no one had died. I was determined not to interfere unless they wanted me to take them to the hospital in Dangriga. But here was Porfilio, looking tired and worried, in front of me.

After checking the trap, I stopped in to examine his sister. She had malaria. I returned to my shack and checked the treatment listed in the medical bible of the jungle, a book called *Where There Is No Doctor.* I gave Porfilio the prescribed dosage for the type of quinine I used and told him how to administer it. Within a few days she was back to the rigors of her life, still weak, but cured until the next bout.

Word spread about her quick recovery, which might otherwise have taken up to a month. That was the start of a two-year medical residency in Cockscomb Basin. I considered hanging a sign: "The Alan Rabinowitz Jaguar Research Station and Maya Medical Clinic." I was soon treating at least two people a week, sometimes as many as five. My next trip to Dangriga, I stocked up on aspirin for headaches, fevers, and body pains; chloroquinine for malaria; ampicillin, erythromycin, and tetracycline for infections; Merthiolate and Betadine for abrasions; codeine for pain; antihistamines for itching and allergies; thiabendazole for hookworm; metronidazole for amoeba and giardia infections; and boxes of Band-Aids for cuts and scratches.

Only twice in the two years I was there did I attempt something that made me uncomfortable. One was sewing up the neck muscles of a dog whose head was nearly severed by a jaguar, and the other was setting a broken leg bone. Most of the cases involved headaches and fevers from malaria, and maladies arising from parasites, primarily hookworm.

The Maya are generally a healthy people. They are small in stature and often eat a diet low in protein. Yet they are strong, active, and exhibit great endurance. Though they look and live very much like their ancestors, much has changed since they were overrun by the Spanish in the sixteenth century.

More serious than the physical abuses inflicted upon them by the Spanish were the European diseases introduced by the conquerors, against which the Maya had no natural immunity. Among the worst were smallpox, influenza, yellow fever, measles, tuberculosis, and amoebic dysentery; many believe malaria and hookworm were introduced as well. The population of some Maya tribes was reduced 75 to 90 percent in the century after the Spanish conquest. Eventually some of the havoc was brought under control, but the swollen bellies of modern Maya children and the constant bouts with malaria attest to the lasting influence of the "white man" on their lives.

The Indians, especially Adriana and her children, continued visiting me regularly, though I no longer allowed them in the house when I wasn't there. The newest item of interest was a set of weights and a piece of equipment called a Bullworker that I had bought for exercising. Though the Indians first thought it was ridiculous to work hard at something for no apparent reason, several of the men liked the effect it produced on their muscles. I wondered what their wives said about it. Soon I had a regular clientele coming by just to work out with my weights.

Porfilio would never stay when the other Indians came by, even children. He was obviously uncomfortable around his own people. Word had reached me that his sister's family wasn't treating him well, but I tried not to meddle. One night he came over very agitated and restless. After I gave him a few stiff rum and Cokes, he started to relax. He told me that his own people barely acknowledged him and that all the other Belizeans distrusted him. Only his older brother from their home village of San Antonio in southern Belize had understood him. But six months ago his brother was shot and killed in an argument over a woman. Everyone knew the killer, but the police did nothing. That's when he came to Cockscomb. In the last several nights he dreamt about the killing and felt he should get an obeah man to help him punish his brother's killer.

I had heard of the practice of obeah throughout Belize, but knew little about it. It was a form of black magic or voodoo that had originated in Africa and had been brought to Belize by the Black Caribs. There were several well-known practitioners within the country, but it was illegal and so they kept a very low profile. Some of the best were said to be Maya Indians, particularly of the Kekchi group, from southern Belize.

Porfilio was a firm believer in this practice and had seen it work. He explained how a good obeah man could send a poisonous snake into your house or make a wax figure, called a *puchinga*, to hurt you.

When the fourth rum drink took effect, Porfilio told me of his life as a young boy; even then he was an outcast, because he didn't want to marry young, live in a hut, and grow corn for the rest of his life. The Maya concept of equality meant uniformity. He had always wanted to learn new things, to work, and to travel, but was stuck in an Indian's body, and anywhere he went, he was treated the same. He didn't know where to turn or what to do.

"You no understand dese tings," he suddenly said to me. "You white, have plenty money, can stay or leave. What you want, you can do." He looked at the floor.

He was right in thinking I could never understand exactly what he was feeling, but I sure understood his feeling of desperation. I thought of my stuttering and the years I had spent hating life for burdening me with a handicap from which there was no escape. I was luckier than he, but I knew something of his pain.

"Porfilio, let's close the trap tomorrow and take three days off to go hiking toward Victoria Peak."

We had talked about trying to climb some of the peaks in the Cockscomb Range since we had begun working together. I hated closing the trap, but I could feel Porfilio slipping away from me. Both of us needed a break from camp anyway, and it was a good opportunity to look for jaguar sign in that part of the basin.

He looked up at me as if coming back from a long trip inside himself. "Okay, tomorrow we go. I come early. But, Alan, soon I leave here."

He left the shack, and the night swallowed him up.

4 THE MYSTERIOUS MAYA MOUNTAINS

One of the earliest documented descriptions of the Cockscomb Range dates from the sixteenth century. While on an expedition through the Maya empire to bring it under total Spanish control, Bernal Díaz del Castillo, one of Hernando Cortez's captains, claimed to have crossed part of the Cockscomb Range. He described it as "not very high, but consisting of stones which cut like knives." In the nearly five hundred years since then, something about these mountains has repeatedly stirred the imaginations of people who have seen them.

The first expedition to the top of the Cockscomb Range was organized in 1888 by Governor Roger T. Goldsworthy of British Honduras, who hoped to survey and report on "that hitherto unexplored district." The members of the expedition claimed to have climbed the highest summit in the range, and named it Victoria Peak. J. Bellamy, a member of the party, in a report to the Royal Geographical Society, described the aura of mystery surrounding the area:

> The top of Mount Victoria is a thorough peak, with but little room for moving about, and an extensive view is obtained on all sides. For some distance the prospect is nothing but alternate ridge and valley, densely wooded. . . . The barometer read a little under 4000 feet. This mountain or hill district we had explored, although so near the coast, had never been visited, and had always been enveloped in a cloud of mystery. The native imagination and superstition had peopled it with evil genii and all kinds of mysterious creatures, and the main peak was said to be surrounded by a lake and unapproachable by man.

In the next half century several British expeditions tried to duplicate this feat. Some claimed to have reached the summit of Victoria Peak, while others, like the Grant Expedition of 1927, could only describe it from a distance:

> Crouching close to the ground and peering through the tree-tops I saw a spectacle which filled me with awe. There perhaps 4 miles away, the tip of a great cone of solid rock shot perpendicularly skywards, seeming to float on the very roof of the forest.

During most of the year, the jagged summit of Victoria Peak is shrouded in clouds, giving the impression of a Mount Olympus inhabited by the gods. Many times I was warned to stay away from the range by the timber workers, who repeated to me some of the superstitions known since the nineteenth century.

All the known attempts to climb the peaks of the Cockscomb Range had been made from the north. That approach was the easiest. You could hike or take a boat about four miles up the Sittee River and then hike south about a mile through the jungle to the base of the mountains. Getting to the peaks from the south meant hiking many miles through dense forest, until timbering operations opened up the Cockscomb Basin. But even then it continued to pose a challenge.

I was told that in the last five years, several groups of British soldiers had tried climbing Victoria from the south and had failed. The roads built by Don Smith's operation could take you within five to seven miles of the peak, but the going from there was anything but easy. Traveling through the thick jungle and up and down one hill after another, you'd lose your bearings and think you were much closer than you really were. A member of the Grant Expedition wrote about the experience:

Progress was exceedingly slow. Half an hour brought us to the end of the cut over ground and thereafter I rated our forward speed at half a mile an hour. . . . For minutes at a time we would make no headway at all. Their banks were exceedingly steep, and here, as might be expected, Nature put forth her heaviest vegetation. . . . Again and again where the sky showed through the treetops we were deluded into thinking the summit was at hand.

The only sure method of reaching the peak from the south is to navigate by compass regardless of the terrain. This takes stamina, strength, and willpower. If you are fortunate enough to make it to the base, scaling to the top from this side is still very difficult. The last three to five hundred feet are straight up over slate rock that crumbles in your hands.

It was not until 1984, while I was in the basin, that a group of fifteen Belize Defence Force soldiers made what was to my knowledge the first successful attempt from the south. It took them two weeks, and only one man, a Maya Indian, made it to the top of Victoria Peak.

▲ ▲ ▲

Porfilio and I followed a similar route before the soldiers made their attempt, though we had no real intention of even reaching the base of the range. I was anxious at least to get beyond the extent of the timber operation into areas where there might still be virgin forest. After sharpening our machetes and loading our packs with rice, flour, and water, we set out.

The hiking was long and arduous but no worse than I had now come to expect from this area. I continually wondered how Porfilio knew that we were going in the right direction.

"You're sure this is the right way?"

"Yes, I sure."

"But how can you tell?"

"I know," he would say, smiling.

One of the early explorers of this region said that in this forest the term "guessing" is more appropriate than "estimating." Porfilio never once hesitated, and we always ended up where he said we would. If he was "guessing," then he was doing a great job of it.

Occasionally we would come upon one of the giants of the forest, towering a hundred and fifty feet into the air, its trunk sometimes six feet in diameter. It stood like a lonely guardian, watching over the destruction of the other members of its species and waiting for the inevitable chainsaw to reach its own base. Such trees were few and far between.

Cockscomb's rain forest did not consist of the classically tall trees that can be found in other parts of the tropics. Hurricanes and nearly a hundred years of selective high-grade timbering had destroyed it. There were, however, small untouched pockets too rugged for exploitation and protected from the onslaught of storms. In these little areas, Porfilio and I would stare up in awe at the towering banak, ironwood, Santa Maria tree, and barba jolote trees, their crowns spreading over the smaller denizens of the forest. Even Porfilio was impressed. He had only seen trees like these stripped naked at the camp.

At the base of a large banak, we talked about these trees. Some of them were possibly hundreds of years old. They had nourished the people and the animals of the forest and watched as generations of jaguars lived and died. Now they, and some of the species that had always grown beneath their canopy, were endangered. I told Porfilio that there was no terrestrial habitat on earth as dynamic and rich as the lowland tropical rain forest and that if we were to lose all this, all our lives would be much poorer.

As we lunched on flour tortillas, sitting against a large banak tree, I wondered how long it would take people to figure out how to exploit these few remaining trees economically. Someone surely was willing to meet any costs for a mahogany dining-room set or a hardwood-paneled den. My thoughts were suddenly interrupted as I realized Porfilio was asking me a question.

"What did you say, Porfilio?" I asked.

He repeated the question with such intensity that I realized it was something that must have been long on his mind. "Alan, why you study tiger? What you get for it? What it do? You like catch tiger? You no 'fraid?"

The questions, one after the other, were direct and simple. I'd often asked myself the same questions. How strange I must look to these people, putting myself through hardship, exposing my life to danger, and for what? I looked over to a small gap in the forest and watched the sunlight sparkle as it hit the web of a golden orb spider. The red breast of a slaty-tailed trogon sitting quietly on a nearby branch caught my eye.

What can I tell you? I thought, looking into his questioning eyes. I could easily tell you part of the truth. I could say I love animals and would like to see them have a chance to survive despite man's often unreasonable drive to destroy them. I could tell you how I love the out-of-doors, how I thrive on adventure, and how I never feel so at home as when I'm close to nature. That would definitely be part of the truth.

Then maybe I could tell you the rest, some of the deeper reasons I only started admitting to myself in recent years. I thought back to our conversation of the previous night and how

Porfilio felt trapped. I too had felt trapped, and the animals were my escape. My fear of people's reaction to my stuttering made me withdraw into a shell. I didn't want people to hurt me more than I was already hurting inside.

I could tell you how I kept a line at a supermarket checkout counter waiting because the words I needed wouldn't come out. People were getting angry so the clerk said I was retarded and dumb, so I acted retarded and dumb, using it as a protective shield. Moments like that still pain me, like thorns that have never been extracted. I don't stutter when I talk to animals. Animals don't make fun of me or think me dumb, and their world often makes more sense to me than the world of people. Would Porfilio understand all that? Did it matter?

"Because I like to study tiger, Porfilio, and they need my help. Come on, let's hike. You lazy today."

We camped that night on a high knoll where the trees seemed stunted and we could just make out the tip of Victoria Peak. It seemed so close, towering above all around it, but there were numerous ridges between us and the peak. I set up my hammock and fell into it, completely exhausted. Porfilio, who had cut most of our trail that day, was as energetic as he'd been when we started out. He ran around camp setting up a thatched lean-to with cohune leaves, then built a small cot from hardwood poles. Just watching him tired me out and I quickly fell asleep.

The next thing I knew I was smelling cooked meat, and for an instant I imagined I was at a barbecue in graduate school. Every other weekend during the time I was conducting my doctoral research, I would leave my study area in the Smoky Mountains of Tennessee to meet with a small group of friends, most of whom were working in the same mountains. For the day we'd drink beer and feast, enjoying one another's company. It was one of the few ways we eased the tensions of fieldwork, though all we talked about was wildlife. Those memories were happy ones.

I opened my eyes and saw the jungle. Porfilio was hunched over a cloud of smoke ten feet away. In the hour I had slept he had set up camp, called in and shot a tinamou, and was now roasting it over a fire. I felt guilty as I watched him cooking the meal. Porfilio held out a leg to me, smiling.

"Gringo no good in de bush. You a city man, not a bush man." He was right. I jumped out of the hammock and grabbed the meat.

That night, under a clear starry sky, the silence of the jungle engulfed us. We sat around the dying embers of our cooking fire sipping coffee as Porfilio hummed a Maya tune and I watched the stars, wondering where the jaguars were that night. Porfilio stopped humming and started talking of things that only a night in the forest around a campfire can bring out.

"You 'fraid in de bush at night?" he asked. Not waiting for a reply, he continued, "If you no 'fraid, you should be 'fraid. Dere plenty bad tings in de bush at night."

I expected to hear more about the master tiger. Instead he spoke the word "*duende*" (some Belizeans call it *ta-da-duende*).

"He a lil man wit only four finger on de hand. He no got tumb. Sometime he wear big hat. If you meet he in de bush, he hold up de hand, show you de four finger, and make you want follow he."

"What can you do?" I was engrossed.

"If you show he you got five finger, he get vexed [angry] and rip de tumb from you hand, or make you lost in de bush and no one ever see you again. But if you hide de tumb, show he four finger, den he happy. He touch he four finger to you four finger and, if he like you, he show you to play any music you want."

"What?" I was not sure I'd heard Porfilio correctly. He repeated that you could learn the musical instrument of your choice from a *duende*.

"Many people, dey see *duende*," Porfilio was saying, "and many chilren gone 'cause of dem and no one see dem again. But I know man in San Antonio—he learn play de guitar from *duende*."

I thought Porfilio was finished, but as I was writing his words in my notebook by the light of the fire, he continued. "Dere also de big hairy man, the Sisimito, in de bush. Two men see he in Cockscomb already." I shivered.

"You know de hairy man close when you hear scream at night, like woman screaming. Long time ago, an old man from de south, he still a boy. He go wit he fadder way back in Cockscomb for hunt. He go different way from he fadder and soon hear crash in de bush. He tink maybe it a tiger and he get scared and hide in de big mahogany log, and look out from a crack. Den, a big hairy man come out from de bush and he have a big bird [hawk] in he hand. The hairy man bite off and eat de head of de bird. Then he go 'way. The man lay in de log and shake because he scared bad. Finally he fadder come out of de bush and dey both go 'way fast. De fadder see de hairy man too."

Then Porfilio went on about how the Sisimito sometimes will carry a person off and keep him as a slave. Just before I arrived in Cockscomb, he told me, one of the workers was hauling a load of logs back to camp and saw what looked like a big hairy man run across the road.

"What do you do if you're captured by one?" I asked.

"You carry matches, and if hairy man grab you, you must make he on fire."

Porfilio continued with stories about the woman spirit, Ixtabai, perhaps the most dangerous and evil of them all. She is an enchantress enticing men into the forest to kill them. She can assume the face of a wife or girlfriend or she might not show her face at all but will bare her breasts to make the man come to her. She never speaks, but you know she's around when the dogs howl for no reason and horses whine. She can change anything about her appearance except her feet, which are shaped like chicken feet. She tries to hide her feet, but if you see them before she touches you, she runs away.

The next morning we decided to cut our trip short and return to Guam Bank. We both felt better from the hike, and Porfilio knew I was anxious to reopen the trap. The hike back to the truck went by quickly since we could now follow our own freshly cut trail.

As we drove back to camp we talked about putting the pig out that evening. Suddenly Porfilio grabbed my shoulder and pointed. No more than a hundred yards in front of us were two jaguars; one lying stretched out on the road, the other sitting over it. Their lack of fear of a large blue truck coming toward them seemed incredible.

I stopped the truck and we watched them watch us. This was the first time I had seen a jaguar since beginning the study, and now I had not one but two in front of me. What luck!

I examined them closely with my binoculars. They looked like a male and a female. Jaguars are thought to come together only when breeding. I wondered if the female might soon be raising a litter. The male didn't seem interested in anything other than sleeping. I inched the truck to within thirty feet of them.

Their fur was a rusty-yellow color paling to white on the undersides. Their heads and undersides were marked with black spots, large ones on their bellies. Their backs had large black rosettes enclosing one or several spots with fur slightly darker than on the rest of the body. The backs of their ears were solid black with a small white spot. Their tails, almost white along the entire length, had black spots merging into rings and finally a solid black tip. Their heads and paws seemed large, especially those of the male, and out of proportion with the rest of their muscular bodies. Though their bodies together took up the entire ten-foot road width, they didn't give the immediate impression of being huge cats. I was anxious to get my hands on one.

Finally, after five minutes of lying there being watched, the cats casually stood up and ambled into the forest. Suddenly I realized something. The cats were within half a mile of the trap. If we baited it that evening, there was a chance of catching one of them within the next few days. Porfilio had the same thought. We both felt we'd have a jaguar soon.

Porfilio was busy during the next week helping his brother-in-law harvest plantains in an effort to improve family relations. I went out alone in the mornings to check the trap. On the third day I pulled around the last curve and stopped the truck. The door to the trap was open but I could see something was wrong. The door was not hanging where it should be, above the entrance.

I jumped out and ran toward the trap. The door lay, ripped apart, six feet to the right of the trap. The pig was alive, crouching in the corner. The mud floor was covered with large fresh jaguar tracks, and the inner walls of the trap were scarred with numerous claw and teeth marks.

"I had him," I screamed out loud. "I had him and he escaped!"

The jaguar had ripped out the lower crossbeams of the door, straightening the bent ends of five-inch nails that held the beams together and ripping them out through the boards. After two lower crossbeams were removed, the door was loose enough to slip from its locking mechanism to be pushed out. The marks on the inside of the trap showed the cat had been caught for at least several hours before finding a way to break out.

I stood back and looked at the trap. I had underestimated this species and could not afford to do so again. For an instant my anger and amazement turned to fear. The jungle seemed unnaturally quiet around me. I wondered how close he was right now. Was he angry and watching, recognizing my smell from the trap? Would he seek revenge when I was alone in the jungle? I tried to push such thoughts aside, knowing my imagination was running away with itself. But what awesome power was locked up in that body! I looked again at the trap. At least I had caught him. I would have to build a better trap, but I knew I could catch others.

Meanwhile, I decided on a new tactic. I would try to catch jaguars by tracking them with dogs, a method used extensively by hunters throughout Central and South America. They chased jaguars into trees and shot them there. Howard Quigley had successfully adapted the method and captured live jaguars in Brazil, using tranquilizer darts instead of bullets. The key to the technique was using well-trained dogs that would follow only a jaguar's scent and ignore the smell of all other wildlife.

Every hunter with dogs claims his are the best, so finding a good pack could be an expensive and time-consuming process of trial and error. But one man, Bader Hassan, a Belizean of Lebanese descent, kept a pack of jaguar dogs that was unparalleled throughout the region.

I had first met Bader during my survey and we had hit it off immediately. His knowledge of jaguars helped me tremendously, and he said he would help again if I returned. I knew that if anyone could catch a jaguar for me, it would be him.

I phoned Bader. He wasn't at all surprised at what the jaguar had done to my trap and sounded excited about the idea of organizing a hunt. Cockscomb was one of the few areas in the country he had not yet hunted jaguars and he was anxious to try. We made arrangements to meet early the next week.

5 THE HUNT

I stood on the zebra-skin rug just inside Hassan's front door and looked around the room. Jaguar, puma, and ocelot skins covered much of the furniture; ocelot and puma skulls were mounted on the wall; and a large jaguar skull sat on the refrigerator. A tame margay and puma wandered in and out of the room, and I could see a wild jaguar caged in the backyard.

Hassan stood in the middle of the room. I have never admired big-game hunters. The idea of killing animals whose value in death is directly related to their magnificence in life is abhorrent to me. But as I looked at Hassan and saw the smile breaking across his deeply tanned face, I knew this personality encompassed strength, kindness, and intelligence.

Before 1974, when jaguar hunting was legal in Belize, Bader had been one of the most sought-after guides in the country.

Hunters from all over the world paid him large fees for the opportunity to take home the remains of one of these animals. Bader led them, and often helped them do the killing, and many cats died as a result of his hunts, but his excitement and love of hunting came from the dogs and the chase, not the kill. He knew that any fool could kill. Our backgrounds and motives were vastly different, but we shared a goal. We both wanted to ensure the future survival of the jaguar.

Bader's knowledge of jaguars, amassed over years of hunting, could fill several books. I just listened as he talked, trying to absorb it all so that I could use his knowledge in my fieldwork. Occasionally, I'd interrupt with facts I had picked up from books and other hunters. I knew, for instance, that the first European documentation of the jaguar was made in 1500 by Amerigo Vespucci, who spoke of "panthers" in Venezuela, and that Charles Darwin was the first to document tree scratching by jaguars. He suggested it might have something to do with the demarcation of their home range.

When Hassan spoke of how adaptable jaguars were to changes in their environment, I told him there was abundant evidence of jaguars at elevations higher than three thousand feet in the Peruvian Andes, as well as throughout the low, marshy jungles of Central and South America. They have been known to occur in the Sonora Desert of North America, at nearly seven thousand feet in northern Peru, and at nearly nine thousand feet in Bolivia.

Bader and I couldn't have been more different. I was a Jew who had grown up stuttering and reclusive, often fighting because of my handicap on the streets of New York. Bader was a Palestinian who was raised in small villages in Belize and was now a cattle rancher. But we got along immediately. He admired my knowledge, training, and drive, and I was awed by his strength, charisma, and deep love of wildlife. Several times I wanted to grab him, pit my strength and will against his, and wrestle him to the ground to draw power from him.

We talked through the night; finally, I collapsed into a bed in one of his guest rooms. At 6 A.M., I was awakened by the barking of dogs. The ranch hands were arriving to work. I had slept two hours. I dressed quickly, anxious to get back into Cockscomb. Over coffee, I said my farewells to Bader and his wife, Mary Ann. I left with half a pad of notes on jaguar behavior, several pages of skull and skin measurements, and a promise from Bader to come to Cockscomb with his men and dogs in the next few weeks.

With my limited budget, I could barely pay Hassan enough to cover the expenses for his men, and I knew Cockscomb would be a rugged and relatively costly hunt. Yet it was the promise of a challenging hunt that lit the spark in his eyes, for Bader had long heard that Cockscomb was one of the most difficult and dangerous areas to chase jaguars. He was most excited by the fact that we would be capturing them alive.

It was three weeks before Hassan could free himself from his ranch duties to plan and organize the hunt. Meanwhile, Porfilio and I were monitoring jaguar tracks and collecting their feces. Sometimes we'd find areas where jaguars had scraped or rested. In the vicinity of the jaguar beds, I'd often see twigs and branches broken and chewed, or small shrubs torn out of the ground. Hassan and other hunters, who had watched jaguars roll on the ground tearing at surrounding vegetation, called this "play" behavior. He told me that you could estimate the head size of the jaguar, and thus perhaps determine if it were male or female, by the spacing of the chew marks on the branches.

Late one afternoon, Bader came driving into Cockscomb with six dogs, three dog handlers, and a Land Rover, which looked like it could go anywhere and already had. His dogs were magnificent. Each had a distinctive personality, and when I later watched them in action, I could see why so much time, money, and energy went into their training.

The leader of the pack was a thirteen-year-old black-and-tan named Timber Jack, or Timber for short. This old hound with drooping, tired eyes didn't look like he'd live through a hunt, but Hassan assured me he could follow a cold trail better than any dog he had ever had.

The next in the hierarchy was a bluetick hound named Blue, nearly deaf but strong and sturdy. Bader kept him close to Timber so that he could lead the pack after Timber met with the big jaguar in the sky.

Then came Duke and Red, a Plott hound and a redbone, respectively. Young and massively built, these two were put into the chase once the trail was warmed up by the more experienced dogs.

Finally there were two very young black-and-tans, who were in training and tended to become overzealous. They were put into action only when the cat was actually on the run so that they wouldn't ruin the trail.

Chief among the dog handlers was Machario, a short, squat mestizo (Maya Indian–Spanish mix) who'd lived much of his life as a chiclero. A chiclero's job involved living in the jungle most of the rainy season and searching for the sapodilla, or zapote, tree, which he would then tap, like a rubber tree, to obtain a white resinous latex called chicle, at one time the primary basis for chewing gum. Chicleros, by far the best and toughest bushmen one could find, were fiercely independent. Some of them seemed like they'd just as quickly cut you with a machete as buy you a drink. It was Machario's job to keep up with the lead dogs while chopping a good trail for us to follow. This was a difficult job once the dogs started running at top speed through the jungle.

Guermo, a handsome young Creole, had trained with the Special Forces of the Belize Defence Force. He was to follow Machario and keep rein on Duke and Red until the trail became hot enough to release them.

Phillip, a Creole, was a complainer and seemed to dislike everything about the hunt except the prospect of the money he would be paid at the end of it. He was to bring up the rear with the two remaining dogs until they could be let loose.

Hassan would stay somewhere in the middle, watching and

coordinating both ends, while I would just have to keep up with everyone, hauling all the drugging and radio-tracking equipment.

Bader and his men moved into one of the empty shacks at the camp. Their presence created quite a stir among the Indians and timber workers. The timber men thought Bader was the ultimate in machismo, while the Indians had eyes only for the dogs. As soon as they arrived, I took the motorcycle back into the jungle to look for fresh jaguar sign.

Each day's hunt began at 3:30 A.M. so that we could be deep in the forest before the sun rose. We needed light to look for cat sign, but we had to work quickly before the heat of the day burned off the scent or tired out the dogs. We usually ended by noon so as not to risk overtiring the dogs for the next day's hunt.

Over the next three days we followed dozens of leads but never treed or even sighted a jaguar. The jaguars were at home in this rugged terrain and we were not. After the first day, I didn't think I had the strength to continue. Running at full speed through the jungle carrying a full backpack was like nothing I'd ever read about in *The Runner* magazine. Yet the more difficult tasks fell to the men in front. After watching Machario chop and run at the same time, I thought that if we could train some of our Olympic athletes this way, we'd see some new records.

The basin proved more rugged than Bader had anticipated, and the dogs were tiring fast. After four days, Bader had to give the men and dogs a break, so he decided to pack up and leave, promising to return in a week. I was discouraged, having hoped to catch a jaguar during this first hunt.

"Do you think we'll still get one, Bader?"

"Are you kidding? We haven't even begun to really hunt." He was still filled with enthusiasm. "Look, the dogs are stronger and tougher from these last few days and now they know what to expect. So do we. We've been close, and the next time we'll have one."

I hoped he was right.

As soon as their Land Rover disappeared down the entrance road, I collapsed on my bed and slept for eighteen hours.

Over the next week I developed a new tactic for the hunt. Hunters had always assured me that when a jaguar makes a large kill, such as a cow, tapir, or peccary, they never stray far from it. Thus the quickest way to tree a cat was from a fresh kill. The day before Bader was to return, Porfilio and I staked out two live pigs, each twenty pounds, in areas of frequent jaguar sign. Porfilio had not been allowed to accompany us on the last hunt because Bader felt he might be in the way. He wanted very much to go, however, so I planned to take him on the next hunt. Maybe it would delay his return to San Antonio.

Bader returned on schedule, with the same men except for Phillip, who was replaced by his father, Jack, a much more colorful character. Jack, a man in his early sixties, was a jungle-tough veteran of many jaguar hunts with Bader. His eyes drooped like Timber Jack's, and his body didn't have the youthful energy of his son, but he was no complainer.

"What happened to your son Phillip?" I asked Jack.

"Phillip, he stay home. He want play with he wife, make more baby. He no want come in de bush," Jack explained.

"I thought Phillip like to hunt tiger," I lied.

"What! Phillip like to hunt tiger?" Jack repeated. "He like to do nutting. Dat lazy shit. De best part of him drip down his mama's leg." He laughed, running his finger down his leg.

June 21, 3:30 A.M. I woke to the first day of the new hunt feeling strong and ready. I looked out the window into a clear, starry sky and knew it was going to be a sunny, hot day. While the others prepared breakfast, I went out to check the pigs. Neither had been taken, but there were fresh tracks along the road where the jaguar had escaped from my trap.

When I brought Bader to the area, he felt the tracks were between six and eight hours old. Timber and Blue had picked up the trail within two hours of starting. By 6 A.M., we were running fast, up and down hills, through thickets and over large fallen trees. By 7 A.M., Timber started slowing from the exertion, which slowed up Blue as well. Bader released Red and Duke, who took off and made me run like I'd never run before. My shirt was already ripped and I was bleeding from several places on my arms and legs from the thorns and spikes of the surrounding vegetation. My heart thumped against my chest.

I now understood why Hassan was hooked on the hunt. It was like a drug, carrying us to a different level of consciousness, one of the most elemental levels of human existence, the hunt and the chase. Bader, Guermo, and Machario were already far ahead, and Jack and I brought up the rear. My last glimpse of Machario was just after I started to run, when I glanced up to see him chopping through the bush with his machete like a lawn mower through grass, silent, intent, and completely at home in this jungle. I climbed another hill and paused for breath, realizing I had been ignoring all the dangers I told myself to beware of. Jack was far behind and I realized I was all alone. The dogs sounded no more than half a mile away, so I rested for a moment, waiting for Jack and conserving my energy for the cat I was sure we'd soon have.

After nearly two hours of running at full speed, the dogs were now barking with the madness of bloodlust. Bader told me that, once on a scent, his dogs would run until they either dropped from exhaustion, treed a cat, or were killed by the cat. If we didn't stay right behind them, we might never see them again. A rustling below told me Jack was hobbling up the hill. Tough as he was, this chase had worn him down. I could tell he was tired when he stopped telling me dirty jokes. As we started off together, all noise ceased.

The abrupt silence was eerie. Damn, I thought to myself, the dogs have lost the trail. I turned to Jack. "What the hell do we do now?"

A broad grin spread across his face. "Dem dogs tree de cat. Now dey look for de tree. We must get dere quick, man."

We backtracked on our trail to cut across the hill where we had heard the dogs barking last. Within minutes we were chopping up a new hill and I heard Bader yelling in the distance, "Alan! Alan! Alan!"

We've got the cat, I thought, and I hollered that I was coming. Then I heard what Bader was yelling about. "Alan! Alan! Come quickly! Guermo's been bitten by a snake!"

There was panic in his voice and I knew it must have been a tommy-goff. I sheathed my machete and was about to run toward Bader's voice when Jack summoned up an extraordinary reserve of energy, jumped in front of me, and started chopping to clear the way.

I stayed so close behind him that when he stopped suddenly and turned to shove me back, his arm connected with my jaw and knocked me to the ground.

"What the hell—" I started to say, but the words died in my throat as I followed his eyes to a spot about nine feet in front of where he stopped. Curled up, shaking its tail rapidly against the leaves and making a sound like a rattlesnake, was a fer-de-lance, head up, poised and ready to strike. I was torn between fascination and all-consuming fear.

"We must kill 'im," Jack said, staring at the snake as if it were the devil incarnate. "He scared. He chase us if we try go round."

I got up, not taking my eyes off that deadly head. Bader's voice came again from the other side of the hill. "Alan, Jack, where are you? Come quickly!"

I turned to Jack and found he had chopped a young hardwood tree and fashioned a long pole. He handed it to me. "Hit 'im wit de end of de pole and hit 'im on de head de first time. If you no kill 'im quick, he jump at you. So hit 'im good."

I was about to ask Jack why he handed the pole to me when a look at his face told me he wasn't about to move one step closer to that snake. I lifted the pole, hoping that Jack was wrong about it jumping at me. I didn't have the greatest confidence in my ability to hit a snake's head with the narrow end of a six-foot pole on the first try. I lifted the pole high above me and brought it down with all my strength, miraculously connecting right on top of the poised head. I smashed it over and over, then pulled out my machete and chopped it into several pieces.

Ashamed at the intensity of my own violence, I looked away from the gory mess at my feet and started running toward Bader, who was still hollering for Jack and me to come quickly. He was only about two hundred yards away, but he was over the next hill in a little ravine.

We finally got there and found Bader kneeling over Guermo, who was lying on cohune leaves in the center of a cleared area, rolling his head back and forth in pain. I immediately loosened his clothes and examined the bite on his ankle. Machario stood off to one side, watching in barely suppressed anguish. A dead fer-de-lance, later found to measure a little over six feet in length and seven inches in girth, with a head nearly the size of my hand, was lying off to the right. I looked above me and saw only a green ceiling. Somewhere in one of the trees above, the jaguar we wanted sat watching us.

"The antivenin is in the truck," were my first words to Bader.

We had decided not to bring it since we thought the jaguar was close to where we had parked. Bader told Machario to get back to the truck as quickly as possible, and I told him where to find the pack and what to bring. Machario took off running.

I looked at my watch. It was 8:30 A.M. An image of my mother just getting up to fix breakfast passed through my mind. I could almost smell the eggs cooking on the stove. I missed her. My father would be off to work by now, and the day's routine would just be starting. Where was Sue, the woman I had left behind? Was she thinking of me or had she finally given up on our seesaw relationship? What was I doing here?

Guermo's skin felt clammy and his pulse was rapid, but he was still coherent, though he showed initial signs of shock. I elevated his legs and told Bader to assure him calmly that everything would be all right; then I peeled off his socks and examined the wound more closely.

The fer-de-lance had been at the base of the tree the jaguar had chosen to climb. Machario had passed the tree but Guermo had stopped right alongside it to grab two of the dogs. With all the noise and confusion, the snake must have sensed danger and must have been poised for defense, like the one I had just killed. When Guermo stepped close, the snake lunged out and sank its fangs into his leg. He was wearing sneakers and the bite was right above his ankle.

Guermo was already feeling the pain moving up into his thigh. The puncture was deep, and over fifteen minutes had elapsed between the time of the bite and my arrival with Jack. There was no point in using the regular snakebite kit; we needed the antivenin.

We tried to comfort Guermo while Jack sat to one side, silent and immersed in his own thoughts. I was sure that the jaguar above our heads was the same one that had escaped from my trap. As I huddled over Guermo, my neck exposed, I hoped this jaguar bore me no ill will.

Thirty minutes later Machario returned. Guermo was moaning in agony, saying the pain was unbearable. Although the situation was critical, I couldn't administer the antivenin immediately. It was made with horse serum, and a person first had to be tested for a possible allergic reaction to the serum. Failure to do so could cause death from the serum alone.

I dissolved the freeze-dried antivenin in the sterile water provided with the kit, then put several drops into Guermo's eyes. We waited fifteen minutes to see if any signs of redness or swelling appeared that might signal a reaction. The minutes ticking away felt like hours.

There was no allergic reaction, so I injected 20 cc of the antivenin deep into the muscle of each buttock using a twenty-gauge one-and-a-half-inch-long needle. His calf had started to swell, and he was bleeding from his tongue. I had heard of cases where Indians bitten by these snakes started bleeding from all the pores in their body before they died. I knew that the venom from such bites could damage blood vessels, affect red blood cells, prevent coagulation, and even damage the heart, kidneys, and lungs.

Jack and Machario built a stretcher of hardwood poles and

cohune palms so that we could carry Guermo. Bader ran ahead to the timber camp to bring assistance and to radio for an airplane. When I finished with the injections, we lay Guermo on the stretcher and started off. Jack walked in back of us, mumbling, "Man di walk, dead di watch am" (meaning death can come any time whether you're ready for it or not).

Carrying Guermo over the hills, through the creeks, and over rocks was an arduous task. We had all been close to exhaustion before we even started, so it wasn't long before our arms and legs began quivering from the strain. Every few seconds Guermo would moan in agony, and every bump or stumble brought additional cries of pain from his lips. Our rests became more frequent, and each time I thought I couldn't lift that stretcher again. But each time Guermo would grab my arm. "Please, Alan, I no want die. Let's go. Get me out," he'd say over and over. Each time, we found the strength to move on.

Soon Guermo became delirious, screaming that he couldn't stand the pain any longer, that his nerves were on fire. The bleeding from his mouth worsened, but he felt no pain above his thigh because of the antivenin injection.

"We're almost out, Guermo," I kept assuring him. "The truck is close." I lied, knowing we were probably still a long way from the truck.

Finally, after having carried Guermo over a mile, Machario and I both collapsed and could no longer force our arms to lift him again. We could only sit and wait, listening to Guermo cry. He begged us to keep going and squeezed my arm until he drew blood with his fingernails. But our energies were spent.

Eventually Bader returned with four men—Oral, Tino, Prudencio, and Ignacio—and we took turns carrying him the remaining distance. Upon finally reaching the truck, we loaded him into the back. Jack disappeared into the bush, reappearing shortly with leaves and branches to cover Guermo's face. On the way back to camp, I could hear him talking to Prudencio. "We not let any woman look on 'im," he was saying. "If she pregnant and see 'im, he dead for sure."

Prudencio agreed.

A plane was waiting on the airstrip outside the camp. Five hours had elapsed since the bite. We rushed through camp, loaded Guermo into the rear of the plane, and Bader and I climbed in front. We told the men we'd be back as soon as possible.

The flight to Belize City was tense and quiet, punctuated by Guermo's moans. The pilot knew better than to ask any questions. At the municipal airport an ambulance was waiting to rush us to Belize City Hospital. I was impressed with the speed of movement from the jungle to the hospital, but my expectations soon plummeted. Though there was a team of doctors waiting, no one seemed to know what to do.

They immediately injected Guermo intravenously with additional antivenin, but then what? Guermo's leg had swollen to the size of a watermelon and he was begging for something to relieve the pain. I pulled a doctor aside and asked him if Guermo should be on an antivenin intravenous drip. Their only drip was clogged and unusable, I was told. Anyway, they were thinking they might have to amputate.

"No!" I said, raising my voice and drawing attention from the beds around me. "We need other opinions." Though I had no medical training, I felt sure that amputation at this point was not called for. I found Bader talking with another doctor, a worried look on his face.

"They're talking amputation," he said to me, his voice breaking from the strain. "We have to get him out of here, get him to the British Hospital."

"I know, Bader, but they won't take him at the British Hospital. He's Belizean and has to stay in a Belizean hospital. That's their policy."

We became increasingly frustrated with the situation. I got on the phone to some officials I knew in the British army. Their response was rapid, and soon I was put in touch with their surgeon-in-residence at the British Hospital.

He told me he had treated poisonous snakebites all over the world and had never had to amputate. "They should not even be thinking of amputation at this point," he said vehemently. In the absence of a drip they needed to continue injecting him and to keep him awake.

I conveyed the instructions to the doctor in attendance. He agreed to try that and seemed relieved that the burden had been lifted off his shoulders. Then I walked out onto the hospital balcony and looked out over the city, feeling an overwhelming weariness creeping through my body. As I was thinking about finding an empty hospital bed to sleep in, a Creole nurse approached me. "Are you one of the men who brought in the man bitten by the tommy-goff?" she asked.

"Yes, is anything wrong?"

"No, he's still being looked after. I just wanted to know why you brought him all the way up here instead of taking him to a snake doctor," she said.

I smiled at her, thinking she was being facetious. Then I suddenly realized she was very serious.

"You should have brought him to a snake doctor," she repeated and turned away, walking back into the hospital.

I wanted to run and grab her and ask how she could say this to me. But my body could hardly move, and my mind said to leave it alone.

Bader and I stayed with Guermo for several hours to make sure the doctors continued with the injections and the nurses kept him from sleeping. After that there was nothing more we could do, so we decided to fly back to Cockscomb before dark. We had no money with us, and we were still in our dirty, sweat-soaked field clothes, with machetes strapped to our sides. We reassured Guermo through his pain that everything was being done for him and that he would be all right. Then I left Bader at his bedside while I looked for the nurse who had spoken to me earlier about the snake doctor. I wanted her name; I wanted to tell her to stay away from Guermo. But I couldn't find her. We left Belize City feeling confident that Guermo would recover with all his limbs intact.

Back in Cockscomb, Bader and I wanted to continue the hunt, but the men, particularly Machario, didn't want to go back into the Cockscomb jungle. "I don't know if I run good back dere again," Machario said.

"I tink dis place bad," Jack added. "It not right chase tiger just for catch and no kill it."

"Maybe we should leave dis place," Machario said quietly. "It real bad what happen to Guermo. I no like it." He looked at the floor.

"Maybe he too salty [unlucky]," Jack said, nodding his head in my direction.

Bader tried to calm them down, telling them Guermo was going to be all right. I felt this was the end of the hunt.

The next morning, feeling tired and depressed, I went out to check and feed the pigs still staked out in the jungle. As I approached the second pig, I stared in amazement. There was no pig—only an empty rope harness and the pig's intestines to tell the story. I was excited but wondered how the men would react to the news. This was exactly what we had hoped for. The jaguar should be close. I sped back to camp thinking of ways to plead with Bader. But as soon as I called him outside and told him the news, excitement flashed in his eyes. "What are we standing around for? Let's go," he said, a big grin on his face.

"But the men," I said, "they're frightened. Will they work?"

"The men will work," he replied.

The men did work but were not happy about it. Porfilio readily agreed to replace Guermo, and Machario wanted Porfilio up front with him. As soon as we got to the harness, the dogs went crazy. The scent was hot, so hot that not only Blue and Timber started barking at the empty harness, but Duke and Red as well. There were no preliminaries. They took off into the jungle and we followed right behind. The terror, anxiety, and weariness of the previous day were forgotten. We were on the chase again.

6 AH PUCH

The younger dogs passed Timber and Blue quickly but were soon confused by the jaguar's having run a circle and having crossed its own path. While Duke and Red chased their tails, Timber circled once, then immediately ran north after the cat. It was clear this was going to be a difficult chase. We were running toward Victoria Peak.

While we were all trying to straighten the other dogs out, Bader suddenly realized that no one was with Timber. We could just make out his faint voice in the distance. Machario immediately took off in the direction of his barks. We finally got the other dogs back onto Timber's trail and followed Machario.

Several hills later, outdistanced by Bader and Porfilio, Jack and I were once again bringing up the rear. The cacophony ahead sounded as if all the dogs were now together. Just as we were closing the distance, the barking stopped. This time I knew what it meant and started running before Bader's excited voice called to me. Timber had treed the jaguar himself and had held it single-handedly until Machario and then the other dogs caught up. Porfilio told me after the hunt he had killed another fer-de-lance as he was catching up with the dogs.

When I arrived, the dogs were already tied up, and Bader, Porfilio, and Machario were talking among themselves.

"He's over there," Bader said, pointing to a small ironwood tree that was leaning at a forty-five-degree angle against a large cotton tree. I walked over and looked up. The foliage was thick, but through that mass of green there was no mistaking the large spotted head and the green piercing eyes that shone golden when the light hit them. I was looking into the face of the animal I had sought for so long.

I heard nothing but my heartbeat. I felt naked and alone, as I confronted wild, untouchable beauty. Those eyes were watching me with no trace of fear or anger, but with thoughts I'd never know, and listening to voices I'd never hear.

A voice in my own mind told me to leave, that I had no right to interfere, to do what I was spending so much time and effort to do. But the scientist in me, trained to capture, study, and analyze, was much too strong and spoke in a different voice. It said that I could walk away if I wanted, but other magnificent creatures like this one were dying every day and I was there to try and help save it from extinction. To leave would have been selfish, for knowledge was the only key to understanding, and understanding could be the only weapon for the battle. And I wanted to win the battle. Do your job, I told myself. Do what you know is right.

The mouth opened, canines flashed, and a low growl brought me back to the matter at hand. It was time to get on with my work. The decision had already been made, not then and not by me. I was merely trying to prevent more damage by a society that was turning its back on the natural, free-living creatures of our world. He growled again and I backed away from the tree.

I don't have you yet, I thought to myself, estimating him to be about twenty feet above the ground. The head was massive. I was sure we had a large male.

"We have to work fast," I said to Bader and the men.

"The first shot has to be good," Bader said. "Otherwise the cat may jump and run again."

Porfilio had already started to prepare the equipment and he handed me the blowgun. We had two means of tranquilizing the cat. Bader had a standard tranquilizer rifle that could shoot a syringe with some speed and force and that was fairly accurate at longer distances. I had a three-foot-long blowgun with a compressed air pistol on one end, which was less traumatic to the animal and delivered the drug more slowly and efficiently. Unfortunately, both of our darts held only 3 cc of drug. I was using a relatively safe drug called Ketaset (ketamine hydrochloride), and injecting 10–15 mg per pound of body weight. This hundred-to-hundred-and-fifty-pound cat might need as much as 10 cc to knock him out. I didn't want to sedate him completely because I feared he'd fall from the tree. I wanted to just make him groggy enough so we could climb the tree and lower him down with a rope.

"Bader, you use the rifle and I'll use the blowgun. We'll both shoot him at the same time, aiming for the hindquarters," I said. "Six cc of drug should make him sleepy enough to handle. You sure you want to climb the tree after him?" I asked.

Bader smiled. "Don't worry, Alan. I've done it with cats who weren't even drugged. I'll climb to a nearby branch, throw a rope around him, and lower him down."

It was all neatly thought out, but I had done this too often with other animals, such as black bears and raccoons, to assume it would go exactly as planned.

Drugging large carnivores in the field can be tricky. An adverse reaction to the drug is always a possibility, and individuals within a species can react differently. Partial drugging was safer for the animal though definitely more dangerous for the researcher. We loaded extra syringes in case more drug was needed. As it happened, nothing went as planned.

As Bader and I approached the base of the tree, the jaguar watched intently our every move with curious eyes. The rear of his body was partially obscured by leaves. It was a difficult shot, but even if only one of us hit him, 3 cc should sedate him enough so that it would be an easy chase if he jumped and ran.

I had to control the shaking in my arm as I lifted the blowgun to shoot. I counted to three and we fired. My syringe was deflected by a branch, but Bader hit him in the hindquarters. The jaguar was up and roaring, but didn't jump. We backed away from the tree and waited, loading two more syringes for a second shot.

Five minutes passed and the cat showed no signs of drowsiness. We later discovered that Bader's dart had pierced the coat but had not penetrated muscle. From where we were, the syringe appeared to be solidly embedded, yet whenever we approached the tree, the jaguar stood and growled. After ten minutes I decided we'd shoot him again. The five of us circled the tree, talking loudly to keep him up there for a second shot. It had the opposite effect, for the jaguar had about all he would stand. As we reached the base, the jaguar started down the tree toward us.

We yelled to keep him up there but I lost my voice as his eyes riveted on mine. I backed away, lifting the blowgun to shoot, when suddenly he leaped over my head and was off and running. I was dazed. It took me several seconds to realize the blowgun had been knocked from my hands and was lying on the ground bent in half. Only later did I think about the danger I had been in, but at the time all I could think of was catching that cat quickly before I lost it for good.

Bader ran to the dogs and released them. They disappeared on the cat's trail, followed closely by Machario, Porfilio, and Bader. I packed the equipment.

"Dat drug no good," Jack mumbled, loud enough so that I

could hear. "And dat tiger, he no want to get catched."

I threw the pack on my back and ran after the others, hoping to leave Jack far behind.

I started wondering if the cat would be treed again when I almost ran into the dogs circling a large dead mahogany tree lying on the ground. I hadn't realized they had stopped barking and thought at first they had lost the trail, when Bader fell to the ground. I ran over and saw him looking into an opening at one end of the tree where the roots had once anchored it into the ground. When Bader jammed a long pole into the hole, there was a growl from within.

The hunt was far from over. When the jaguar turned his head toward the opening, we could see the golden eyes looking out from the darkness. We couldn't just shoot into the hole. We needed a flashlight, but our only flashlight was in the truck.

While Bader and the men stayed at the site to keep the jaguar in the cavity, Porfilio and I followed an old skidder trail back to the main road. Though Porfilio was much more at home in the jungle than I, as soon as we hit the timber road he couldn't keep up with my running. The muscles in my legs were tired, and as they started to tighten, I thought of other things to keep my mind off the pain.

I imagined myself back in the triathlon I had entered while in graduate school. The race had included swimming, running, and solo white-water canoeing on the Nantahala River in North Carolina. I had trained six months for that race and learned to push my body to its limit for the first time in my life. I never kept track of the other competitors in the race and never took the time to find out how I had placed. I had just wanted to pit my body against the elements. It had taken a month for my system to fully recover but I had learned what I was capable of and knew anything short of that would be easy. We had pushed ourselves to the limit the previous day trying to carry Guermo out of the jungle. Now I was doing it again.

Finally, I topped a hill and the truck was in sight. Its light blue color stood out against the omnipresent green of the jungle.

I rummaged through the glove compartment, grabbed the flashlight, and started running back. Porfilio was still half a mile down the road, bent over, trying to catch his breath. I shouted the expected greeting as I ran by, "Let's go Porfilio; you run like a woman," and was soon back in the jungle.

Porfilio promply caught up with me. "City gringo no good in de bush." Porfilio laughed as he passed me. "Go home and make tortilla, gringo." Forty minutes had elapsed before we arrived back at the site. The jaguar had retreated deeper into the hole and was now completely out of sight. It was our move.

I loaded the rifle as Bader cut a stout pole. We needed to bring the jaguar closer to the opening so that I could get a clear shot into the neck or shoulder region. Bader gently stuck the pole into the hole and probed. There was a roar and the pole flew from Bader's hands and danced in the air. Bader flashed the light into the opening, revealing the jaguar's head and part of the shoulder. I resisted the urge to run, for no more than three feet in front of me was that massive head and those angry shining eyes again. I aimed at his neck and fired.

Porfilio jammed a second dart into my hand and I quickly loaded and fired again. With the second shot, the jaguar charged the opening. I screamed and fell backward. Bader and Machario each held poles across the hole to prevent the jaguar's escape. We waited.

After five minutes, no sounds were heard from within the cavity. We removed the poles and probed the darkness with the flashlight. Nothing—no sound and no sign of the jaguar. He had retreated deeper into the cavity and had fallen asleep. I calculated we had about thirty minutes before he'd start to awaken, so we needed to get to work. The problem was that none of us was eager to go into that hole and pull him out. I turned to Porfilio. "Porfilio, if you a man, you crawl in and pull the tiger out." Porfilio didn't smile.

"Why you no pull he out?" he asked.

"Porfilio, I think you afraid to go in that hole. I pay you ten dollars if you pull that tiger out."

Bader laughed. Porfilio smiled. Then he removed his hat, took the flashlight, and dove into the hole.

Everything but the soles of Porfilio's shoes disappeared from sight. Soon Porfilio yelled for us to help him out. We grabbed his feet and pulled. His legs reappeared, then his body, then his smiling, dirty face, then his outstretched arms, and finally his hands pulling a beautiful sleeping jaguar.

We gathered around to admire the animal. How soft its coat felt to the touch, how large its paws, how menacing those one-and-a-quarter-inch canines protruding from its slack jaws! We'd come a long way for this animal. I looked over at Bader. He was elated.

The jaguar's body was a bit stiff. I knew that the drug, a dissociative anesthetic, could cause muscle rigidity, spasms, or even convulsions. So I injected 2 cc of a tranquilizer, Valium, to reduce the cat's anxiety and relieve tension in the muscles. I pulled out my data sheets from the pack and started following the procedure I'd developed for this occasion.

Jack, Machario, and Porfilio watched with undisguised amazement as I took body measurements, obtained the head circumference, checked tooth wear for a general age estimate, and examined the coat for external parasites and general wear. I placed opthalmic gel in the jaguar's eyes to prevent the lenses from drying out because the eyelids remained open during Keta-set-induced sedation. Machario and Jack brought over a pole and we attached a scale to weigh him. Meanwhile, as I called out numbers, Bader filled in the blanks on the sheet:

Sex—male
Age—mature adult
Total length—70 inches
Tail length—20 inches
Head circumference—22 inches
Height to shoulder—18 inches
Height to hip—22 inches
Weight—125 pounds

There is no accurate method of determining the exact age of a jaguar. But tooth eruption, attrition, and coloration, as well as coat condition, can help determine whether it is a subadult (two–three years old), mature adult (four–ten years old), or an old adult (over eleven years old). Using skeletal material, you can be more accurate. You can examine the cranial sutures and compare them with those from African lions of known age.

Jaguars are smaller than lions and tigers, and heavier and more powerfully built than leopards. Their large heads, deep-chested barrel-like bodies, and short but massive limbs make them look larger than they are. Their almost legendary strength comes from their powerful jaws and limbs. Their teeth and jaw musculature are so developed that, relative to their size, their bite is the most powerful of any of the big cats.

We unhooked our jaguar from the scale, laid it in the shade, and I began to attach a radio collar around its neck. The collars are adjustable so they can fit an animal comfortably but can't be pulled off when the animal is freed. Twenty minutes had elapsed and the jaguar was beginning to move again, so I injected an additional 1/2 cc of Valium to keep it relaxed for a while longer. Bader attached a cable around its chest and hooked the other end to a tree so the animal wouldn't stumble off partially drugged into the jungle. I tightened the four small bolts on the collar and checked its fit, making sure it moved freely around the neck. These radios were the most important tool of the project, for they would help me learn more about the behavior of this animal than had ever been learned before. This was the first jaguar ever to be tracked by means of these collars in the rain forest.

As I felt the power emanating from the warm body beneath me, I once again stifled the thought that I was venturing into an area I had no right to be in. What would the jaguar feel from now on? Was I affecting its chances for survival in a world already rugged and harsh? I had been involved with radio-telemetry long enough to know that, properly applied, the collar should not hurt the animal or even permanently affect its out-

ward behavior. Still, it was a bit like breaking a wild stallion—
it would never be the same. So my victory, as all victories might
be, was tinged with a little sadness, even a sense of loss. But I
had to keep in mind that the alternative was to do nothing and
thus accomplish nothing.

When I had finished, we backed off about ten yards and waited
for the jaguar to recover. Now that I could relax, I looked at the
jaguar more closely. There was a large scar on his nose, and both
ears had been torn. What do you do out there in the jungle? I
wondered. Did you fight to get and keep this territory? A big,
battle-scarred male like you, how many young have you sired,
how many females are under your watchful eye? Maybe I'll find
all that out. As long as that radio keeps working, we're tied
together now, you and I.

I turned on my radio receiver and tuned in the frequency for
this collar. The characteristic beeping told me it was working
properly. These collars had been designed specifically for this
jaguar project. They consisted of a white polyurethane band
measuring two inches in width, with a small rectangular radio
hanging perpendicular to the ground. Each radio was powered
by lithium batteries and was built to emit individual frequencies
to distinguish the animals from one another. Within the radio
was a tip switch that changed the pulse rate of the signal if there
was any head or body movement. Since the vegetation and topography also changed the quality of the signal, making it
louder or softer, I could also tell if a jaguar was traveling. If the
jaguar was resting, I would hear a slow pulse. When it moved,
a faster pulse would be transmitted. If the fast pulse was steady
and consistent, I assumed the jaguar was awake but not traveling much. If the pulse was fast but shifted between loud and
soft, I assumed the jaguar was moving. The radio package was
shockproof and waterproof, and weighed less than half a pound.
A larger radio would have allowed me to hear the cat at greater
distances, but I wanted to minimize the weight and the potential
interference with the animal's behavior at all costs.

I turned off the receiver, put my head back against a tree, and waited. Jack and Machario were squatting under a cohune tree talking about Guermo, and my thoughts drifted to the events of the previous day. It seemed so long ago.

"Dis ting wrong for do," I heard Jack say. "It no good." I stared at him icily, but he ignored me. "It not right catch tiger like dis. Guermo in hospital. Should be wit snake doctor." He looked at me accusingly.

Damn you, Jack, I thought, you're not making it any easier. A rustling made me turn back to the jaguar. He was standing and trying to walk. Bader walked over and loosened the cable, allowing him to slip through the harness. Jack and Machario, holding long poles, stood to one side, while Bader and I had the tranquilizer guns loaded just in case something went wrong. The jaguar looked at us for several moments, then turned and walked into the jungle.

The following day Bader and the men packed up early and left for Belize City Hospital to check on Guermo. Porfilio decided to ride with Bader to the highway and then catch a bus to his home village, San Antonio. He promised he'd be back soon. I went back out into the forest to make sure the jaguar was gone from the capture site and returned to camp by early afternoon exhausted. I lay down to rest for a while and slept until 9 A.M. the next morning.

By the afternoon of the following day I felt renewed and decided to go into Dangriga and combine a shopping trip with a phone call to Bader. As usual, several Indians accompanied me into town. I reached Bader at his home and was surprised when the voice on the other end sounded so weary.

"Haven't caught up on your sleep yet, Bader?" I asked.

"No, still haven't slept much, Alan," came the curt response, barely audible.

"How is he, Bader?"

There was a long silence. "He's dead, Alan."

I held the receiver to my chest, hoping the sick feeling in my stomach would go away. I leaned back against the wall for support and looked out the window of the phone station. A Carib woman was passing with a load of plantains on her head. A blue Datsun pickup truck pulled up to the bank across the street and parked. A dog was eating garbage in an alley next door. The world looked as normal as ever. Maybe I had heard wrong. I lifted the receiver to my ear again.

"Dead! How the hell is he dead, Bader? What do you mean, dead? He was just here. We just left him . . ." My voice trailed off.

Bader told me what little he knew of the circumstances at this point, and I hung up.

It was weeks before I got the full story. After we had left the hospital, Guermo's condition stabilized. Although still in serious condition, he was expected to make a full recovery. The doctors had operated on his leg, drained the fluid that was building up, and began administering blood and glucose solutions. But the day after we left, his wife brought a snake doctor into the hospital from one of the outlying rural areas. The snake doctor stood by Guermo's bed and told his wife that he should be taken out of the hospital. He would cure Guermo.

The doctors were outraged but legally could not prevent his wife from removing him. Guermo was under sedation and could not make the decision himself. He died the night we caught the jaguar. The snake doctor, of course, blamed the hospital for killing him, saying he had gotten to him too late. His wife blamed us for taking him to the hospital instead of directly to a snake doctor. Bader's men blamed Bader and me for having brought him to the hospital.

When I heard the news of his death from Bader, I got into the truck and started back for Cockscomb immediately. I didn't feel like staying in town any longer. All I knew at that point was that Guermo was dead and it involved his wife and a snake doctor. I thought back to the nurse who had suggested we bring him to a snake doctor and wondered if the Indians might be right in telling me that our fates are predetermined. I broke the news to the timber men, explaining that I didn't have the full story about his death. I wished Porfilio had been there to share my grief and tell me that I had done the right thing.

Word of the death spread quickly through camp. By the next day, the consensus was that Bader and I had helped kill Guermo by bringing him to the hospital instead of to a snake doctor. By the third day, the Indians were saying that I was jinxed by something in Cockscomb. On the fourth day, I decided it was time to search for the jaguar. Nobody wanted to go with me, even when I offered them more money. Porfilio still had not returned, so I went alone.

Though I stayed out all day, I made only a halfhearted attempt to find the cat. After an hour of listening for the signal, I parked the truck at the side of the road and lay in the back looking up at the sky. I felt desperately sad and lonely. While I was building the first trap, I had decided to name the captured jaguars after ancient Maya gods. A name for this jaguar sprang instantly to my mind as I lay in the truck thinking about it. I called him Ah Puch (pronounced Ay Pook), after the ancient Maya god of death.

Porfilio returned two days later, distraught and distant. He had already heard of Guermo's death from Indians outside of Cockscomb, and I felt he too was blaming me. It was a crushing blow. When he came back out into the field with me, it was like being with a stranger.

I sat in my house that night waiting for Porfilio to come over for our usual coffee and conversation, realizing how much his friendship and approval meant to me. He never came. By the second day in the field, I could no longer stand the tension between us. I decided that if he blamed me that much, then we shouldn't work together for a little while. After we had searched unsuccessfully for Ah Puch, he was the first to break the silence on the ride back to camp. But the words I heard were not what I'd expected.

"I must go back to San Antonio," he said, looking out the window of the truck. "My family need me."

"What happened there, Porfilio? When can you come back?"

I realized that my self-pity had made me insensitive to his problems. I wanted to comfort him, touch him, share an understanding that I knew would soon be lost forever. But I didn't, and the moment was lost.

"I no come back, Alan. I must go wit my people. You can stay, you can go, you do what you want. I must go back."

There was nothing for me to say. Certain patterns of our lives are set when we are born and we can never be truly free of them. Some people just have more choices than others. I had just held back from comforting Porfilio. I would always regret it.

The next morning I drove Porfilio to the highway to wait for the bus. We had not spoken since the previous day. I stood with him on the side of the road for a while, then shook his hand and wished him well. He stood there, a young Maya whose total possessions filled half a flour sack flung over his shoulder, going back to a life he felt trapped in. I turned the truck around and started back to Cockscomb. I looked in the rearview mirror and saw him watching the truck. Should I go back and try to stop him? Would it make a difference? Did I have a right to even try? I had no answers, so I let him go.

Porfilio was alone. I was alone. Ah Puch was waiting for me.

7 SNAKE DOCTOR

The weeks that followed were terrible. The rains were increasing in intensity, and there was no sign of Ah Puch. I couldn't hear his radio signal or find his tracks in the areas I'd followed him earlier. And it was hard to overcome the depression brought on by Guermo's death and Porfilio's departure. It was more and more difficult to go into the jungle alone. Cockscomb seemed different, the jungle more ominous.

The Indians avoided me, and even the children stopped their regular visits. I realized how much I missed the sound of their laughter. On days when I forced myself to go into the jungle, I jumped at every noise and imagined fer-de-lances beneath every clump of branches. I even began to wonder about the reality of the Master Tiger.

I started thinking how life and death are continuous acts in the tropical rain forest and equally necessary for nature's balance to be maintained. Why should my death be any different or more important? Why shouldn't protective forces have evolved within the forest that might work against me, the way our own body's internal defenses work against the intrusion of foreign matter? This vibrant rain forest was not simply a world of wonders; it was a menacing force, a world of fear, of death.

I knew I was close to an emotional crisis that needed to be dealt with if I wanted to continue the project. Under different circumstances, I could have talked to people who would understand. But in Cockscomb people lived with a completely different outlook on life. If I wanted to continue to stay in Cockscomb, I needed to change my outlook. The Indians said I had *macobe*, or the Maya blues, and all I needed was a woman. The Creoles in camp told me that the jungle wasn't made for gringos and that I'd better leave before I lost my mind completely.

I stopped going into the jungle. The heavy rains transformed the area around the camp into a swamp, and when the bridges weren't flooded, the timber road was barely passable. I thought I should leave Cockscomb for a while and go to Belize City or Mexico; but the Indians couldn't leave, so why should I?

Then I realized it was an opportunity to get to know the Maya better, so I began spending almost all my time with different families in the village. As they did with me, I just walked into their huts, sat down, and watched them go about their lives. By now they were all accustomed to my presence and I was usually treated like just another Indian come to visit.

The furnishings in the Maya's huts were sparse and very much the same. On one side of the hut, the hammocks were slung and seemed always to be occupied by the man of the house or a young child. There was usually a small hand-built table in the far corner, where the store-bought meat grinder for corn had replaced the old grinding stone of their ancestors. In the other corner, closest to the table, was usually the earthen hearth built no more than a foot off the dirt floor. Behind the hearth the woman of the house was most often found. If she was not to be found here making corn tortillas for breakfast, lunch, or dinner, she'd inevitably be at the creek doing laundry. I'd rarely stay long in a hut alone with the woman. It was not considered proper. But I often watched them go about their chores as I talked with the men.

Most of a woman's daily routine appeared to revolve around making corn tortillas. First, she soaked the corn in a lime solution overnight. The next morning she washed and ground it several times until it was a fine flour. Then she added water to it, squatted on the floor, and took a piece of the damp dough to flatten it into a tortilla, usually on a banana leaf. Then she placed a little lard on it so that it wouldn't stick, and put it onto the hot comal (a slab of sandstone used as a griddle) over the fire. When it was finished, she put it in a calabash with a cloth on top to keep it warm. The tortillas were almost always eaten warm, and there were usually fresh tortillas for every meal. The women were up first every day, before daybreak, to start the fire and prepare the morning's tortillas. They served the men first.

I became quite close to Cirillo Chun, who had already been a frequent visitor to my house. He was a handsome man of twenty-one years and, unlike Porfilio, he had no desire to break from the typical Maya way of life. Yet he showed an avid interest in learning anything that would help him deal better within his own world.

His wife, Florencia, was sixteen years old and the most beautiful Maya woman I was to see in Belize. She and their little baby Petrona quickly melted into the background whenever I came to visit. This kind of humility was common among the women, especially the older ones. Whenever I'd meet old Mrs. Bolong coming in the opposite direction along a trail, she'd turn away from me and bow her head till I passed. This practice was first reported in the sixteenth century by Fray Diego de Landa, one of the early Franciscan fathers and the second bishop of Yucatán, whose extensive writings serve as a principal source of later Maya history.

It was Cirillo I first talked to about my newly acquired fear of the forest. He laughed, his shining white teeth nearly bursting from his mouth. Then he changed the subject, talking about his milpa, his boyhood, his animals. I came to realize that this was his way of comforting me. He had some similar fears, I later learned, but they were not for discussion. Talking did not change anything. Bad events were a manifestation of evil forces, forces he explained through a strange combination of Maya mythology and Christianity.

I sat on the floor listening to Cirillo and remembered someone telling me that the modern Maya were a defeated, dispossessed, dependent people. Not all of them, I thought. Though they sometimes gave that appearance, clothed in their tattered North American garments, it was what went on in their minds that was important. There was more to them than met the eye, especially those who preferred to remain in the jungle. There was still a spark of their ancestors in these Mopan Maya of Cockscomb.

Much of my understanding of the Maya came from the works of J. Eric S. Thompson, a noted archaeologist, ethnohistorian, and ethnologist. Thompson divided the ancient Maya of Belize into three groups: the Yucatec Maya in the north, the Chan Maya in the central part, and the Manche Chol in the south. He called the central group Chan Maya, meaning "the valiant Maya," as a tribute to those who held out so long against Spanish rule and remained relatively independent. A subgroup of the Chan Maya were the Mopan. The Mopan were distinguished from other groups by geographically determined cultural features rather than linguistic features. The Maya of the coast and of the Sittee Valley in the vicinity of Cockscomb were originally Mopan.

The conquest, or "pacification," of the Mopan by the Spanish began in the seventeenth century, when Captain Díaz de Velasco of the Cortez army traveled to the Mopan area. They never completely subjugated the Mopan of Belize, whom they labeled Indios del Monte, the Indians of the Forest. Of the present-day Maya in Belize, only the Mopan are descendants of the Maya who once inhabited the country.

I spent two weeks virtually living with the Indians, and they helped me see Cockscomb from a new perspective. I also came to view them with new respect. Since the rains kept us confined to camp, they again started coming to my house. I still often ignored them and would ask them to leave, but I could feel a difference in their demeanor. They came to sit with me instead of opposite me.

There was something I felt I had to do before continuing the project. I decided I should visit a well-known snake doctor in the area, a Creole man named Saylor, and decide for myself whether there was any reason for such a firm belief by the locals in these practitioners.

Saylor lived in Sittee, a quiet little town situated where the Sittee River empties into the Caribbean Sea. When you enter the village, you are confronted by two signs. The top sign says "Front Street," with an arrow pointing to the right, and the bottom sign says "Back Street," with an arrow to the left. Saylor lived in the first house on Front Street.

He wasn't surprised to see me. In fact, he intimated that he'd been expecting me. He had heard of Guermo's death and was pleased that I had finally come to my senses and visited him. We walked to a small cleared area bordering the forest behind his house and he told me to sit on a large tree stump. He stood opposite me, looking very serious. I felt like I was back in grade school.

Saylor's appearance didn't fit the role of a snake doctor. He was a heavyset, very black man over six feet tall, and his puffy face had almost a comical appearance. His personality seemed shy, almost subservient, until he started talking about snakes. Then he became aggressive.

"I tell you dis, first ting," he started off. "If a man get bit by a tommy-goff, you no take he to de hospital. In hospitals dey chop you body. A good snake doctor, he cure you whole. But you must be careful. Some snake doctor, dey play wit de devil. Dey bad. You no want dem doctor. If dey no like you, dey make snake bite you." He paused to see if I had anything to say. I wasn't going to argue at this point. I wanted more specifics.

"How can I make sure I don't get bitten by a tommy-goff?"

"If tommy-goff want bite you, he bite you, even if you in de house. If you wear high boots, he jump over de boot or bite tru de boot. But if he no want bite you, you can nearly step on he and he no bite. But no carry de snake medicine in de bush. It make de snake vexed and he bite you for sure."

"But is there anything I can do so tommy-goff no bite me?"

"If you smoke cigar, or chew tobacco and spit when you walk in de bush, den tommy-goff no come close. He no like tobacco," Saylor told me. This was good information. I had to remember to buy cigars.

"If a man get bit by a tommy-goff, and I'm far in the bush, what can I do?" I hoped he'd tell me of a plant or tree that could be used.

"If you see tommy-goff or if tommy-goff bite someone, be very careful," he said. "Dere always a next tommy-goff close. Dem snakes, dey stay in twos. But if man get bit, you kill de snake, first ting. If de snake dead, de poison go slow. If de snake no dead, de poison, it move fast and de man dead. Make sure no woman look on de man," he said. I thought of how Jack had covered Guermo's face. "If a woman bleeding [menstruating] or she wit baby [pregnant], de man surely die. Or if de snake wit babies, de man surely dead."

I went on to question Saylor about exactly what he did if a man bitten by a fer-de-lance was brought to him. He explained how he treated the bites with an herbal broth to induce vomiting and with a poultice applied to the wound. Usually the poultice consisted of herbs, but sometimes of the snake's brains. The poultice apparently reduced the localized symptoms, such as pain and swelling at the site of the bite. Vomiting, to get the poison out, was induced in a darkened room or hut and seemed more ritualistic than therapeutic, although it may serve to calm the patient.

Nothing I could learn, from Saylor or later from other snake doctors, seemed to have any effect on the toxin itself once it was in the bloodstream. Faith in the snake doctor might be psychologically beneficial, but the bottom line was how much poison the snake injected into the body. From all accounts, the success of snake doctors, measured in the number of people that come to them after having been bitten by a snake and then survive, is incredibly high. However, I was convinced that the true explanation had to do more with the ecology of the fer-de-lance than with the skills of the snake doctor.

The fer-de-lance is a viper, a member of the Crotalidae family, which includes rattlesnakes and water moccasins. These snakes have hollow folding fangs that function like hypodermic needles when injecting poison. However, the fangs and the poison have been designed by nature only for killing animals that the snakes can eat. The venom is a complex protein-rich mixture that is energetically costly for the snake to produce. It would be wasteful and potentially detrimental for the snake to use the venom on prey it couldn't eat.

To determine potential prey while hunting at night, these snakes have a special organ in a pit between their eyes and nose that is sensitive to infrared radiation or heat given off by passing animals. If they can sense that something is not a meal, there is no reason to strike. However, if the snake feels threatened, it may strike anyway but conserve its venom. These snakes can control whether their fangs are lowered and how much venom, if any, to eject. They can even control the amount of discharge from each fang. They rarely eject the full contents of their glands. As in any good defense system, they protect themselves at minimum cost.

Someone can be bitten by a poisonous snake and not be poisoned. In fact, in up to 40 percent of poisonous snakebites, no symptoms develop. It is probably only in rare situations, such as that which occurred during our jaguar hunt, that a snake strikes with everything it has against something that it cannot eat.

I was aware of the scientific facts before visiting Saylor, but I wanted his view of the matter. Before I left, he asked me to wait about thirty minutes while he went off into the jungle to get me something special. He returned carrying a piece of root, about nine inches long, with a rough scaly bark that made it look rather like a snake.

"You take dis," he said, handing it to me with great ceremony. "Dry it in de sun for maybe a week. Den you take de bark and mash it up. Mix de powda with garlic and sweet oil. Dat good snake medicine."

"Do I drink it?" I asked. The thought was nauseating.

"Nooo." He laughed. "You put de medicine on you boots or pants. It make tommy-goff no want come close."

I thanked him profusely and he was very pleased. Then he said he had something else I should carry in case of snakebite and rushed off into the house. I expected to see a magical amulet, but he returned holding a Cutter's Snake Bite Kit.

"Dis good for snake too," he said solemnly.

At camp I repeated my conversation with Saylor to the Indians and timber crew, showing them the root. They shook their heads reverently, acting as if I had brought the word of God down from the mountain. Only Jorge claimed it was nonsense. Several days later he came by to get some of the antisnake mixture I had prepared so that he could apply it to his boots.

Despite the endless rains, I started feeling good about myself and Cockscomb again. Don Smith returned for the last time to pay off the timber crew and close down the operation. Only a skeleton crew, consisting of Nari, Tino, and Jorge, was asked to remain to watch the equipment and sell the remaining lumber. Don came by my house and I was surprised to find myself resenting his presence and considering him an intruder. He tried to make conversation, telling me some of the latest news in the United States, and I realized I didn't want to hear about what was happening in the outside world. Cockscomb had become my world.

During the first week of July, the rains stopped and the sun burst forth, drying some of the roads and the forest. It was time to resume my search for Ah Puch. Several days later, however, I still had nothing—no signals, no tracks, no evidence that he had ever existed. I explored new areas of the basin and followed sign of two other jaguars—an adult male and a female—near the entrance to the east of the camp. But I worried about Ah Puch.

It was difficult to assess what was happening, as I had no idea of the extent of his home range. He could be out of receiving range of my equipment or, given the topography of Cockscomb, he could just be in an area from which the radio signals weren't getting through. I needed to get higher in elevation, above the signal, so that the hills and vegetation wouldn't obstruct it.

The timber roads I was using were in some of the lowest-lying areas of the basin. I looked at some of the surrounding mountains and planned to set up antennas on the top of some of the more accessible ones. But for now, it seemed an aerial survey was the best alternative if I didn't locate him soon. It would be expensive, but I had to find him.

Just as I was becoming comfortable going alone into the forest again, two incidents brought my fears back. The first occurred a day after the rains let up as I was exploring a new area of the basin. I rounded a curve on the motorcycle and saw a six-foot-long fer-de-lance stretched out, sunning itself, across about two thirds of the road. I swung the bike to its right, through a three-foot space between its head and the forest edge.

As I approached the snake, its body coiled and its head came up. I sped the bike up and as I passed it, there was a blur in the corner of my eye as it leapt at the motorcycle. I lifted my legs up onto the handlebars and drove another fifty feet before stopping and looking back. There it sat, in the tracks of the bike, coiled and shaking its tail.

The second incident occurred three days later. I was looking for jaguar sign along the roads, measuring tracks and marking where different cats had traveled. I had just climbed back onto the motorcycle and started off, when my eyes focused on a large dark-colored snake coming out of the forest and crossing the road in front of me. With the previous experience still fresh in my mind, I jammed on the brakes trying to stop the bike before reaching the snake. The bike went out from under me as if I had hit an oil slick and I sailed over the handlebars.

I landed with a hard thud on my back, my legs pinning the tail of the snake briefly before it squirmed out and shot for the jungle. It was a large black snake, known locally as black tail. They can give a painful bite but are not poisonous. My heart missed a few beats. As his tail disappeared in the undergrowth, I lay my head back in the mud and looked up at the sky. A roadside hawk, disturbed by all the activity in his area, screamed and swept low over my head. I don't need this, I thought.

When Irma left with the rest of the timber crew, my dietary habits went into a nosedive. I was always too tired to cook after a day in the field, so now that I was eating alone again my evening meals involved opening a can of whatever I had on hand and eating it cold. Adriana would bring me corn tortillas every evening, and Cirillo would occasionally bring over a dish of stewed meat made from wild game they had just killed. Finally, I was saved from malnutrition when Jorge told me that, if I bought the supplies in town, he would cook chicken, flour tortillas, beans, and rice for us every evening.

Jorge was an enigma, a tough, jungle-hardened man with a past he never liked to talk about except in one of his drunken depressions. He had fought in the Vietnam War after making a deal for a United States passport, but deserted when brought up on charges of beating up an officer. He had a sharp mind and a quick tongue.

Though he liked to stay around me, he was angry because he did not have the opportunities I had in my life that he felt cheated out of. Sober, he was a calm, gentle, generous man. When he was drunk, though, his frustrations surfaced and took the form of physical aggression. He was even more angered by the fact that I was not only more educated than he, but was physically stronger too because I worked out regularly with weights. Yet, if there had ever been a reason for me to fight him, I would have tried to avoid it. Strength alone could not overcome what was brewing inside him. After a few drinks our conversation always took the same turn.

"You tink you strong, no?" he'd say to me. "I not go to college in de States and I no have money like you, but I tougher than you. We fight, you and me, see who more tough."

"You more tough, Jorge. I know that." I always tried to put him off.

"No, I not stupid. You got big muscles. You tink you tough. We fight. I try not hurt you too bad."

Finally, after putting him off repeatedly, I drank too much rum one night and agreed to an arm-wrestling match, the best of five. I won all five times and rubbed it in. Jorge didn't come around for days and I was never that foolish with him again.

Toward the end of July the rains came again and continued for a week, day and night. Creeks became rivers, and rivers, overflowing their banks, became miniature lakes. These prolonged downpours carried over into September. Again and again we'd be trapped at the camp at Guam Bank, sometimes for days at a time, until the creek at the entrance road would go down enough to allow us to drive out for supplies.

When cabin fever started setting in, I exercised for hours at a time, sometimes twice a day, just trying to relieve some of the anxiety. Jorge drank more and became more morose, sitting in my house talking to himself. My house was a refuge for a steady stream of Indians afflicted with fevers and colds, often the result of their sleeping on the bare earth. I had not a moment's privacy.

What worried me most when the timber camp closed was our lack of radio contact with the outside world. If an emergency occurred, we'd simply have to wait until the water went down and then drive to Dangriga or the nearest phone at Silk Grass, fifteen miles away. If I wanted to live like the Maya, I would have to take the chances they took.

This was made clear to me when I suddenly fell ill with severe cramps and diarrhea. I couldn't leave the house for more than a few minutes at a time, and I spent hours doubled up in agony on my bed. The Indians' reaction to my illness was simply to stay away, except for Adriana, who brought me some strange-tasting soup I never questioned.

I thought I might have amoebic dysentery. Nari had hooked up a rope and pulley system so that he, Tino, and I could continue getting our water from the timber camp's well. I foolishly hadn't been taking the time to boil it.

Within days of my illness, Tino and Nari came down with similar symptoms, and I put us all on medication for dysentery. It helped but wasn't curing us. After two weeks of suffering, one of the Indians told me he hadn't seen his dog for a long time and thought a jaguar might have come into camp and gotten it. I had a strange premonition, and a quick inspection of the well confirmed it. No one had thought to look into the well while drawing water. There, floating on the surface against the wall was a rotting dog carcass. I nearly vomited. From then on, I drank only rain water.

The prolonged rainy season in Cockscomb, generally from June through February, seemed a terrible inconvenience to me. Yet I soon saw that these rains were a key element in the survival of the Maya, who practiced slash-and-burn, or milpa, agriculture. The milpa system involved the growing of crops in small temporary clearings in the forest. The farmer was called a milpero, and his success depended on the accurate prediction of weather patterns.

Toward the middle of the dry season, late March or early April, the Indians cut down the standing vegetation with axes and machetes. After several weeks, when it has dried sufficiently, they burn the fields, and a perpetual haze hangs over the area. Sometimes the Indians wait for a strong wind, then start a fire on the windward side of the milpa. Shortly after, in May, before the weeds can take hold, they plant the corn. A feast is usually held before planting. Then the Indians make holes in the ground with a sharp, pointed stick and drop kernels of maize in them. Planting is work-intensive and done communally, most of the men getting together to help one another plant.

If the burning or planting is done too late, the rains that come leave the foliage so wet that it can't be properly burned or wash away the seeds before they take hold. If planting is done too soon, the soil is baked by the sun and the plants die. A milpa is usually used only two seasons before it is abandoned and a new clearing made. During the second season, burning doesn't take place as early as the first year because the weeds and the maize stalks dry more quickly, and if they are cut too early, more weeds will grow.

The main harvest occurs in late September and early October. In August, the Indians harvest small amounts of green corn to prepare a delicacy called *dukuno* (pronounced dukunew), or corn tamales. The Indians in Cockscomb also have a smaller second planting in November or December, with the harvest in March. There is no new burning or feasting during this time. Two kinds of corn are planted—white and yellow. The white corn is preferred for tortillas, and the yellow, for *dukuno*.

A combination of factors, including decreased soil fertility and increased growth of weeds, makes it more efficient for the Indians to cut a new milpa than remain on the old one. After a milpa is abandoned, it lies fallow until second-growth forest chokes out the shrubs and weeds, usually after seven to nine years. An average milpa in Cockscomb was about five acres.

When I asked the Maya how they knew when to cut, burn, or plant despite constant variation in weather patterns, they were amused. "We look and see what happen wit tings round us," they'd tell me.

It seemed so obvious to them. When I'd ask what those things were and how they watched them, they didn't understand what I was asking. Such things were not explainable in words. I realized that they were still in touch with the earth, as their ancestors must have been two thousand years before.

8 CIRILLO

The cultivation of corn was a major factor in the development of aboriginal civilizations in the New World. In the Maya culture, corn has always been at the center of their existence. The time of planting corn is a cause for celebration, each family holding a feast before planting. For months they fatten their domestic pigs and chickens for the occasion, or they hunt wild animals for meat. This is the one time of year when the Maya rejoice and eat to excess.

All else takes second place to the planting and harvesting of the corn. Indians working at timber operations or elsewhere simply walk off or stop coming to work in order to go to their fields. It's difficult for outsiders to understand this when the Indians can make more money by working at "real" jobs than by growing and selling their corn. But it's not a question of money. Corn is more than a food for them or a source of income —it represents a way of life, it is their reason for being.

Unfortunately, the modern Maya seem completely out of touch with the historical reasons behind many of their actions and have lost many of the traditions associated with them. Gregorio was the only Indian who admitted to me that he burned copal in his fields after planting. Copal is a resin from special trees that were cultivated by the ancient Maya. The resin was used for ceremonial purposes. Gregorio didn't know why he burned copal, just that his family had always done it. Others burned copal too, he told me, but wouldn't speak of it. No prayers, no songs, no thanks to the gods accompanied the burning as in earlier times. I wondered how much longer they would be driven by these deeply buried spiritual forces that were not yet dead, but were quickly dying. I often hoped that they would always hold on to those last threads of their culture.

In 1930, J. Eric S. Thompson, studying the Maya living to the south of Cockscomb, observed that the old prayers were retained by only a few members of the older generation. In 1984 only Jesus was God and the missionaries said he'd be angry if the Indians continued the pagan traditions, such as burning copal. If any of the old ways were still in the minds of the older Maya in Cockscomb, they kept it to themselves.

When I went on my weekly trip into Dangriga for supplies, I always ended up carrying a truckload of Indians wanting to "take a walk" or sell their produce. Sometimes I would plan to sneak out of camp, but they always had a "feeling" the day or hour before I planned to go. They'd ask if I would take them and "a few tings," which usually included sacks of corn or rice and the entire family. I had a hard time refusing them.

At first, they'd all pile into the rear of the truck and no one would sit in the front with me. I thought they were ashamed to be seen with me. Of course, the opposite was true: they believed that I'd be ashamed to be seen with them in public. When I'd invite them into a restaurant for a meal or soft drink, they'd immediately go to a separate table until I pulled them over to sit with me. Apparently the hard-working saviors of their souls, while teaching them how evil their old ways had been, neglected to instill in them a pride in themselves as people.

After dropping them off at the marketplace, I would stop at the post office, one of my last remaining contacts with the outside world. I would collect my mail, find a quiet corner in the nearest restaurant, and order a cold beer.

There was always at least one letter from Sue. Sue and I had first met while we were in school together at the University of Tennessee and continued our relationship for three years, until I left for Belize. She was a wonderful woman, but I had tried to end our relationship when I left the United States. Now, as I read her letters telling me she wanted to come to Belize, I realized how much I missed her and wanted her with me. I had thought of her often since coming to Belize. But Cockscomb was a hard life. Should I really let her come?

My next stop was always the local telephone station. Here I'd put through a call to my parents to tell them I was alive and well, or to Dr. Carr in New York to bring him up to date on the project and request that additional funds be transferred to my Belize bank account. On one trip I was calling Belize City, trying to locate a good bush pilot who would agree to fly over Cockscomb and help me find Ah Puch. I had already paid several Indians to clean up the airstrip.

After several calls, I finally located John Fuller, a native Belizean, who agreed to work with me for U.S. $100 per hour. His plane was a Cessna 172, which could cruise at fifty-five miles per hour and fly slow, tight circles, ideal for pinpointing radio signals. He agreed to fly in that afternoon. I cut short my shopping, gathered the Indians, and rushed back to Cockscomb, glad to be distracted from making a decision about Sue.

John landed at our airstrip an hour after my return to camp. I attached a small portable antenna to each strut of the airplane and hooked them up by coaxial cable to a switch box attached to my receiver. Once I'd hear the signal, I'd use the little switch box to alternately turn on and off each antenna so that I could find out which side of the airplane the signal was coming from. Then I could zero in on it. I jumped into the passenger seat, put on my headphones, and gave the thumbs-up signal.

Cockscomb from the air looked completely different and truly rugged. An unbroken expanse of undulating hills filled the basin. To the west, the hills became larger and merged with the Maya Mountain divide separating Cockscomb from the Chiquebul Forest Reserve, bordering Guatemala. I could see steep canyons with no obvious access and wondered if anyone had ever penetrated these mountains. As we circled over the northern boundary of the basin, we flew over Victoria Peak and I looked upon its sheer rock face rising from the sea of green. It took my breath away. The whole area was magnificent.

We flew low enough to see the colorful naked heads of king vultures soaring above the treetops. We continued a search pattern over the basin and surrounding area for the next hour, but there was nothing but silence. I really hadn't expected this and my mind groped for explanations. Wherever he was in the area, alive or dead, I should hear the radio signal from the air. What was happening? I could not afford to fly any longer, so I signaled John to land.

I returned to the house perplexed. My only recourse was to forget about Ah Puch for the time being. It was time to catch the other jaguars that were roaming within the basin. Bader's men refused to return to Cockscomb after Guermo's death, so I'd have to try trapping jaguars again.

I decided to drive north immediately to visit Bader in Belize City. I wanted his opinion on different trap designs, and it provided an opportunity to pick up supplies that were unavailable in Dangriga. Besides, I hadn't seen Bader since Guermo's death and wanted to know if, for any reason, Bader blamed me.

Bader and his wife, Mary Ann, welcomed my arrival with their usual warm hospitality. We spent the first few hours drinking rum and flattering each other. Then we rehashed the jaguar hunt, taking comfort in each other's perception that we had done everything possible to save Guermo's life. Bader and I talked through the night, with me rambling on about Cockscomb, Ah Puch, and jaguar conservation and him talking of jaguar behavior and his hunts. Finally, toward morning, we talked of trapping and different trap designs he'd seen.

The next day, while Bader worked on his ranch, I visited some nearby villages to check out illegal jaguar kills. This was not a formal part of my research, but I wanted to take every opportunity to learn how intensive the illegal hunting pressure was on these animals. Repeatedly I was told of a man in the small town of Maskall, situated on the old Northern Highway. He was a forty-five-year-old Creole who bragged of killing numerous jaguars and pumas in the area. When I finally located him, he was only too happy to talk to me.

Most of his kills, he said, occurred while he'd be out hunting smaller game. He'd come upon the cats sitting or lying in the road. They'd usually just stay there and watch him approach, unaware of any danger. It was easy, he said, to get close and drop them with one shot. There was no market for puma skins, so he'd leave the pumas where they died.

"But dese tiger skins, I can sell to American for maybe hundred dollar," he told me. "You want one?" We were walking toward a thatched lean-to against his shack.

I saw a beautiful seven-foot-long jaguar skin stretched between two poles.

"I cum close to dis one 'fore I kill it," he bragged. On the ground, beneath the skin, was a second jaguar skin, ripped apart and barely recognizable. He saw where I was looking.

"De dog get to dat one," he said, laughing. "You want? I sell cheap; in fact, I give you de head wit it for nutting 'cause de dog chew dat too."

He pointed under the house where his mongrel dog lay gnawing at a jaguar skull. I turned, hoping to hide the disgust on my face. Anger would do no good. The real problem went far beyond Maskall.

"No, I'm not buying skins today," I said. "Thanks anyway."
I turned and left quickly.

That evening I ranted to Bader about the hunter in Maskall.
He listened patiently, agreeing with me but explaining that
killing jaguars was simply not wrong to most people. Bader felt
the real waste was that no money was being made from these
killings because jaguar hunting was illegal. If such hunting were
legalized and controlled, he said, it might benefit everyone. I
said nothing. Bader's feelings made some sense, but I was not
convinced that such hunting could be controlled. Not as long as
there were large sums of money at stake. We had argued about
this many times. On some issues, there would always be differences of opinion between Bader and me that could never be
bridged.

Our last night together, Bader took me to a nightclub in
Orange Walk. Apart from Sue, I hadn't thought much about
female companionship because there was always too much work
occupying my mind and body. But in the club, all thoughts of
jaguars left my mind. I had forgotten what it was like to be
among so many women, and my eyes immediately fastened on
an extremely attractive Chinese-Spanish woman standing at the
bar. After a brief conversation, during which I learned her name
was Rosita, I left the bar with her, telling Bader I'd see him in
the morning.

Her little shack was on the edge of town. As we walked in the
darkness I started having second thoughts. This was not really
what I wanted, I said to myself. We reached her door and I
hesitated, but she took my hand and led me inside.

When our naked bodies came together, feelings burst forth
that I had long subdued. Passion turned to anger, then to frustration, as I made love with a ferocity I didn't know was in me.
We were worlds apart, this pretty woman and I. As her eyes
closed and her spasms carried her into her own thoughts, I
looked into the face of a stranger and became frightened. She
opened her eyes, digging her nails into my back, and I found

myself looking into the eyes of Guermo digging his nails into my arm. I lost control and the world exploded, the visions gone. When I awoke several hours later, she was caressing my chest and smiling. I felt sad and depressed.

On the drive south I tried to locate another well-known jaguar hunter named Littlejohn, who was said to have built several jaguar traps. After many inquiries, I finally found out where he'd last lived. Turning down a narrow rock-strewn path, I drove four miles through creeks and swamps before pulling up to a little hut. Ten very serious-looking Spanish men came out to greet me. Four of them held guns.

"Hi there," I said, smiling and showing both my hands, feeling a little like I was in a John Wayne movie. "I'm looking for Littlejohn, the tiger hunter."

"Dat son of a bitch, he gone," one man said vehemently. "He beat he wife till she crazy, he beat he son, make he simple, now he gone off marry a tirteen-year-old Mennonite girl. He crazy fucker."

I was at a loss for words. I explained who I was and that I was looking for an old jaguar trap he had once used. At first they didn't seem to know what I was talking about. I described what I was doing in Cockscomb in more detail and explained what the trap probably looked like. They started speaking rapidly in Spanish and were soon all laughing.

I couldn't believe it. They had heard about me on the radio. There was only one station in Belize City and they had talked about my project. Now these men seemed flattered to meet this crazy gringo. I suddenly felt everything was going to be all right. One of the men with a gun signaled me to follow and I walked behind him down the road and into the forest. I was more than a little nervous, especially when we came into an open area and he stopped.

"Dat what you want?" he asked, pointing in front of us and laughing.

I started laughing with him. At the edge of a small field of marijuana, which I pretended not to see, was a large iron-bar trap, about six feet long, three feet wide, and three feet high. On top lay a large board, used as a drying rack for the plants.

"That's what I want all right," I answered. "You think you could sell it to me?"

He shook his head in disbelief, then took out a cigarette and lit it. "You really want dat ting for trap a tiger?" he asked.

"No, I want that thing to catch plenty tiger," I replied, smiling.

"Take it, gringo. It yours for nutting." He put his fingers to his mouth and whistled. Two of his men suddenly reappeared. They had been nearby all along.

We dragged it to the side of the road, and I drove the truck over. We loaded it into the back, and I gave the men Bze$100 for their trouble. Everyone seemed happy.

I was anxious to get out of there while they were all in such a good mood, but they seemed intent on having me visit for a while. It was not often someone whose name they heard on the radio came into camp, they said. After several cups of rum, I said I must leave. They walked me to the truck.

"You no see nutting here right, gringo?" one of the men asked as I got into the truck.

"I don't even know where I am," I lied. "All I want to do is catch tiger."

He laughed and waved another man over. "You okay, gringo. Take dis," he commanded, giving me a half-filled shopping bag his friend was holding. I put it beside me and drove off. When I was out of sight of the hut, I stopped the truck and opened the bag. It was filled with marijuana. I scattered it.

Back in Cockscomb I examined the trap closely. It was built of quarter-inch-thick horizontal iron bars spaced six inches apart and welded to vertical crossbars eight inches apart. There was a rear compartment for live bait, visible but inaccessible to the jaguar. The main compartment had a clever triggering mechanism that would close the front door only when a jaguar was turning in the trap. Its entire body had to be inside the trap before the door closed. Parts of the triggering mechanism had been built of wood and were completely eaten away by insects. Some of the welding was also broken. Otherwise the trap was in good shape. Within a week, I could have it ready.

Cirillo was the first person in camp to ask about the trap, though everyone who passed by looked at it with curiosity. I wanted Cirillo to work for me but I knew I had to broach the subject carefully. He was interested in what I was doing but did not understand the reasons behind it. The Indians were not yet convinced that what I was trying to do wasn't bad.

"What dat?" he asked thrusting his bottom lip outward, a pointing gesture commonly used by these Indians.

"With that, Cirillo," I said, practicing pointing with my lips, "I catch the next tiger."

He went outside and walked around the trap. He was intrigued. I thought it might be a good opportunity to interest him in working with me. I knew that despite our friendship, the work still had to be judged acceptable by his own criteria.

"Cirillo, I need help bringing the trap into the bush after I fix it. Please help me. I pay you the same I pay Porfilio," I said.

He didn't answer immediately. "I see," he said eventually and walked back to his hut.

Three days later the trap was repaired and I found fresh feces and tracks no more than two miles outside the camp. I walked to the Maya village and found Cirillo digging out a tree stump. He called me over and seemed glad to see me.

The tree stump contained a nest of fire ants, and the insects, not happy with the destruction of their home, were literally swarming around the site. The Indians respect these ants, which can kill small animals and make people very sick from their bites.

Cirillo stopped working and pointed to the nest. "Alan, if you put you hand easy into de ant nest, dey no bite you. Try it and see."

"Cirillo, I've been in Cockscomb long enough. I know how these ants bite. They hurt bad. I'm not putting my hand into that swarm of angry ants."

A small crowd of Indians—men, women, and children—started to gather around.

"Watch, I make you believe," he said, sticking his arm gently into the nest. Then he held his arm out for nearly twenty seconds, teeming with ants up to the elbow. I watched his face closely for any change in expression. I saw none.

He brushed them off and looked at me. I had no choice. I placed my hand into the nest, then lifted it out. Within seconds the ants were biting me furiously—between my fingers, on the palm of my hand. I yelled, jumping up and down and shaking them off. My hand, throbbing from at least twenty bites, felt like I had stuck it into an open flame. I was furious.

Looking around, I saw all the Indians laughing at the joke. I looked angrily at Cirillo. His hand and arm, a mass of bites, were swelling to one and a half times their normal size. Being in pain myself, I could imagine the incredible pain Cirillo must have been in, yet his face showed nothing other than pleasure while he laughed with the rest.

Then I realized. Pain was nothing new to their lives and was probably not even felt in the same manner as my mind had been taught to experience it. They were testing me. I wanted to hit Cirillo, but I turned and went back to my house.

Cirillo followed within minutes of my return. He stood outside waiting by the trap, acting as if nothing had happened. He was ready to go to work. I thought I had started to understand the Indians but realized how little I actually knew them. Could I ever adjust to them? Then I looked out at Cirillo and the surrounding forest. This was their world, not mine. I needed their help for this project to succeed.

We took the trap into the jungle. At the site I wanted it set, Cirillo cleared an area so that the trap was placed in the forest with its entrance along the roadside. He cut large cohune leaves

and spread them around the trap to make it blend into its surroundings.

I watched Cirillo, thinking about the different purposes the
cohune palm tree served in the jungle. It is one of the common-
est and hardiest jungle trees. Its ironlike trunk makes it virtually
impossible to chop down with a machete. Its leaves are used for
thatching huts and lean-tos. Its nuts, hard as stones, serve as food
for squirrels, pacas, agoutis, and a host of other animals. The
smoke from burning cohune nuts keeps insects away.

Cirillo disappeared into the jungle after more cohune leaves.
Soon I heard him calling me. I followed his trail and found him
staring at the ground.

"See dis here?" he asked, pointing to a large three-toed track
about six inches long. "You know what dat?"

"It's a mountain cow, Cirillo. This is the first time I've seen
their tracks back here."

"Dere plenty back here. But you no see dem much. See where
it go?" he said, pointing out a well-defined trail that the mountain cow, or tapir, had made.

Though I'd heard much about this stocky, short-legged animal, I hadn't yet seen one in Cockscomb. An endangered species, Baird's tapir is the largest indigenous terrestrial mammal
in Central America. Adults can weigh as much as six hundred
pounds yet can run faster than a man through the jungle. With
a prehensile, elephantine nose they are known to feed on at least
ninety-five species of plants in Costa Rica alone, yet rarely gorge
on any single plant. Their nibbling is thought to minimize the
effects of toxins present in any single plant.

Tapirs appear to be the perfect prey for jaguars, yet I never
found evidence of them in a single jaguar feces sample. When
attacked by jaguars, tapirs often run headlong into thick jungle
brush or into a river. Their leathery skin seems unaffected by
the vegetation that usually obstructs the jaguar. I'd heard of
tapirs being killed by jaguars, but it was far more common to
hear of tapirs exhibiting claw marks on their sides, a sure sign
of an unsuccessful attack by a large cat. Unfortunately, tapirs,

like jaguars, are now only found in abundance in remote areas or in areas where hunting is restricted. They are usually shot on sight, sometimes for the meat, often because they are feared, albeit unnecessarily. Cirillo had killed two in Cockscomb while he'd been out hunting.

I asked Cirillo if he would continue working with me to help me catch tiger. He didn't answer. When we got back to camp, he got out of the truck and left.

That night Cirillo came to my house after dark. He said that the next week he would be working on his plantation, but then he could work for me for a while. I looked at Cirillo's face by the light of the kerosene lantern and felt strangely thrown back in time. His face could have been carved in stone for all the expression I could read.

Among the modern Maya, virtually nothing seems to remain of their ancestors' cultural achievements, such as their knowledge of astronomy, mathematics, and architecture. On the surface, they seem like a dead or dying culture, simply waiting to be swallowed up by the world around them. In a study of the Maya Indians of Yucatán, M. Steggerda, an anthropologist, noted in 1941:

The present day Maya although interesting, tranquil and clean do not reveal special attributes of any kind as far as intelligence is concerned. They maintain themselves as a group burdened with superstitions, pursuing ends aside from progress, allowing themselves to be led submissively, and living a conservative life.

What about you, Cirillo, with your curious mind and independent ways? I wondered. Are you an anachronism? I don't think so.

I went to my shelves and pulled out several books on Maya history. Without explaining what I was doing, I opened the books to the black-and-white pictures in the center and handed the book to Cirillo. "Look at these and tell me what you think,

Cirillo." I watched him turn the pages slowly. Every now and then he'd laugh.

"People tell me of dese tings," he said, referring to the pictures of large excavated Maya temples. "But I never see dem like such. I see small ones, still under de ground. Dey got plenty like dis." He pointed to the pictures of various artifacts.

My heart started beating faster. "Where you see these things, Cirillo?" I asked.

"I find tings back in bush sometimes," he said. "We all find tings like dat when we cut bush or we hunt. Tomorrow I show you tings. It late now. I go."

"Cirillo"—I stopped him—"people know of these things?"

He laughed. "Yes, all of we know of dese tings."

"No, Cirillo. I mean white men. Any gringo know about these things found back here?"

"We tell Mr. Smith once. But he no care. I go."

I went to Cirillo's hut the next evening. For several hours I sat with him by the cooking fire examining ancient Maya artifacts. He showed me several flint blades, a stone chisel, and an axhead made of a black stone I couldn't identify. They were beautifully crafted. Cirillo knew that these came from Indians long before him, but knew nothing of their use or how they were made.

I told him what I knew from my reading. Florencia sat sewing in the corner, Cirillo lay in his hammock, and Petrona was asleep by the door. I talked about how and why some of these old tools were made and how many years they might have lain beneath the earth before Cirillo uncovered them. When I looked into his face I thought I may have struck a chord deep within.

A week after putting the trap out, Cirillo and I went to Santa Rosa to buy another pig. The one that remained from the jaguar hunt I had given to Adriana. There were no small ones to be had this time, so we purchased one from a nearby rancher who raised them. This new pig was totally white, unlike the mottled Indian pigs, and exhibited a calm, unaggressive personality, which was a pleasant change. It was soon labeled the gringo pig by all the Indians in Cockscomb. We put him in the trap that afternoon with food and water and wiped away all traces of our tracks from the area with a cohune leaf. The trap was set.

We then proceeded into the basin for Cirillo's first introduction to tracking and data collection. Until now, only Porfilio and Jorge had seen me collect the cat feces often found along the roads. But everyone knew about the practice after seeing bags of it lying in my house for analysis. Still, Cirillo couldn't believe it when I'd suddenly slam on the brakes to the truck and say, "I smell tiger shit!"

I would swing the truck around and return the way we had just driven. There it would always be, in the middle of the road or off to the side where we hadn't seen it. I definitely had the nose for it. I'd stop the truck, jump out, and kneel by the side of the road to measure and scoop up the fresh jaguar feces into a plastic bag. There were usually four to six large pieces, each three inches long and a little over an inch in diameter.

When it was very fresh, the smell was awful. At first, Cirillo wouldn't even approach the feces. When he finally did, he couldn't stand near it or watch me handle it without spitting constantly on the ground, an action he continued throughout the entire time we worked together. It also took him a while to get used to riding with it in the truck. Even when I put it outside in the back cab, the smell was overpowering.

A corner of my house was set up for the fecal samples. When it was fresh, I set aside a portion of the sample for parasite analysis. I preserved some in formalin solution and mailed some to a laboratory in the United States. Parasites that inhabit the digestive canal and the biliary and urinary tracts produce eggs, larvae, or cysts, which leave the body of the host by way of feces or urine. Occasionally I found adult parasites in the feces. I wanted to get some idea of the parasite load of these cats in the wild. It was data that had never been collected before.

I used the remainder of the feces to determine what the cats were eating. The four other species of cats—margay, ocelot, puma, and jaguarundi—would also occasionally walk the roads and trails. Their feces were not as common and could be distinguished by their size and the tracks in the surrounding area.

I dried the feces in the sun, then carefully teased them apart to look for prey remains. After several months the Indians had brought me enough body parts in the form of hair, nails, hooves, scales, and bones from other animals in the basin for me to amass a reference collection I could use to identify remains in the feces. This bizarre collection of body parts from at least twenty different species sat in labeled jars on my shelves. This was always an item of interest for visitors to my house.

I'd collected twenty-two samples of feces so far from at least three different jaguars. Over half had armadillo scales in them. I wondered why a predator with such teeth and muscles, feared throughout Central and South America, should feed so frequently on such an animal.

One day, while crossing the last bridge leading into camp with Cirillo and another fresh fecal sample in the truck, a board gave way beneath us and the right rear tire went through the planking. The rear differential grounded on the bridge. We were almost three feet above the water and needed to lift the tire out of the hole so that the front wheels could pull us off the bridge.

I ran back to camp and returned with Tino, Nari, Jorge, and a large iron pipe. The five of us still could not move the truck. A group of Indians had converged on the scene and were standing on the bank watching. Four times we failed, and the Indians laughed louder each time. Frustrated, I ran to where they were standing and started pushing them angrily toward the truck, telling them where to stand and what to do.

Fourteen of us lifted the truck out in seconds and I drove slowly over the bridge. I wanted to thank and apologize to the Indians. It was one of Cirillo's first days in the field with me, and I was worried he might never work with me again. They were all laughing again, talking in Maya and pointing at me. I was reminded of my first day driving into Cockscomb. Then Cirillo came over and told me proudly that everyone thought I was one mean guy.

9 CHAC

My problems with the Maya were to take many forms, one of the more serious being their attitude toward the wild cats. One afternoon, when I was trying to get a few hours of sleep, Adriana came over with Agapita and Formenta in tow. At first I ignored them, hoping they'd be gone when I awoke. Just as I began drifting off, Adriana called my name and started talking about a tiger-cat, the local name for the smaller spotted cats. Now I listened, though I still feigned sleep.

"Our dog chase tiger-cat up de tree near de house," she repeated.

I jumped out of bed. "Where is it?" I asked, starting to gather my equipment.

"Ignacio shoot it. It dead; we got skin. You want see it?"

I thought this must be another joke. Her face said it wasn't. I ran out of the house to find Ignacio.

Their hut was apart from the main body of the Indian village. It stood at the edge of the forest about a hundred yards west of the timber camp. While I slept, the cat had been treed by a scrawny little Indian dog that it could have killed and eaten as a snack. Ignacio was tacking the skin to the side of their hut when I got there. I recognized it immediately as a male ocelot. When Ignacio saw me, he waved me over to see his prize.

I had brought several small radio collars with me to Belize in case I came across some of the smaller cats. I had told all the Indians that I'd pay them if in any way they helped me catch a cat alive: Bze$100 for a small cat and Bze$400 for a jaguar. It was much more than they could have sold the skins for.

"Ignacio, why'd you kill that cat?" I asked.

"My dog, he tree it, so I kill it."

"Ignacio, don't you remember I said I'd pay you a lot of money if you help me catch a cat like this?"

"Yes."

"Why didn't you come tell me?" I was starting to get frustrated.

"My dog, he tree it, you sleep. I no want wake you, so I shoot it. It no kill my chickens now."

"Was it killing your chickens?"

"No, but it want kill chicken. Tiger-cat always want kill chicken. It look pretty hanging in house, no?"

"Didn't you want a hundred dollars?"

"Yes, dat nice," he replied.

"Why didn't you come get me, wake me up?" Now I was shouting.

"The cat in de tree, it near de house, it pretty. I shoot it."

That was the end of our conversation. My anger quickly dissipated and in its place there was only frustration. Would any of my work ever mean anything? Could attitudes change before it was too late?

I rubbed my hand through the black-spotted white fur of the

ocelot, then pulled the measuring tape from my pocket. The total length of the skin was fifty inches, including the tail, which measured fifteen inches. The elongated spots almost gave the appearance of black lines in the fur. Ignacio watched me as I caressed it. He walked over, took the skin down, and handed it to me.

"You like, you take," he said, thinking it would please me. I took it, knowing it was offered as an act of friendship. He had not killed the animal to sell or keep the skin. He killed it because it was pretty and he saw little difference between live and dead beauty.

During my initial jaguar survey I had been told that I wouldn't find jaguars around Maya villages. A Creole snake doctor had said that the Maya "do someting" around their villages to keep cats away. Now I realized that that "someting" was not magic. It was killing any cat that came near. They feared these cats, yet no one to their recollection had ever been hurt by them. I learned that some Indians collected the jaguar's fat, which they would then either melt down and spread or burn in the milpa to keep other pest species away from the corn.

People serious about killing jaguars had little trouble given the cat's curiosity. I met a man south of Cockscomb, Irenayo Chinchia, who claimed to have killed over one hundred jaguars by calling them in. In his little shack he showed me a strange-looking instrument that looked like a drum. It was made from a large calabash, one end of which was covered by deerskin. A piece of banana peel hardened by beeswax hung inside the gourd, one end knotted through the deerskin. It was a jaguar caller, he told me, and could be "played" by gently rubbing two fingers down the banana peel. I had heard of such callers when I first came to Belize. It was said that an expert could simulate the calls of either sex and thus attract either males or females.

He showed me the technique and I tensed involuntarily. It was the deep, guttural grunting of a jaguar. It sounded as if one were in the room with us. He played it for several minutes, subtly changing the tonal qualities and the rate with which the sounds were made. It was too easy, I thought. I wondered if the cats had a chance.

The proper technique is important in using jaguar callers, but often a cat may come in simply out of curiosity upon hearing the sound. One man claimed to have called in and shot a jaguar by putting a bucket over his head and grunting. I was also to see callers made of plastic milk jugs and cardboard boxes. Whatever was used, it was always advisable to stay up in a tree when calling, I was told. Often, hunters said, a male jaguar will come in very angry thinking another male is in his area.

The hunting of jaguars in this fashion is well documented throughout their entire range. Such a hunt, the experience of a man who lived among the Indians of the upper Amazon in Peru, is vividly described in Bruce Lamb's *Wizard of the Upper Amazon* (1971). In that case the jaguar caller was in the form of a small earthenware jug.

> It was necessary for the caller to get above the forest canopy if his calls were to reach any distance. . . . Soon a wavering, wailing call of a wild cat floated out over the forest from our treetop caller with his jug. This weird sound made one's spine tingle and stopped every other sound for some minutes. The call was repeated intermittently for an hour or more, and as time passed the tension built up in our bodies as we perched in the low trees.
>
> Suddenly from nowhere a tremendous spotted animal was in an open spot just below us, looking up into the trees and growling. Almost in unison the bowstrings twanged from different directions.

The week after we set the trap, Cirillo didn't want to work, so I checked the trap myself every morning. I carried a cup of black coffee in one hand, while with the other I tried to negotiate the ravines. It was several days before I was able to drink more coffee than I spilled on myself.

During the first four days, no jaguars came near the trap. I started to worry. On the fifth day I pulled up in front of the trap as usual and looked out the passenger window to check on the pig. I found myself staring once again into the eyes of a jaguar.

It had rained hard during the night and the cat was covered with mud. When he saw me, he roared and lunged at the door of the trap, paws against the bars, claws extended. Mud splashed through the open window and into my face as I fell back against the steering wheel.

The trap works! was my first thought as I threw the truck into reverse and backed quickly out of sight of the jaguar. I raced back to camp to get the drugging equipment and to find Cirillo. "It works!" I yelled out loud. "The project will work!"

I sent a passing Indian boy to get Cirillo while I loaded the truck. He returned to tell me that Cirillo had gone off to his milpa. I'd have to work with the jaguar alone. I was frightened and excited. Within thirty minutes I was back at the trap. It was 6 A.M. I parked about fifty feet away, around a bend in the road. I got out of the truck and grabbed my three-foot-long jab pole with a syringe attached to one end. Ideally, all I had to do was walk up to the trap and inject the cat.

I walked through the forest to within twelve feet of the trap, then got on my hands and knees and started to crawl the rest of the distance. The jaguar, a large male, was not so easily fooled, and I saw two eyes peering at me through the cohune leaves as I reached the side of the trap. I was sweating profusely and took several deep breaths to calm myself while looking at the angry eyes peeking through the leaves.

Alexander von Humboldt, a German explorer-naturalist traveling throughout the American tropics in the early nineteenth century, found himself unexpectedly face to face with a jaguar. "No tiger had ever appeared to me so large," he had said. I had similar feelings now.

I judged the jaguar to be about a hundred and twenty pounds, so I loaded the syringe with a gram of Ketaset. I could see his footprints in the trap and knew this was one of the jaguars I'd been following east of the camp. Five inches long and nearly four and a half inches wide, the prints were the largest I'd yet seen in the area.

I got to my feet and he leaped at the bars as if they weren't there. I jumped back, nearly jabbing myself with the syringe. I looked at the pig and saw that he had turned over the water bucket and had hidden his head underneath it, his rear end facing the jaguar.

As I moved, the jaguar followed, lunging at me constantly. This was an angry jaguar. I needed to jab him in his hindquarters, but he wouldn't allow me to maneuver around him easily. Finally, I grabbed a branch and banged it on the door. As the jaguar swerved toward the noise, I pushed the syringe through the bars and injected him in the rump.

Within five minutes he was asleep and I pulled him out of the trap. His nose was scraped and bleeding from banging into the bars. I opened his mouth to examine his dentition, and his tongue licked my hand. It felt like someone was rubbing sandpaper against my skin. The upper surface of a cat's tongue has sharpened papillae, directed toward the back and used for cleaning the fur or removing remnants of flesh from bones. The jaguar's teeth were cream-colored and the tips of the canines were just barely flattened, characteristics of a mature adult. The canines in these cats serve to hold and often kill larger prey by crushing their bones. Another more sharpened pair of teeth toward the rear of the mouth, called the carnassial teeth, are adapted for cutting into the meat. These teeth are the reason cats often turn their heads sideways when feeding.

I took his measurements:

Sex—male
Age—mature adult
Total length—72 inches
Tail length—21 inches
Head circumference—22 inches
Height to shoulder—23 inches
Height to hip—22 inches
Weight—110 pounds

Although he appeared in excellent condition, there were numerous breathing holes of botfly larvae in his coat. I squeezed several out, each of them one and a half inches long, and dropped them in alcohol.

The hardest part of working on the cat alone was trying to weigh him. I fashioned a harness around his chest and attached it to a scale tied to a long pole. Jamming one end of the pole between the top bars of the trap, I pushed up on the other end until the jaguar barely cleared the ground.

I attached a radio collar around his neck and tested the signal with my receiver. He was still sleeping soundly when I treated the abrasions on his nose with antibiotic and then placed him back in the trap. I tied the door of the trap so that it was slightly ajar, about eighteen inches. I wanted him recovered enough to maneuver out the narrow opening. I packed up the equipment, went over to the side of the road, and sat down on a rock to wait.

I was covered with mud, sweat, and insect bites, which now began to itch. The cat had been walking the road during one of the heaviest rainfalls so far this season when he got trapped. I decided to name him Chac, after the ancient Maya rain god. Chac was a prominent figure in the Maya pantheon, a benevolent deity associated with creation and life. His intervention was sought more frequently by the Maya than that of all the other gods combined.

Chac tried to get to his feet, swayed, and lay back down. It was sad to see an animal like this so vulnerable. I thought of Ah Puch somewhere out in the forest, maybe close by. The sites where Ah Puch and Chac were captured were only a few miles apart. I wondered if the animals were neighbors.

An hour passed and Chac finally crawled out of the trap and started walking down the road. He was unsteady but had recovered most of his muscle coordination. He was walking toward me, his head down. Remembering his anger, I stood up, wondering how close I should let him come and what I could do anyway if I decided he was too close. My boots scraped the rock and he stopped and looked up at me.

"Hello, Chac," I said nervously, not knowing what else to do. He turned, stumbled, and fell, then stood up and started walking away from me. I followed him down the road, staying about thirty feet behind. I wanted to keep him moving away from camp. I would not have followed so close had he not been partially drugged.

Occasionally he'd stop and look back at me. Once, I watched as he clawed at the dirt, making a scrape that I was later to find was part of a whole system of communication among these cats. Why did he do it then? I later wondered. Finally, he walked to the side of the road, rolled in the grass, and lay quietly, his eyes fuzzy with the drug but watching me as I watched him.

It was the first opportunity I had to observe jaguars make what I'd been calling beds, areas of flattened grass where they apparently rested. I'd been finding beds averaging forty inches in length and twenty-two inches in width along the roadsides where jaguars walked. These beds seemed to indicate that jaguars in Cockscomb rested mainly on the ground instead of up in trees, as they are thought to do elsewhere. Later, when I was unable to pick up the radio signals of resting jaguars, I became more certain of this. Had they been resting in trees, the radio signals should have become stronger, not weaker.

I almost started to drift off, listening to the clicking of some red-capped manakins nearby and watching the occasional group of toucans fly overhead. A noise in back of me made me jump, and I swung around. There stood Cirillo with his bicycle, the characteristic smile gone from his face. He was looking past me to where the jaguar lay. I wondered what he was thinking.

"You been there long, Cirillo?" I asked quietly.

"No, not so long," he replied, still keeping his eyes glued to the cat.

"See the radio around its neck, Cirillo?" I asked.

"I see radio," he said. "What dat for? You talk to cat with dat radio?"

I hadn't thought of it that way, but it made more sense than many other explanations. "The cat talk to me with that radio,"

I answered, glad that Cirillo was even curious about such things. "He tell me if he sleep, he tell me if he awake."

I looked back at Chac, who was now watching us both. Then I looked at Cirillo watching Chac. Two worlds so intertwined yet so foreign to each other, I thought. You're not as far apart as you think. And I'm right in the middle.

"Let's go back to camp and leave Chac alone," I said, confident that the jaguar would now be all right.

Cirillo looked at me strangely and I realized he hadn't heard the cat's new name.

"That's Chac," I said, pointing to the jaguar. "Chac, the old Maya god of rain." My finger pointed toward the sky. For an instant Cirillo's eyes followed my hand, then quickly returned to the jaguar.

"Chac," he repeated slowly, almost as if he were savoring the words. From his mouth the name sounded better than ever.

Word soon spread around camp that I could talk to the jaguars with my radios. It was not what I had originally intended them to think, but I knew that if Cirillo continued to work with me, he would eventually come to understand. For now, however, I decided to use that belief for my own ends.

10 ITZAMNA

Four days later Cirillo and I went looking for
Chac. We spent several days scouting the surrounding ridges for
high, accessible areas to radio-track from. I had brought six large
antennas to Belize, each six feet long, with five receiving elements. They could pick up signals more efficiently than the
portable three-element antennas I carried around, but, unlike
the smaller antennas, they had to be permanently mounted. I
had held off unpacking these until I was sure we'd catch more
jaguars. I no longer had doubts.

One particular peak, called the Outlier, rose almost fifteen
hundred feet above the basin floor. Cirillo said he could get me
to the top despite the mountain's sheer granite cliffs. He had
never been up there before, but it looked like a good place, he
said, to "take a walk."

We drove six miles west of camp when Cirillo suddenly told me to pull over. He jumped out and disappeared, and I could hear him chopping into the forest. I assumed this was where we should start. He was constantly to amaze me with his sense of direction in a jungle where it's sometimes difficult to see the trees through the lianas and epiphytes. I remembered that J. Eric Thompson had noted that the "Maya have an uncanny knack of locating any such feature in what seems to a gringo a thousand square miles of monotonous forest where the only difference is between high ground and swamp." It was true.

It took us two and a half hours to reach the top. Half of the climb was on slopes so steep we had to grab roots or shrubs to pull ourselves up. I could tell we were gaining in elevation when the soil became rocky, and the trees, elfin. When we came out onto the first series of rock ledges overlooking the basin, the pain of the climb was forgotten. It was a spectacular view, better than flying over the area because we had worked hard to get up here amid all the greenery. We climbed the last hundred feet to the top and sat against a boulder, drinking in the air and scenery.

I could have been on the top of one the highest mountains in the world, I felt so isolated and peaceful. I saw jungle as far as the eye could see. It was my first intimation of what the earliest explorers of Cockscomb must have felt. During one expedition, in 1928, two British forestry officers, J. N. Oliphant and D. Stevenson, noted how the ridge vegetation created an eerie effect, like an illustration for a fairy tale, making it easy to understand the legends concerning "the Cockscombs of Duendes and Sessimites." Later, the noted zoologist Ivan Sanderson, traveling through the area in the 1930s, called it "terra incognita": "The summits of tropical mountains are always mysteriously intriguing places. There is about them a quietness and purity occasioned by the rarefied air. . . . You almost expect to see little gnome-like faces peering at you from behind the boles of the trees. Sometimes you do see them."

I hooked up the portable antenna to the receiver and tuned into Chac's frequency, pointing the front of the antenna toward the basin. There it was, the unmistakable beeping of his collar, loud and clear. It was a fast pulse: active. The quality of the signal was changing, alternating between loud and soft. He was moving. I looked down into the green sea of vegetation and pictured Chac slowly walking through the underbrush. Perhaps he was on the trail of a herd of peccaries, or perhaps he had just eaten a paca and was looking for a place to rest. It was 9 A.M.

I put the headphones on Cirillo and watched his face light up. I explained that the jaguar was telling me what he was doing by the change in beeps. He seemed to understand.

I thought I might as well try Ah Puch while up here and started to alter the frequency dial when my hand froze. It was Ah Puch I was listening to, not Chac. I had been trying to find Ah Puch for so long that I automatically tuned into his frequency. I couldn't believe it. He was out there, he was back! "It's Ah Puch, Cirillo!" I yelled. But where the hell had he been?

The strongest signal was coming from the direction of a creek that crossed the timber road, no more than five miles west of camp. Although I knew he was within a certain area, I needed a second reading from some other point to get an accurate fix and thus determine his exact location. I looked down into the area where we could hear him moving. I had been through there dozens of times listening for him. Where had he been?

Switching to Chac's frequency, I picked up his signal immediately. The pulse rate was slow, with no change in signal quality. He was resting. Moving the antenna in a complete circle I keyed in on the strongest-sounding signal for each cat and took compass readings. At least I knew their general areas and could search again once we got back to the road.

On our way down, Cirillo wanted to follow a different route, and I wasn't sure why. Walking quickly through the forest, Cirillo stopped using his machete to clear a trail. He started marking his trail by breaking a twig here, notching a tree there, or, to indicate a change of direction, cutting small branches. I said nothing at first, concentrating on keeping track of his marks.

I soon found myself alone and disoriented. I floundered for a while. I began cutting a new trail, then realized I had no idea where I was going. Tired and frustrated, I yelled for Cirillo. He stepped from behind a tree not twenty feet in back of me, smiling and silent. I knew my anger would only amuse him more, so I held it in check.

He played the same game with me several more times on the way to the truck, and each time I'd have to call for him. He was to do this countless times during our first months together, especially when he was annoyed with me. I became better at following his trail, but he could always lose me when he wanted. By the time we reached the truck, Cirillo was in great humor and I felt like taking my machete to his head. I laughed, but it took a while before my laughter was real.

I attached a whip antenna to the roof of the truck so we could listen for signals while driving. Now that I had two cats with collars and the hope of several more, I decided to plant a seed in the minds of the Indians to protect my jaguars and my research. The incident with Ignacio was still fresh in my mind.

Driving along the road with the receiver and headphones attached, I heard nothing but static. I pretended otherwise. At first I started to laugh, then to talk to myself. Then I started rapidly turning a knob back and forth that did nothing but change the volume of the static. I took off the headphones and told Cirillo that the jaguars were telling me in beeps where they were and that they had seen us on top of the mountain. I was telling them, by turning the knob and sending beeps back to their radio, that we were looking for them. Cirillo said nothing.

Soon I actually heard the signals of both jaguars within a mile and a half of each other along the road. I stopped the truck several times and hooked up the directional antenna, taking compass readings of the strongest signal. I took out a map and plotted the compass readings showing the directions of the strongest radio signals to see if they crossed or if I'd have to continue taking readings from other places. After a few stops, I had my first locations of the two male jaguars.

I continued to act as if the radios were controlled by the jaguars and I could send information back to them. As we pulled into camp, I told Cirillo that he must tell the Indians that they could not hurt the jaguars anymore in Cockscomb. I said that the jaguars with radios would tell me if anyone shot at or injured them. They would also tell me if any jaguars without radios were shot. I could see that Cirillo wasn't sure whether to believe me or not. That was all I wanted. I had additional plans to convince him.

After the capture of Chac, I moved the trap two and a half miles west of Chac's capture site into an area where there were tracks from another jaguar. It was sometimes hard to differentiate between the tracks of different male jaguars, but this new set of tracks had one toe that was crooked and proportionally smaller than the others. A set of small tracks where Chac was captured, different from the tracks I'd noted on the entrance road, east of camp, also told me there was at least one female jaguar in the area. It could not be a subadult male here. Only a female would occupy the same area as another male.

Before setting the trap again, Jorge helped me attach hardwood boards around the walls and floor of the trap. I hoped this would prevent the next captured jaguar from banging himself against the bars and might allow us to approach the trap unseen. Then we put the gringo pig, who had recovered from the trauma of angry Chac's capture, back to work enticing a new jaguar into the trap.

I returned with Cirillo to Sittee, where there was a large patch of bamboo, some nearly sixty feet tall, by the river's edge on Front Street. The weight and flexibility of bamboo made them ideal antenna masts. I wanted to bring several back to camp and start constructing permanent radio-tracking sites. The first would be erected against the side of my house, from which I hoped to occasionally hear Chac and, possibly, Ah Puch.

I ran into "Dr." Saylor and told him that I had made a batch of the snake medicine and had already used it on my boots in the jungle. He was pleased. I didn't tell him that I had stopped using it because the smell of garlic kept people as well as fer-de-lances away from me.

While Cirillo and I were cutting some bamboo, a well-known hunter I knew from Sittee walked over and stood to one side, watching us. Finally, during a break in our work, he approached me. He said he had been hunting along the entrance road into Cockscomb the night before when two large green eyes appeared in the light of his flashlight. He fired into the darkness, thinking it was a brocket deer. When he went into the bush after it, he saw that it was a little tiger-cat.

I started cutting the bamboo again, thinking what to say to this man who had probably killed an ocelot in my study area. But he went on. "I know you get vexed when people kill tiger or tiger-cat. And I hear you maybe pay for tiger. Dis tiger-cat, she very little but have big green eyes like tiger. Maybe you want she?"

I stopped working and looked at him. There was something more here than I had thought.

"How big is this cat?" I asked. When he held apart his hands to indicate the size, I knew there was only one cat he could be describing, a margay, the smallest spotted cat in Belize. I had never seen one in the wild, and virtually nothing was known of their behavior.

"The cat dead?" I asked.

"No. She no dead. She hurt, I tink, but maybe you still catch she."

"You show me where you see it?"

"I show you," he said. "She run under a log and I go 'way. I no want kill she because I know you no like it."

We loaded up the truck and raced back to camp. After dropping the bamboo off, I collected the drugging equipment in case we found the cat alive. Halfway back out the entrance road, the hunter indicated I should pull over. A trail marked where he had cut into the bush.

We walked in about twenty yards before he pointed to a narrow space beneath a fallen tree. I peered in with a flashlight and was greeted by two large eyes and shining white teeth hissing back at me. It was a margay, and it was definitely alive. I backed away and loaded the blowgun without attaching the air pistol. I was close enough to use my mouth to propel the dart. I handed Cirillo the flashlight, and he shined it beneath the tree. When I saw the cat's body, I shot the dart into its hindquarters.

Suddenly, my mind registered another sound in the underbrush. It was the sound of a twig tapping quickly against the forest floor. Cirillo and I jumped back simultaneously, backing quickly down the trail. There was no mistaking that sound. It was a fer-de-lance, telling us we had come too close and had only seconds to back off. We knew where the sound was coming from, but the undergrowth was too thick to see anything. Cirillo looked at me. I knew he wanted to leave, but he would do whatever I said. We had to stay. I had to get that margay, but right now the snake was between us and the cat.

We rushed back to camp for help. Jorge, Tino, Nari, Martin, and Cirillo all returned with me carrying their long machetes. They insisted I give them the snake medicine to rub on their legs before they went into the jungle. Nari also brought a cigar to smoke while near the snake. We formed a wide semicircle around the fallen tree and started chopping inward. I thought of Saylor's words to me about how a snake either wanted you or didn't want you. I hoped this snake didn't want any of us.

I wondered what was most frightening to the snake—the overpowering smell of garlic, the cloud of cigar smoke, or six men chopping with frantic terror. Whatever it was, the fer-de-lance beat a hasty retreat. Jorge pulled the now-sleeping margay from beneath the tree. It was a male.

Many people who have spent years in the forest have never seen a wild margay. Those who have often don't even know what they are looking at. These cats are usually mistaken for ocelots and the Indians don't differentiate a third species of spotted cat in the jungle.

As everyone stood around in awe, I showed them how the margay was more slimly built, stood higher on its legs, and had a relatively longer tail than the ocelot. Then I saw the bullet wound in the head. The cat had been injured by the shotgun blast of the hunter but still seemed in good condition. I decided to bring him to camp for observation before putting a collar on him.

Back at my house I laid the margay on the floor and looked him over carefully while taking measurements:

Sex—male
Age—possibly young adult
Total length—40 inches
Tail length—14 inches
Head circumference—9 inches
Height at shoulder—11 inches
Height at hip—12 inches
Weight—9 pounds

His half-inch canines were white and showed very little wear. His teeth and coat were in excellent condition. There were no external parasites.

I put the margay in a cage I had brought down for capturing small cats. While he was under sedation, the entire Indian community came by to look at him. I even convinced some of the women to stroke his fur. I wanted them to see that these wild animals were not inherently bad.

When he started to awaken, I chased everyone away and put the cage in the back room, covered with a blanket. I wanted to hold him for twenty-four hours before releasing him. I had found only a single hole from a BB in his scalp but could not feel the BB beneath the fur. This might be a bad sign, I thought. The pellet might have gone through the skull into the brain. In any case, there was nothing I could do now but clean the wound.

The margay cried through the night and drank some milk I left in the cage. By morning, he seemed fully recovered but not at all pleased with his surroundings. Whenever I tried to come close, he'd slam himself back and forth against the trap. His behavior made me decide that, despite the injury, it was worth putting a radio on him. I calmed him with Valium and attached one of the smaller radios around his neck.

That night I released him at the capture site. Back at camp I could hear his signal, loud and clear, from the newly erected mast antenna outside my shack. I named him Kan, after the god of corn. Like corn, Kan was believed to have had many enemies. His destiny was controlled by the gods of rain, wind, drought, famine, and death. He was a benevolent deity, a god of life, prosperity, and abundance.

The day after I released Kan, I captured a new jaguar. It was another adult male, larger than the previous two. This time, however, the sedation didn't go well.

Upon first seeing the jaguar in the trap, I felt something was wrong. His coat seemed dull and his eyes lacked the fire of Chac and Ah Puch. Despite an adequate amount of drug, he would not go under. Instead, he seemed to fight the drug's effects, shaking his head against the drowsiness and trying to remain on his feet despite the loss of muscle coordination. I administered additional Valium to calm him down, and finally, after twenty minutes, he succumbed to sleep.

> *Sex—male*
> *Age—mature adult*
> *Total length—79 inches*
> *Tail length—21 inches*
> *Head circumference—21 inches*
> *Height at shoulder—21 inches*
> *Height at hip—24 inches*
> *Weight—117 pounds*

His sparse fur was covered with numerous ticks and botfly breathing holes. His canines were more worn than those of the previous two jaguars, and though still classified as a mature adult, he appeared to be at least eight years old.

Despite a dull, weary look in his eyes, his body had the hard, firm musculature I had been seeing on these males. He had torn the wooden walls to pieces and then bent seven of the horizontal iron bars that made up the walls and door of the trap. At least two of the bars were bent at one-hundred-twenty-degree angles, presumably from pulling them with his jaws in an effort to break out.

He reminded me of an old king, and while I was attaching the radio to him, I decided to use a name I'd been saving for a special jaguar. I called him Itzamna, after the lord of the heavens, the most important Maya god, usually represented as an old man with toothless jaws and sunken cheeks. Said to be the first priest and inventor of writing, Itzamna dated back to the beginnings of Maya history and probably was always at the head of the pantheon. A benevolent deity, he was known as a friend of man.

After testing the radio, I put Itzamna back into the trap and left the door partially open. This time I didn't care to watch the jaguar wake up. I knew he'd recover without incident and I wanted to remember him as I saw him now, a sleeping king.

All the three adult male jaguars—scar-faced Ah Puch, angry Chac, and old Itzamna—were captured along the timber road within a five-mile radius west of Guam Bank. This seemed curious, since male jaguars were thought to be somewhat territorial, with relatively large ranges. Virtually all the feces I'd collected so far had also come from this same stretch of road. Something interesting was going on and I needed to follow these cats closely if I was to find out what it was. How many other cats were in this same area?

John Fuller agreed to fly into Cockscomb in two days. Aerial radio tracking should give me locations on all the collared animals simultaneously, something that would be very difficult to achieve on the ground. This would give me information on how close the male jaguars stayed to one another. I hoped to fly at least once a week, as long as I could afford it.

While I was waiting for the plane, Cirillo came with me on a twenty-four-hour radio-tracking session from the top of the Outlier. It was August and we were in the midst of a dry period between rains, called the *mawger* season by the Indians. It was a good time to get work done.

Rains and shifting cloud cover affected the radio signals, and it was tempting fate to hold an antenna during one of the many electrical storms that often accompanied the rains. All the permanent mast antennas that I set up were attached to lightning arresters. But during this short dry period, the roads were more passable, so I collected more data, Jorge drank less, the Indians didn't come to my house as much, and sickness declined. Life was fairly pleasant.

I gave Adriana and her family free reign of my house while I was away. Anticipating Cirillo's games in the jungle, I made his pack at least twice as heavy as my own, without his knowledge. It had no effect on his speed up the mountain, though he seemed to stop and wait for me more often. Anyone who thinks that the Maya are lazy should spend some time with them in the forest.

At the first rock ledge I listened for the cats. Chac was in the vicinity of camp; Ah Puch was forty degrees east of him. Both were resting. There were no signals from Kan or Itzamna. It was 1 P.M. Cirillo munched on corn tortillas, the only food he brought for the next two days. I opened a can of Vienna sausages, and we shared our fare.

While working with the Indians I had learned that they had no set times for eating. They would stop along the trail and eat their tortillas when the urge struck. Sometimes Cirillo would stop two or three times within several hours, clear a space, put his machete down, and inform me that he was hungry. At other times he might go all day and never touch food or water. Eating for Indians was an activity in response to the body's needs rather than to a timetable.

As the sun went down at 6 P.M., Chac turned active but stayed in the same area. By 8 P.M., Ah Puch and Kan became active. All three cats were on the move, presumably off on their night's hunting. I could not pick up Itzamna. The cool night air and the radio signals revitalized my tired body. I took readings of the cats' activities every fifteen minutes and compass bearings of their locations once an hour.

Margays are thought to be relatively arboreal, preying upon birds, small to medium-sized mammals, and some reptiles. Sometimes Kan's signal changed rapidly, and I imagined him walking along a creek or forest edge, moving to some other part of his range, hunting along the way. Other times, I picked up a loud, active signal hardly varying in intensity. I had tested these small collars and knew that such a loud signal could only be coming from up in a tree. Maybe he was stalking some unwary prey.

The night passed quickly. At 3 A.M., the jungle below me was dark and silent. All the cats were inactive and Cirillo was asleep in a hammock fifteen feet away. I owned the world. I thought back to the night with Porfilio and wondered how he was. Did he ever think of me? It seemed so long ago now. I looked back over the basin bathed in moonlight. It was a land of contradictions.

During the 1888 Goldsworthy expedition to Cockscomb, a member of the party wrote: "I feel sure there is a prosperous future for British Honduras." In a 1972 *National Geographic* article about Belize, the country was described as "one of emptiness —a land untended, overgrown, unutterably lonely." I looked out now over some of the same areas in 1983 and little had changed in nearly a century. That feeling of timelessness was part of its beauty.

The cats became active again just before sunrise. Kan became inactive as soon as the sun came up, while Chac and Ah Puch remained active, though not traveling, until about 9 A.M. Throughout the day all the cats were primarily inactive, though the jaguars showed occasional signs of movement. All of the jaguar sightings in the basin so far had been of cats walking during the daytime.

In the course of the study it became obvious that the activity patterns of individual jaguars could vary greatly, both daily and seasonally. Though they could be found active any time during a twenty-four-hour period, the jaguars were predominantly nocturnal, usually traveling just after sunset. They showed intermittent periods of traveling throughout the night and rested most during midday. Overall, the male jaguars were active nearly 60 percent of the time.

I followed the margay for twenty consecutive hours and obtained forty activity readings. This was the first data of its kind ever on a wild margay. From 9 P.M. one day until 5 P.M. the following day, the margay was active only 35 percent of the time. He rested mainly during the day, between sunrise, at 6 A.M., and sunset, at 6 P.M. All of his activity occurred during the night hours.

It was a very busy two days, but I obtained a lot of data. Soon after we had returned to camp, John flew in and we went looking for the cats again. Ah Puch was one and a half miles away from Chac, who was now just to the east of our camp. The two males were obviously neighbors. I could hear Itzamna now. He was near the southern extremity of the basin. His transmitter had probably been out of range from the Outlier. Kan was a mile from where he'd been captured, probably along a creek that paralleled the entrance road.

I decided to reopen the jaguar trap at the location where I had captured Itzamna. I was hoping that the collared jaguars would not readily walk back into a trap after experiencing the trauma of capture. The crooked-toed male and at least one female were still in the area. I wanted to catch them, especially the female. The gringo pig, now a veteran of two jaguars, seemed well adjusted. His head had not been under the bucket when Itzamna was in the trap, and he had gained five pounds since I'd acquired him.

A few days later I was telling Adriana about how I was now trying to catch a female jaguar, when she told me that Ignacio's brother at Maya Center had recently killed a "she-tiger" along the entrance road to Cockscomb. The innocence with which she related the story indicated that the Maya still had no conception of what I was trying to do. There was still no distinction in their minds between my capturing them alive and their killing them.

I raced to Maya Center with Adriana in tow and went straight to her brother-in-law's house. He wasn't at home, but Adriana took me inside. Beams of light penetrating the wooden slats of the walls fell on the rosettes of a stretched jaguar skin tacked on the wall. It was a female, eighty inches long. I knew it was the female whose tracks I had followed earlier along the entrance road.

When I later spoke to the man who killed her, he told me more bad news. A kitten had run off into the woods when its mother was shot. I knew how slim the chances of its survival were. Two jaguars dead from one shot. This female had been killed within what appeared to be Chac's area. The kitten was probably his. The man looked at me with complete innocence.

"You no kill more tigers, you hear?" I said to him wearily. He nodded.

"My tiger with radio tell me of this anyway. I vexed bad. You no do this again," I repeated. "Why you shoot she anyway?"

"She walk on de road in front of me when I hunt armadillo. I get fright. I no shoot tiger again." He seemed upset by my disapproval. I shook his hand. I had no idea if anything really changed as a result of the encounter, but what else was there for me to do?

Back at camp I went right for the weights and worked out until I was exhausted. It was my only outlet for frustration. Then I started questioning people in camp about any cats killed before I'd arrived. It was something I hadn't even thought about until now. What I found out shocked me.

Compiling independent reports from Tino, Nari, and Jorge, I learned that during the last four years of the timber-camp operation, nine jaguars—six males and three of unknown sex—as well as two pumas and three ocelots had been killed by timber workers or Indians in Cockscomb. This latest killing made jaguar number ten. Jorge told me that one of the pumas was killed by Cirillo the year before.

When I later extended the survey to Kendall, a small village just outside Cockscomb, I was devastated. Four jaguars, one puma, four ocelots, and one margay had been killed there within the last year. No one had thought to tell me anything of these killings until I had asked about them.

I questioned people carefully because I knew some people called large male ocelots white tigers, thinking they were a lighter, more aggressive version of the jaguar. And the Indians found it difficult to differentiate between an animal's being killed last month, last year, and three years ago. Past and future were not distinguishable categories. Yet whatever the accuracy of some of the reports, I felt that the numbers were gross underestimates of the true situation. It was likely that many killings were not widely known and that I was not always talking to the right people.

Suddenly I was frightened. Was there still a chance to save these animals, even in relatively untouched areas like this? Or was I simply playing "a rich man's game," as many of these people thought? Would they kill my radio-collared animals even before I could find out enough to protect them? I started working harder and longer hours to capture more animals and to track the ones I had collared. It was also time to further perpetuate the rumor I had started about talking with my animals.

A week after I had tracked Kan from the Outlier, his signal was inactive for over twenty-four hours at a point nearly four miles from where he'd been captured. I feared the worst. I asked Cirillo and Gregorio to come with me into the bush. I told them Kan had been telling me with the radio that he was sick and getting weaker. Now he had stopped talking to me, but I had already learned where he was. They said nothing.

Using the direction of the strongest signal, I found Kan. His partly decomposed body lay by the bank of a creek. There had been heavy flooding in the area for three days and I couldn't tell if his death was at all related to that. I peeled away the fur on his head to reveal the skull. It showed what I had suspected. The BB had penetrated into the brain.

I packed the remains into my pack and looked at Cirillo and Gregorio. They both stood quietly to one side, Cirillo's face set in a grim expression. I knew they wouldn't tell me what they were thinking. All I wanted was to plant a question in their minds. They had seen me walk right to the dead cat. How had I done that? I now hoped that the story of this incident would spread to others in Cockscomb and Maya Center and, hopefully, beyond.

11 SUE

At the beginning of my jaguar project, I agreed to make a monthly telephone call to Sharon Matola, a friend in Belize City who had helped the government establish the country's first zoo. This was to assure everyone in the outside world that I was alive and well. About this time, as I became fully immersed in trapping cats and in the activities of Cockscomb, I forgot about calling. She didn't. One day, while I was out searching for my jaguars, a British helicopter swept low over Guam Bank. Thinking they were planning maneuvers in the area, I raced back to camp just as the aircraft was landing on the runway.

As I pulled up alongside the helicopter, four paratroopers in full jungle combat gear jumped out.

"What do you want?" I asked abruptly of the man who appeared to be in charge.

"We're looking for Dr. Alan Rabinowitz," he replied. "We were told he might be lost back here in the jungle. We came to find him."

I knew immediately Sharon had been at work.

"I'm Dr. Rabinowitz," I said, laughing, "and obviously I'm not lost, at least not in the jungle."

They looked at me with disbelief that quickly turned to annoyance. Then it occurred to me how I must look. They came searching for a scientist and found someone in torn jeans and a shirt that had been worn for three days and smelled like five days, a man with unkempt hair and a two-week growth of beard.

So much had been going on that it was seven weeks since I'd last left Cockscomb and contacted Sharon. I should have known better. I had run out of food a week before but had been eating armadillo and corn tortillas with the Indians. I was so involved in my work that I gave no thought to anything else.

The soldiers followed me back to the house. They told me that their orders to search for me had come from high up in the chain of command. Sharon had more influence than I realized. They thought they'd be pulling a body out of the jungle, and I could tell they were a little disappointed. I felt almost apologetic for not being lost or dead.

I started telling them about my jaguars, the Indians, and why I'd forgotten to phone Sharon. I suddenly realized I was babbling, speaking partly in broken English, jumping from one thing to the next, asking them questions and not giving them a chance to answer. I stopped talking. Silence hung between us and I could see they were uncomfortable in my presence. Less than half an hour later, I walked them back to their helicopter, where a crowd of Indians had gathered to admire this powerful machine. They had never seen a helicopter up close before.

When it left, I felt despondent. The next day, after checking the trap, I drove to Dangriga. I needed to stock up on supplies, and I also needed to get to a phone. I decided to ask Sue to come down.

At the post office a two-week-old telegram was waiting for me. It read: "Either Belize or Alaska. Need to hear from you in three days. Then I leave for Alaska. Sue." My deadline had passed a week ago. Maybe it was too late. I left the post office and drove immediately to the telephone station. Along the way I was surprised by the number of people "hailing" me. Word of the jaguar captures and, unfortunately, of Guermo's death had spread. Few people knew me by name. Instead, the most common greeting was "Hey, tiger man," or *"Yo, el hombre tigre."* I knew that none of them really understood the meaning of what I was doing. But they all thought I was one helluva guy.

I dialed the only number I had for Sue. It rang eight times. I held my breath.

"Hello?" It was Sue. I let out my breath.

"It's me, Sue." There was silence on the other end. I continued, "I just got your telegram. I haven't been to town for weeks. I didn't think you'd still be there. I miss you, Sue. I'd like to see you, if you still want to come. We can give it a try."

"I was planning to leave for Alaska in two days," she said. "I would've been gone by now but, knowing you, I decided to wait a little while longer. I'd finally given up." There was a pause. I didn't know what it meant. "I miss you too," she said quietly. "I still want to come see you." I could hear her holding back tears.

We made arrangements for another phone call so that I could find out the details of her arrival. I asked her to come in no less than three weeks' time so I could continue uninterrupted trapping. She agreed.

"Sue, be prepared for a different way of life here," I said.

She said she was, but later she told me that she never could have imagined just how different a life it would be.

Two Carib boys that day tried to sell me canines from a jaguar they'd killed. It was not uncommon for people to be seen wearing these as ornaments around their neck. I didn't doubt that this behavior stemmed from the basic belief that to possess a part of something more powerful than oneself imbues one with some of its power. Jaguar teeth and claws were prized trophies among some of the Amazon Indian tribes. They sometimes collected jaguar blood after a kill to anoint a newborn of the village, thinking it would impart hunting prowess and leadership abilities later in life.

For a week no jaguars came near the trap and I wasn't picking up radio signals from any of the collared animals. When John finally flew down and we conducted an aerial search, all the cats were located in areas where I should have heard them with my receiver. The terrain was so irregular that the signals were unable to travel even short distances. Radio tracking from the Outlier was one solution to the problem, but it was too rough a climb to do every day. I decided to erect another mast antenna, on a ridge to the south of Guam Bank. Though half the elevation of the Outlier, it was only a thirty-minute walk and should allow me to pick up the signals of any cats moving through the eastern section of the basin. What I really needed was a network of high antennas that would enable me to pick up any signals whenever I wanted. There were no other easily accessible ridges, but there were several tall trees, some over a hundred feet, still standing near the timber road. We could set up the antennas high in the trees. I told Cirillo my idea; he smiled and said nothing. I took that as a good sign.

Our first problem was how to get safely to the top of these trees. The vegetation was too dense to easily sling ropes over large limbs, a technique used elsewhere, so I decided to try building a ladder up the trunk. For our first attempt we chose a tall banak tree located where both Chac and Ah Puch traveled. Securing three-foot-long hardwood slabs with five-inch nails, we started climbing.

The first sixty feet were easy, but then Cirillo and I started getting nervous. We were secured by a rope wrapped around our waists and the tree trunk, but we had to keep the rope taut by leaning back. If the rope became loose, we could slide down the tree. Hammering the nails with our arms above our head while leaning back into space was not exactly the safest thing in the world. But I insisted we keep climbing. All we had to do was get to the top once. Then I could fasten a rope to one of the large limbs that would keep us secured on subsequent climbs.

By ninety feet, I was terrified. We had already had two close calls. The first was when Cirillo disturbed a nest of bees under the bark of the tree. Caught off guard, he started flailing his arms and nearly lost his balance. The second occurred when half of a wooden step broke beneath my feet. I reacted instinctively by hugging the tree, which rendered the rope around my waist useless. Almost immediately I started losing my grip and sliding down the tree, but the rope caught on the step below and stopped me. We continued to inch our way upward and finally made it to the top.

After all that, we found that we still couldn't hear the cats' signals from the treetop any more often than from various locations on the road. Obviously we weren't going to go through the same exercise on dozens of trees in the area. I tried radio tracking from the top of the banak tree for a while anyway, but found my time was better spent on the ground.

The Indians couldn't help me for two weeks while they harvested their corn crop. This was to be their major source of food for the coming year, though they planted other crops as well. Most of the Indians had small patches of beans and rice, and everyone had a piece of land near their huts under permanent cultivation for things such as plantain, chili, or cacao. This was in stark contrast to their ancestors, who, when first encountered by the Spanish, were cultivating beans, squash, sweet potatoes, cacao, cassava, chaya, chili, native tomatoes, and maize as well as such wild fruits as papaya, avocado, and guava. They had also grown tobacco for smoking, gourds for making containers, and henequen for weaving coarse cloth.

It was the domestication of maize that allowed the early creation of large agricultural complexes. However, some think it might have been the later domestication of beans, as a major protein source, that helped stimulate the blossoming of the Maya civilization. The diet of the modern Maya appears meager in comparison to that of their ancestors, but it still utilizes these two food sources, which seem to adequately meet their nutritional needs.

While waiting for the end of the corn harvest, I decided to start building a second jaguar trap to enable me to cover more ground. For the first time, I had discovered the tracks of a female jaguar near the trap, but she seemed reluctant to enter it. How different from the male jaguars. I decided to wait this cat out while going after another. For two weeks I worked alone, radio-tracking the cats and looking for new sign.

By the second week, I felt something was wrong with the old king, Itzamna. For three days he remained in the same location, and his radio was always in the inactive mode, day and night. I remembered my last view of him and the strange feeling I had about the look in his eyes. Maybe the collar came off somehow, I thought, knowing that the chances of that were slim.

I called in John and we obtained an aerial location. We then buzzed the treetops to make the jaguar become active. It had worked with the collared cats before, but this time there was no change in the signal. I feared the worst. He was deep in the southern part of the basin, far from any old timber roads or trails. I wanted to find him immediately, but I needed Cirillo's help.

Cirillo agreed to leave the corn harvest for a day to help me find Itzamna. I learned later that this helped elevate my status among the other Indians because they knew Cirillo would not abandon his work without good cause. I also thought he wanted to see me find the jaguar the way I had found the margay.

I couldn't pick up Itzamna's signal on the ground, but the aerial search had given me an indication of where to look. We drove as far as possible on the timber road, then started chopping trails to higher ground. Frequently I'd hear a faint signal, but as soon as I'd try to follow it, I'd lose it. Sometimes we'd follow a signal only to find out it was a reflected sound wave originating in the opposite direction. This process of hit or miss continued for three hours, until I got a strong signal that I could zero in on.

We passed through a beautiful virgin bog between two large streams that met downriver to form South Stann Creek. A mist hung beneath the canopy, vines pulled at our arms, and a dark, sulfurous mud gripped our boots. Cirillo seemed nervous. The area was unearthly, almost evil, and it was in here that the signal was the strongest. I almost expected to see a *duende* step from behind a tree.

The signal was loud now and I knew we were close. I unhooked the antenna, and the signal was still being picked up from the two-inch-long metal connector on the receiver. The cat or the radio must be within a thirty-foot radius. My eyes scanned the trees, hoping he was alive, while Cirillo scanned the ground. He tugged at my arm and pointed, his eyes wide.

Fifteen feet away, beneath a large cohune, lay the clean, white skeleton of Itzamna, virtually all the bones in place. The radio lay undisturbed behind the skull. It looked as if the skeleton were simply asleep and upon seeing us might stand up and walk off. I shivered. Food in the rain forest does not lie untouched for long. Itzamna had been picked clean by ants, vultures, and whatever other meat eaters were in the area.

I had no idea why Itzamna had died, but I suspected natural causes. I had felt there was something wrong with him when I'd first seen him in the trap, and from the position of the skeleton, it seemed Itzamna had just lain down in a shady, comfortable place to die. It bothered me that I'd never know what went on with this animal king before his death. I knelt down and gathered up his skeleton.

On the hike back to camp my thoughts were interrupted by a rare sighting. Hearing loud raucous calls, I looked up to see fifteen to twenty scarlet macaws flying overhead. I shaded my eyes, noting how their colorful red, yellow, and blue plumage stood out in stark contrast against the sky and the forest. One of the largest neotropical parrots, these birds are considered an endangered species in Belize. They reside in areas of tall deciduous trees, usually in lowland forests, in savannas, and along watercourses, and will often abandon them when they are disturbed by man. It was a good sign for Cockscomb.

Cirillo told me that the Maya kill macaws on sight; they eat the meat and use the feathers for dusters and decorative purposes. He had not seen them in several years and was excited, but for a different reason. He wanted to return to kill them. I was not feeling very good about Itzamna's death and told Cirillo that if I ever caught the Indians killing these birds or the cats, I'd tie them up and bring them to the police. It was against the law. He laughed, but I was very serious.

Over the next few days I reconstructed Itzamna's skeleton, wiring it together to hang in front of my house. The day after I hung it, many of the children didn't come by the house as they usually did. Among some of the men I heard the words "obeah" and "evil spirits" spoken about the skeleton. Again I realized how much their attitudes had changed from those of their ancestors. Some of the ancient Maya hung animal parts, such as antlers, jawbones, and wings, in their huts as a sign of respect for the "souls" of the animals they had killed.

One morning I found the trap that was in the area of the female closed but empty. From the tracks I saw immediately it was the crooked-toe male jaguar. The wooden walls were torn to pieces, the bars were bent, and the ground was dug up where the jaguar could reach through the trap. He had pulled at the bars until, through trial and error, he had found that the door could slide up. It was the only possible way out of the trap. Once again I had underestimated the jaguars' abilities. I had never thought they could lift a heavy iron door upward. Only luck had prevented the previous jaguars from escaping.

"Damn," I said as I kicked the trap in anger. I looked at the gringo pig curled up in the corner. "This is your third jaguar," I said out loud as I saw the blood on his rear leg. I looked closer.

His tail was gone, bitten off by the jaguar. This time, when he turned his back to the cat, his tail must have gone through the grating. The jaguar had gotten a tidbit after all.

Over the weeks he'd been in the trap, the gringo pig had gotten tamer than any pig I'd bought from the Indians. He had served me well and I decided to retire him. I brought him back to camp, cleaned his wound, and set him free around the house. He became my first pet pig.

On the day of Sue's arrival, I closed the traps and arranged to have John fly me to Belize Airport to meet her. But first we had to locate the jaguars. In return for Cirillo's help with Itzamna, I offered to take him up in the airplane. At first he was unsure whether to accept, but he finally gave in to his curiosity and nervously agreed. It was the first time any Indian from Cockscomb had flown in an airplane, and the others were impressed. It helped to cement the bond between us.

It was like giving a child his first ice cream cone. I had John fly low over Cirillo's house before going deeper into the basin. Occasionally I'd turn and see Cirillo's mouth open in a smile, his face glued to the window. When I heard the signals from the cats, I let him listen and showed him how I used a switch to shift between antennas on the right and left sides of the plane. Then we'd fly smaller and smaller circles, zeroing in on the animal until I pinpointed its location. Cirillo kept expecting to see the jaguars running below us, but the forest canopy was too thick. Finally, we dropped him off at camp and went to get Sue.

Waiting for Sue's plane to land, I was both excited and frightened, wondering if I had made a mistake in letting her come. Was it loneliness that had influenced my decision? I waited like a kid on his first date, wondering how she would look and how I looked. All doubts left my mind when I saw her get off the plane. She looked so pretty, with her new hair style and despite the strain of the previous months showing in her eyes. She seemed almost a stranger to me. I felt self-conscious, wondering if she could still see into me, the way she used to do. Could she see the changes I felt inside?

That night, in a hotel room, we talked nervously, trying to become friends again before we could be lovers. It didn't take long. She told me about the months of uncertainty, first waiting for me, then resigning herself to a new life without me. Just as she had come to terms with her feelings, I had called. She then changed the subject and brought me up to date on the lives of some of our friends and described how the Smoky Mountains had last looked when everything was in bloom. I told her about the project, how I feared for the lives of my jaguars, and how I'd never understand the Indians. Then we talked about the things we had done together—the hikes, the trips—letting the good memories block out all else. We laughed and reminisced. Our touches turned to caresses, then to passionate embraces. By morning, I felt I had risen from a great depth.

Any doubts I had had about Sue's adjustment to Cockscomb vanished after the first week. Not only did she love my cluttered little house, but she accepted the Indians as if they were family. She also helped me realize how much my perception of reality had changed. By the third day she finally told me to stop treating her like a Maya woman, expecting her to do all the work and then fade into the background when no longer needed. She also pointed out that I never spoke in complete sentences anymore and that I'd fly off the handle at the slightest and strangest things. Obviously Cockscomb had affected me.

The gringo pig and I started eating better. Sue immediately took to this tailless, chubby little animal and started feeding it at the front door. Soon the pig was sleeping under the house and begging at the door, snorting and pushing at the screen. I drew the line at the pig coming into the house. He started to think he was part of the family, and Sue had to hit him over the head with the broom to keep him out. When I brought other pigs into camp to use for the traps, he'd bully them into submission and eat all their food. Then he'd come to us and want to be rubbed behind the ears.

We acquired another member of the family when Sue's heart was won over by a scrawny white Indian dog that began eating the pig's leftovers. All the dogs in camp looked the same, emaciated and covered with open breathing holes of the botfly larvae. It was not unusual to see these dogs yelping and running in circles trying to bite at some of the holes as the larvae chomped inside. When Sue first saw this bizarre scene, she said that of all the things that could happen in Cockscomb, she hoped never to get one of those larvae in her.

The dogs had perhaps the hardest life in the jungle. They had been the only domesticated animal of the ancient Maya. One type was barkless; the males were castrated and fattened on corn, to be eaten or sacrificed. Modern Maya use their dogs for hunting and for protection when working at the milpa. They believe that jaguars are extremely fond of eating dogs and will take them in preference to many other animals. I was repeatedly advised to use dogs in my traps, and one Indian, no longer wanting his dog, tied it in the forest to be eaten by a jaguar. Alfred Wallace, a British explorer and naturalist journeying through the Amazon in the nineteenth century, described how the Indians tied their dogs to trees so that the howling would bring in jaguars to be shot.

This particular dog happened to be the same young female that had greeted me on my arrival at Cockscomb. Sue started bringing her into the house while I was in the field, letting her sleep under the bed. After that it was ours to the death. Sue named her Cleo and started teaching her tricks, which greatly impressed the Indians. Whenever they tried to make Cleo do tricks by commanding her in Maya, the dog simply got confused. Soon they thought it was only something that could be done by Sue. She quickly gained their esteem. Within a very short time I had gone from living alone to having a woman, a gringo pig, and an Indian dog.

The first hardships Sue learned she'd have to cope with were the omnipresent bugs waiting for an opportunity to get at her. An early page from Sue's journal after a day with me in the field revealed some of her frustrations:

The bugs are so bad. I sprayed my arms and face with insect repellent but the little bastards found some spots that didn't get covered. One bit me just below the cuticle of my fingernail, another bit me on the bridge of my nose. Then when I had to pull down my pants to go to the bathroom, alas, one got me on my upper thigh, another my right butt, and then one flew up my pants and bit me on the knees. One hand was swatting them off my buttocks while the other was waving them from my face.

But she was finding contentment in Cockscomb. While I was in the field, Sue would often remain with the women and children, learning to speak Mopan Maya. Soon she was naked to the waist in the creeks with the others, beating our clothes against a washing rock, or in one of the huts kneeling over the hearth, helping make corn tortillas.

I had forgotten to tell her about the washing rocks, and her first day doing laundry she made the mistake of using any available rock. It was Adriana who soon told her that the woman standing by watching was not doing so out of curiosity, but was waiting for her rock. These large, flat rocks, about two and a half feet long and two feet wide, were not easy to find and "break in" and, once obtained, were treated like any other household item. When a family moved, they left their hut behind but took their washing rock.

Sue's interests in cultural anthropology were given free rein in Cockscomb. As she got closer to the women, she was able to broach subjects I could never talk about. Others who have lived among the lowland Maya have described their childbirth practices as extremely simple, an everyday occurrence causing little trouble. Sue was to find out otherwise.

As our most frequent houseguest, the rotund but jolly Adriana became the major source of information for Sue. Sue quickly came to love her and her family as much as I did. One evening Sue told me some of the things Adriana had said.

For her first child, she had hung a rope from the ceiling for support. When the time came, she simply grabbed the rope and squatted. Her mother had instructed her and helped with the first birth. After that her husband, Ignacio, was the birth attendant, standing by to assist if necessary. The children were kept away. When the pain of delivery became more than she could bear, Ignacio prepared a drink of hot water and black pepper to help alleviate it. After delivery, she'd cut the cord herself with a heated machete. Afterward, Ignacio buried the afterbirth. The "old people" said that the afterbirth must be planted far in the forest because that is where lightning strikes first.

In order to have a normal healthy pregnancy and birth, Adriana told Sue that certain rules must be followed. A woman must not get angry with her husband or there'll be more pain in the delivery. If she's mean to anyone during pregnancy, the baby will "get something" on its back that will make it cry all the time. If she's too mean, the baby may even die.

It is very bad for a pregnant woman to watch anyone or anything else die or give birth. Adriana said she had once watched a fox die, and one of her babies died a month after its birth. If a woman watches an animal give birth, she herself might have her baby like the animal observed. A pregnant woman must never look upon someone bitten by a snake. It could kill that person—the unborn baby makes the poison of the snake stronger. When Sue questioned her about contraception, since she already had numerous children, Adriana simply replied that the old people said that it's not good to stop oneself from having babies.

In September the heavy rains returned. I soon came to see how much work went into maintaining roads and bridges in the jungle. When the timber camp had been in operation, the maintenance had been done by big machinery, which made it look easy. Now things were quickly deteriorating, and I spent increasing amounts of time repairing bridges and patching or draining roadbeds. Done manually, it was arduous work and nothing could be fixed properly. I could only patch, not build, roads and bridges. But as long as I continued using the traps, I needed access by road into the basin. I decided to move the two traps as far back as the roads permitted, knowing that eventually the truck wouldn't be able to get back there anymore.

Jorge still helped me in the field sometimes, but his visits had become less frequent when I became closer to Cirillo and especially when Sue arrived. He was morose, even jealous of Sue's presence, and continued drinking heavily. However, Sue quickly charmed him and he soon resumed his evening visits. While I'd compile the day's data, he would drink rum and Coke with Sue and tell her dirty jokes.

As I collected data, I saw some interesting patterns emerging. For two weeks Chac and Ah Puch stayed within a two-mile radius of camp. I was convinced by now that Guam Bank was within an area where the territories of these two males overlapped. Whenever I tracked them within this area, I could almost always predict accurately when and where I would find feces or scrapes the next day. When they were near camp, either Sue or I would remain awake all night to monitor the cat's activity patterns using the mast antenna on the side of the house. Sometimes, we would both stay up all night at separate locations. The hourly data began to reveal the patterns of their nightly movements.

One evening, while Sue was preparing dinner and I was readying the equipment for another all-night radio-tracking session, she told me that it was becoming increasingly difficult to cook and eat meals with the constant foul smells around the house. When I asked her what she meant, she pointed to ten piles of feces I was drying on the windowsill, two animal carcasses I was cleaning for my reference collection, and a skull, not yet picked clean, of a jaguar killed outside Cockscomb. She was right. The house stank. The problem was that if I put them anyplace outside, the dogs or pigs would get at them. So I shifted them all into one corner. Now only part of the house stank.

When Chac and Ah Puch moved, I decided to get some aerial readings to see how far they had separated. The day was overcast, with an unbroken cloud cover over the western part of the basin. It was always tricky predicting a break in the rains during these months, but I took a chance and called John. He said we could still fly despite the weather. We might just have to weave in and out of the clouds and avoid going near the Cockscomb peaks. I was still foolish enough to put data collection before my own safety, so I told him to come.

By the time John landed in Cockscomb, the clouds had formed a solid cover over the basin at about fifteen hundred feet. The little Cessna bounced up and down trying to alternate between going above and below the blinding white clouds. I was scared but I tried to keep my mind on the radio signals.

We found Chac three miles east of camp. Then I picked up Ah Puch's signal deep in the basin, so we dropped below the clouds to pinpoint him. The forest canopy seemed at our feet. The signal started getting louder, as did the beating of my heart. We were still dropping and I motioned John to level off, because I could detect him from this altitude. We weren't leveling off. I pulled off my headphones to talk with John and heard a buzzer sounding in synchronization with a red light flashing on the instrument panel.

I knew that sound from our landings. It meant the plane's engines were stalling. I looked at John to see a concerned expression on his face. To our right was Victoria Peak rising through the clouds; to our left was the open basin. Below was the jungle and Ah Puch.

We were caught in a downdraft. John kept on trying to bank the plane to the left, throttle full open, hoping to get out of the downdraft as we dropped toward the trees. Fortunately, he resisted the impulse to pull the nose up, which would've probably stalled the engines completely. Finally the stall buzzer stopped and we started gaining altitude. We were out of the downdraft. I looked out the window and could see water droplets on the leaves of some of the trees.

I wiped the sweat from my brow and leaned my head back against the seat. "Let's go back," I said to John. He nodded.

12 IXCHEL

When I returned to camp, Sue was crouched on the floor in a corner of the house with Cleo's head in her lap. Cleo was delivering her first litter of puppies. She had been so malnourished, I hadn't noticed she was pregnant. The first puppy was born shortly after I arrived, a small hairy ball still in its amniotic sac. Cleo walked in circles whimpering in pain. Then she tore at the sac with her teeth and the water gushed forth. One died, but three solid-black puppies were born alive and well. Sue was smiling, tears running down her face. Not the time to tell her about my plane trip, I thought.

That night Jorge and several Indians joined us in celebrating Cleo's puppies. They couldn't care less about more Indian dogs being brought into the world; Jorge came over for the free rum, and the Indians, for the soft drinks. Jorge became very drunk, but his machismo was tempered by Sue's presence. He started reminiscing about the good old days at the timber camp.

By 10 P.M., everyone had left but Jorge. Sue cleaned up the shack, while I planned my work schedule for the next day, trying to shut out Jorge's rambling. When I heard the end of a question he was asking about Indian things, I looked up and saw him holding one of my books, *The Ancient Maya* by Sylvanus Morley. He was pointing at some pictures of Maya temples.

"We find big Indian ting back in de bush, me and Boogle, while we driving de skidder," he mumbled.

"What did you find, Jorge?" I asked and saw Sue had stopped her work to listen.

"We find big hill of dirt wit dese tings under dem," he replied, pointing to a picture of an excavated temple from Palenque in Mexico. "We know dere plenty rich tings dere. We no tell no one so we can cum back and dig. Now everyting finish and no one go back dere. You my good friend, so I tell you," he said, walking over and putting his arm around me.

In his drunkenness, Jorge was telling me of a Maya ruin far back in Cockscomb, where, as far as I knew, there were no Maya sites on record. The fact that the basin was granite bedrock with no outlet to the west and no large navigable waterways had led some to wonder whether the Maya had ever really occupied the basin. The artifacts that Cirillo and other Indians in Cockscomb had found indicated that they had, and a temple set back in the basin would add a whole new dimension to the picture.

"Where you find this thing?" I asked, hoping he was drunk enough to tell me.

"It far back where you and me go one time, see track of tiger," Jorge said, pointing to an area on one of my maps. I remembered the area. "Sometime I go back and dig it. You and me go back, we both dig, make plenty money," he said, smiling.

That week the Forestry Department of the Belize government unexpectedly sent word to me that they wanted my help with their jaguar-livestock problem. For nearly eight months I had tried to work with this department toward a jaguar-management plan but had been continually rebuffed. I therefore thought it best to concentrate my efforts on obtaining as much data as possible for them. If they were contacting me, I knew something bad must have happened.

I was right. A mare belonging to the son of a high-ranking civil servant had been killed by a jaguar. Demanding that something be done, he proposed the reinstatement of legal jaguar hunting. Fortunately, the Forestry Department didn't want to do anything rash and was not anxious to reopen jaguar hunting. They had given me permits to study jaguars and now they expected answers.

It's often difficult to explain to government officials that research takes time, and that even when all the data are in, it may still be difficult to draw firm conclusions. However, I'd learned from my work elsewhere that when you're dealt into the game, you play with what you've got. It may not be the best hand, but you'll definitely lose if you fold. Governments continue to steer society with or without qualified advice. I feel strongly that a scientist's duty is to use insight and available data, however sparse that data may be, to give opinions if requested by those in power.

I told the chief forest officer I'd have my initial assessment and recommendations on his desk in two weeks and a comprehensive management plan by the New Year. I wasn't quite sure how I'd find the time to do that, but it was an opportunity I wasn't about to pass up. He was relieved. I had taken the burden on myself.

I examined my sparse data on jaguar depredation of livestock to see what I could come up with. Since beginning the project, I had had little time for anything other than capturing and tracking jaguars in Cockscomb. However, I had tried to investigate jaguar problems in the Stann Creek area when I heard about them. Some obvious patterns emerged.

It seemed that the most vocal complaints about jaguars came from absentee ranchers. Bader had first told me that many rumors of "jaguar problems" were actually acts of thievery by local people or ranch workers. One incident I investigated involved an eight-hundred-pound bull that was supposed to have been killed by a jaguar and dragged into the jungle. I was immediately suspicious because most jaguar depredation I had heard of involved calves, pigs, and an occasional sick cow or small horse. When I arrived at the ranch to investigate the killing, there was no sign of the bull carcass.

Though a jaguar could kill a large bull, it could not drag it very far. Jaguars usually eat their meals in the vicinity of the kill. If a jaguar made the kill in an open area, it might drag it to the nearest cover. The ranch foreman in this case insisted that the jaguar had taken the bull far into the bush. There were no jaguar tracks in the mud surrounding the supposed kill site, nor were there any in the nearby forest. I made no accusations, but I told the rancher I had doubts that this was the work of a jaguar. He insisted on believing his foreman. Not long after, the foreman was caught stealing other cattle and blaming it on jaguars.

Nevertheless, the fact remained that jaguars did kill cattle, sometimes frequently. Humboldt wrote of jaguars taking goats, cattle, and pigs brought into the Amazon forest by missionaries. Since then, they have been documented as livestock predators throughout their range. Why some jaguars caused problems while others didn't was the mystery.

I learned that much of the livestock depredation occurred when the jaguar could approach the livestock under the cover of the forest. Except on forest roads and trails, jaguars didn't seem too anxious to travel through wide-open areas even under cover of darkness. In the case of the young mare, the corral bordered extensive forest. When I went with the government official to investigate the killing, the cat's tracks indicated it had traveled along the forest edge. The kill was made no more than fifty feet from the woods and dragged back to the closest cover. The canine puncture holes in the braincase confirmed it had been the work of a jaguar.

In another case, a four-hundred-pound cow was killed in a

pasture a little more than a hundred feet from the Southern Highway. A worker who waited up in a tree over the kill the following night saw the jaguar approach the dead cow by skirting a narrow strip of scrub forest bordering the road instead of cutting across the pasture.

In Santa Rosa, where I bought my pigs, a jaguar was killing one Indian's pigs but not his neighbor's. When I went to investigate, I learned that the man whose pigs were being killed allowed them to roam freely in the adjacent forest. His neighbor had trained his pigs to stay near the huts. Any pig going off into the forest was quickly eaten.

It was a common opinion that once a "problem jaguar" was killed, there'd be no more depredation for a while, even when there were numerous jaguars in the surrounding jungle. One rancher watched a jaguar walk along his field then disappear into the forest without even glancing at his cattle. Ranchers who stayed in close touch with their animals all experienced occasional depredation problems, but admitted that jaguars rarely caused severe economic loss. In Brazil, George Schaller found that jaguars accounted for only a small percentage of annual cattle loss.

I had also obtained important information observing the Cockscomb jaguars. By now I knew that part of Chac's range bordered a cattle ranch at the entrance to Cockscomb. Yet he was rarely located in that vicinity, seeming to prefer the interior of the basin. Whenever he was found to be near the cattle, I monitored him closely. He never went into the fields and usually moved farther into the forest by the next morning. There was no reported cattle depredation when Chac was in the area.

Another interesting observation was that seven out of eight carcasses of problem jaguars that were examined revealed previous shotgun wounds in the skull. Hassan had told me that among the recent cattle-killing jaguars he'd shot, all but one had old bullet wounds and most exhibited some broken teeth. I didn't yet know how all this would fit together, but I felt I was assembling important pieces of the puzzle.

I could give the government something useful to work with. Some jaguars definitely killed livestock, though I was still not sure of the reasons. Part of the problem appeared to be proper management practices. Not all jaguars that were near livestock were cattle killers, and because livestock might be dead or missing didn't necessarily mean jaguars were responsible. Jaguars most frequently took young or sick animals.

Jaguar kills could be identified by examining the skeleton of the animal killed. With larger animals, punctures or at least chipping was usually found on the upper spinal vertebrae. With smaller prey or the young of large prey, the cranium was often punctured by the canines or the skull was crushed by the jaws.

If the old shotgun wounds I'd been finding in the skulls of problem jaguars were related to their depredation of livestock, then ranchers might be making matters worse by engaging in cat-killing sprees. After the mare of the government official's son was killed, farmers in the area killed four jaguars trying to get the problem animal. A man who owned the cattle pasture at the entrance to Cockscomb offered a standing reward for any jaguars killed on his property, whether they were causing problems or not. This was not uncommon.

If the ranchers paid more careful attention to what was going on, they might not feel so angry toward jaguars. At the very most, the evidence suggested that the government might continue its policy of allowing ranchers to legally kill only problem jaguars. However, there was absolutely no evidence to suggest that the government should declare open season for jaguar to solve a problem caused by aberrant individuals or poor livestock management.

The last time I had talked with Bader I told him that I hoped eventually to capture a healthy, cattle-killing jaguar that I could relocate to Cockscomb. It would not only be the first translocation attempt with jaguars but would help to determine if it was at all feasible to trap and move problem animals to other locations instead of killing them. Shortly after submitting my report

The Cockscomb Range, with Victoria Peak in the distance. (All pictures taken by the author except where indicated.)

Prudencia, Cleo, Agapita, and Formenta waiting for my return from the field. (Photo by Ben Nottingham)

Adriana nursing Formenta in my shack.

Adriana making corn tortillas in her hut.
(Opposite) The dense greenery of the Cockscomb jungle.

Machario, Guermo, and Phillip on the afternoon before Guermo died.

Porfilio disappearing into the hole after Ah Puch.

Ah Puch waking from sedation and cabled to a tree.

Pinto waking up. (Photo by Richard Foster)

Chac waking up from sedation. Purple is medication used for parasites.

Pinto yawning. (Photo by Richard Foster)

Repairing the timber road. The Outlier
mountain is in the distance.

Sue wading across a bridge flooded out during a rainstorm.

Cirillo watching a king vulture as we stand atop the Outlier.

Florencia, seventeen years old, wife of Cirillo.

Chac leaving the trap. (Photo by Ben Nottingham)

The obeah man burning copal by candlelight in a ritual to bring a jaguar near my trap.

The wild eyes of young Xaman Ek.

The author putting a radio collar on Ek Chuah. (Photo by Susan Walker)
(*Opposite*) Plane crash.

The skin of Ek Chuah at the home of the man who killed him. (Photo by Ben Nottingham)

The author examining radiotelemetry data on maps to plot the movements of the jaguars.

Jane Alexander trying to play the jaguar caller as Julian laughs.

Pinto sleeping, Maya resting. (Photo by Richard Foster)

Ixchel, skinned, decapitated, and left to rot where she was shot.

Maya emerging from the forest. (Photo by Richard Foster)

to the government, Bader sent word that I should contact him.

When I called he told me he'd been asked to kill a problem jaguar in the Orange Walk area. After he treed it, he saw that it was a female and decided not to kill it. He captured it alive, using the tranquilizer drug I had given him. Did I want it? I went back to camp, closed the traps, and, leaving Sue in charge, left for Orange Walk.

Bader already had the cat in a small cage. We loaded her onto the truck and I returned immediately to Cockscomb. Once in camp, I drugged her again and took a closer look:

Sex—female
Age—subadult
Total length—67 inches
Tail length—20 inches
Head circumference—18 inches
Height at shoulder—19 inches
Height at hip—20 inches
Weight—80 pounds

She was a small jaguar, with tiny pink nipples and sharp-cusped white teeth. She appeared to be a subadult who had not yet raised her first litter. Although in excellent condition, she was missing the right upper canine. I wondered what circumstances had caused that.

I thought that the chances of a subadult female being accepted by the resident adult jaguars, both male and female, might be good. I released her where Itzamna was first captured, within the ranges of both Ah Puch and the uncollared crooked-toe male, who had escaped my trap.

I informed the government of her capture and release, but otherwise kept it quiet. The Indians had seen the cat in camp but had no idea where it came from. The ranchers in the area would not be happy to know I was bringing in cattle-killing jaguars. I named her Ixchel, after the goddess of floods, child-bearing, and weaving. Ixchel was the wife of Itzamna and was often portrayed by the ancient Maya as an angry old woman.

During the first week, Ixchel stayed within a half-mile radius of her release. Then she started moving southwest, deeper into the basin. Toward the end of the second week she turned and traveled north. Two days after starting north, she crossed the Cockscomb Range and settled in an area adjacent to the Sittee River. Then I lost her radio signal. I called John for an immediate aerial search.

After an hour of flying over the basin and the area north of the Cockscomb Range, I still heard no signal. Finally I signaled John to go in. As we circled camp preparing to land, I caught a barely audible signal coming through the headphones. We aborted the landing and flew east over Chac's range. It was impossible for her to be in this area, I thought, checking the frequency to make sure I was following the right cat. But as we flew toward the ocean, the signal became stronger. It was on the slower pulse, an inactive signal. There were only two explanations. She had either followed the Sittee River downstream, or someone had killed her and taken the collar to his house.

We located the signal around the cattle ranch at the entrance to Cockscomb. As we flew low over the area, it turned active. She was alive, in the forest between the cattle pasture and the Sittee River. I started to have doubts about translocation as a potential management technique.

On the way back to camp I asked John to fly over the southeast corner of the basin where one of the major rivers in Cockscomb, the Swasey River, came out of the basin through a cut in the hills. I had never seen the area before. We made several passes, then started back, flying along the southern border of the basin. Suddenly, I spotted some large cleared patches of forest at the base of the mountains where South Stann Creek flowed out of the basin. It was far from any Indian settlements.

"What the hell are those fields doing all the way out here?" I asked John.

"I don't know," he answered. "Let's take a look."

He turned the plane back and circled the area. There were no huts, no people, no evidence of settlement—just small green plants starting to sprout. Suddenly I flashed back to the day I picked up the first jaguar trap.

"Shit, it's a marijuana plantation!" I yelled.

I thought again of those men with guns. They had been nice to me as long as I posed no threat, but I knew they were not to be fooled with. Unfortunately, this time I could not walk away so easily—it was too close to home. Situated between an Indian village on the Southern Highway and the Cockscomb Indians, it was in the only valley area that made access into the basin relatively easy, besides the entrance road itself. I had to report it to the police.

I told Sue about my day, and she took my mind off the potential problems by presenting me with a more immediate one. After catching up on some long-overdue bookkeeping for me, she figured out that I was nearly out of funds. In fact, by now, I was probably overdrawn at the bank. The project had been more expensive than anticipated and I still had four months left.

I decided to return to New York for two weeks to bring Schaller and Carr up to date on the project's progress and to request additional funds. I plied Sue with several rum and Cokes and asked her if she'd remain alone in Cockscomb and track the jaguars while I was gone, particularly Ixchel. She agreed. Not much could happen in two weeks, I thought.

During the night, we had the third torrential downpour of the rainy season. We were stuck in camp for a week. No jaguars were near enough to collect data, so, while Sue entertained the constant flow of Indians, I listened to classical and folk music on my portable tape deck and thought of snow-covered mountains.

Sue had fallen into the typical "Maya woman" role. She'd gossip, cook, and clean with the Indian women and remain stoically silent when I'd have a tantrum. It was the way of Cockscomb, and our relationship seemed strong. Sometimes the strangeness of the place hit me with full force, as it did one afternoon while writing in my journal after three days of continuous rains:

1800 hours: Right now, five Maya children are sitting in back of me, Bob Seeger is blaring on the cassette, and Sue is gaily preparing popcorn as if the world around her was completely normal. The Maya baby just peed on the floor, three scroungy dogs and a pig are begging for food at the door, the jaguar skeleton hanging outside is being blown against the house by the wind. My back is killing me and I haven't gotten any data in days.

Before I left for the States, Sue and I radio-tracked Ixchel for twenty-four hours. We stayed at two different locations and followed her activity and movements closely. Sue stayed next to the cattle pasture in the cab of an abandoned bulldozer. I went up on a ridge to the east of her. There was hard rain that night and lightning, and it was Sue's first night alone in the bush. Before the sun even went down, two men with guns tried to get past her to go hunting in Cockscomb. She turned them away. Her field notes show that the night didn't get any easier:

It's 2:00 A.M., dark and stormy. I'm sitting alone on a bulldozer. To my right is a cattle pasture, to my left jungle. I can't see past the edge of the bulldozer, it's so dark. It's raining very hard now. Everything—my pillow, the Vienna sausages, my book—is getting soaked. Something crashes on the roof of the bulldozer. Different parts of the bulldozer look like grotesque creatures. It's raining so hard now. Lightning is right over me. I unplug the antenna from the receiver. I'm no longer connected to the tiger.

Ixchel had not gone into the cattle fields but had stayed across the road in a wooded, swampy area the entire night. Her twenty-four-hour activity pattern was similar to that of the male jaguars. What was she up to?

When the storms let up, John flew me to Belize City several days before I was scheduled to fly to the States. I needed to meet with government officials and the Belize Audubon Society, the country's only conservation organization. I asked Sue to maintain daily contact with Ixchel and to track her closely.

Ever since I had first visited the Cockscomb Basin, I felt it was an area that should be protected despite a long history of selective timbering. The Goldsworthy expedition to the Cockscomb peaks had recorded mahogany camps in the basin as early as 1888. But until the Maya settled in Cockscomb five years before my arrival, there had been no permanent settlements, clear-cutting, or large-scale agricultural endeavors in the basin since the time of the ancient Maya. Parts of the area were still untouched. Jaguars and other wildlife regularly used the roads and trails made by the timber operation, and their prey species abounded in the second-growth and edge habitats. If we could control hunting, Cockscomb would make an ideal jaguar preserve.

Such a concept had to be presented carefully. At the time, there were virtually no preserves in the country, and the word "conservation" was not well established in the vocabulary of Belizeans. The government of Prime Minister George Price was struggling to stay in power. Economic growth and development, primarily through agriculture, was his party's number one priority.

Despite various existing laws, wildlife protection was not taken seriously. No wildlife or parks department even existed in the government. Any protective action had to be approved by the Forestry Department and ultimately the Ministry of Natural Resources.

Belize's Forestry Department, established by the British in 1923, was the first such department in Central America. However, it was set up strictly for the management of harvestable timber. Many believed that conservation, though well intentioned, was the antithesis of their mandate.

Fortunately, there was a nongovernment alternative in the form of the Belize Audubon Society. The volunteers in this society were some of the most prominent members of Belizean society, and their advice was often sought by the government.

I needed their endorsement if I was to succeed with Cockscomb.

I made a trip to Belmopan, the country's new capital, carved out of the jungle in the early 1970s after a hurricane destroyed much of Belize City in 1961. It was designed after an ancient Maya ceremonial center, and the name was derived from the Mopan who had once inhabited the area. When I visited the Forestry Department, they thanked me for my initial jaguar-livestock assessment. I planted the seed in their minds of designating Cockscomb a preserve. When there was no response, I considered it a step forward. I felt they would tell me immediately if it were out of the question.

Before leaving the capital, I was informed that the United States ambassador to Belize, Malcolm Barnaby, had requested my presence at a cocktail party he was holding the next evening. I was surprised he knew that I even existed, and felt it might be an opportunity to push conservation issues. As soon as I got back to Belize City, I went shopping for new clothes.

When I arrived at the party, I realized that I was viewed as an interesting oddity among the white foreign-service community, just as I was among the Indians. But the Indians asked better questions. Many of the people had heard about the events in Cockscomb and simply wanted to meet me and hear adventure stories.

It started when I walked in the front door and was introduced to the ambassador's wife. "Oh, so you're the man that studies jaguars," she said. "Well, I guess someone has to do that sort of thing. Tell me, do you really *like* doing what you do?"

My conversation with her was cut short by the arrival of another guest, and I moved on to talk with an American liaison officer.

"Charmed to meet you, Dr. Rabinowitz," he started off. "Yes, I've heard a lot about you. You're starting to acquire quite a reputation in Belize. I've only seen people like you on television. What's it really like out there?"

I grabbed a drink from a passing waiter and started explaining about Cockscomb, but the ambassador's wife pulled me over to meet one of her friends, the wife of another embassy official. "This is who I was telling you about," Mrs. Barnaby said to her friend. I looked into a pair of arrogant eyes that were giving me the once over.

"I expected an older, more dignified-looking person," were the woman's first words to me, "but I guess it takes someone like you to endure the hardships of the jungle." I thought I had dressed well for the occasion.

My ideas about conservation and a park system in Belize fell on deaf ears. Large-scale economic endeavors were the only thing that interested these people, and their plans showed no regard for the Belizeans themselves.

"Just took a man around who'd like to hunt a jaguar while he's here," an official from the U.S. Agency for International Development said to me. "Do you know where I can tell him to go?"

"What's wrong with you? You know that's illegal," I said to him.

He smiled. "He probably won't get one. He puts a lot of U.S. dollars into this country. I gave him a few names of people to see."

"I can tell him where to go!" I said angrily.

The next day I was on my way to the United States. After eight months in the field, I boarded a plane and two hours later arrived at Miami International Airport. Walking through the terminal, surrounded by crowds, I suddenly became self-conscious of my appearance and mannerisms, wondering if I was behaving properly. I spotted a bar and went over to order a beer.

"You look starry-eyed. Where are you coming from or going to?" a female voice asked beside me. I turned to see an attractive dark-haired woman.

"Belize, I come from Belize. I'm going to New York."

"That sounds interesting. What do you do?" she asked.

"I study tiger," I said, before realizing what I was saying. It was my standard answer to a frequent question I was asked in Belize. I became flustered. I excused myself, left the beer, and found a table in a little restaurant where I could sit by myself. An hour later, I boarded a plane for New York City. It was all happening too fast.

The first week in New York I visited with my family and met with officials at the New York Zoological Society. Carr and Schaller were extremely pleased with the project's progress. They were both field researchers themselves and realized how expensive such a project could be. But what mattered to them was that I was collecting good scientific data and contributing to the conservation and management of the species.

We all agreed on the need to continue the project for a second year. I remained in New York for several more days before flying on to Knoxville, Tennessee. I was scheduled to conduct a seminar on my work at the university and hoped to visit some friends in the Smoky Mountains.

One hour before the presentation, my former professor Mike Pelton handed me a telegram. It was from Belize. I knew Sue wouldn't contact me unless something was very wrong. I ripped open the envelope nervously and read its three words: "Ixchel dead. Sue."

13 AH KIN

The landing in Cockscomb was rough. As the wheels kept hitting rocks and the plane swerved from side to side, I thought John was really having a bad day. Sue was waiting in the truck at one end of the airstrip after having heard us buzz the camp. She had been watching the plane with trepidation, hoping there'd be no mishaps. We soon learned the reasons for her fears.

Before leaving for the States, I had submitted a report to the local police department that marijuana was being grown in Cockscomb. They inferred from the report that my airstrip was probably being used to fly out the marijuana. I had deliberately filed papers early, showing that I had authorization to use the strip for jaguar research. Apparently, my papers were ignored.

This was just one in a series of incidents that made me wonder about the police in this area.

The day before we landed, the Belize Defence Force, under the supervision of British officers, dug trenches three feet deep and six feet wide at thirty-foot intervals along the runway. There would have been no way to see these trenches in time to abort a landing. John thought it could have flipped the plane and injured or killed us.

Sue, realizing the danger, had rushed to Silk Grass to call British army officials. She explained I'd be flying in at any time. At her dogged insistence, they returned and filled in the trenches. Sue looked tired and haggard.

That night, she lay in my arms, detailing the week's events, occasionally stopping to wipe the tears away. I had felt the pain in the three words of her cable and had cut my trip short.

Ixchel had started killing livestock as soon as I left. She had killed two calves, one weighing a hundred and fifty pounds, and she probably killed a dog at Maya Center. I examined the two calf skulls, which Sue had managed to collect. The younger calf had its cranium entirely crushed. The second calf had a single canine puncture mark above the eye orbit on the left side. It was damning evidence for Ixchel. Several people immediately started to hunt her, wanting to collect the three-hundred-dollar reward being offered by the absentee owner.

Sue continually monitored Ixchel's movements despite heavy rains and bouts of dysentery, knowing others were closing in. She had taken on a new Indian assistant, Pablo, who lived with his wife and children across the road from Maya Center. Cirillo didn't want to work with a woman. Pablo, a part-time caretaker of the cattle ranch where Ixchel was killing livestock, had once expressed interest in working with me. Sue finally hired him, although he said he'd been given orders to shoot the jaguar on sight. He had been holding off at Sue's request. Two days before my return, Ixchel was seen in the pasture again. Pablo told Sue he must kill the cat. Sue asked for one more day of readings.

Sue tracked Ixchel all that night, and the strong signals indicated she was right beside the cattle pasture. Just before dawn, at 4:30 A.M., she heard a gunshot nearby. Her first thought was that someone had shot Ixchel. She turned on the receiver and got an active signal. As she continued to listen, the signal faded quickly, as if Ixchel was quickly moving away from the area. Fifteen minutes later Ixchel's location was nearly a mile away from where she had been prior to the firing of the shot. She was still alive.

Sue scanned the darkness to see who was out there. Suddenly she saw a flashlight approaching. Feeling nervous, she moved toward the truck. She yelled out asking who was out there, but there was no reply. Suddenly the flashlight disappeared. She waited in the truck for thirty minutes but heard and saw nothing more.

The next day Pablo told Sue that a man named Algene, living in a nearby shack, had bragged to him of shooting the collared jaguar the previous night, but the cat had run off. He said that he had heard Sue calling while he was coming out of the jungle, and he got scared and waited in the forest until she left.

Sue asked Pablo to help her find Ixchel, to make sure the cat was all right. That was a mistake. As she was recording the compass bearings on the cat, she turned to see that Pablo had been watching closely the direction of the antenna. He picked up his gun and said he had to go in after it. Heartsick at the realization that she had already shown him the direction, Sue insisted that she go along. The rest happened quickly. She recorded the incident in her notes that night:

He now had a general idea of where she was. I told him I would not help him anymore but of course he said it didn't matter now. I went with him and tried to talk loudly, hoping Ixchel would hear me and get away. No such luck. She was easy to find, standing in the open, on the crest of a little hill. When we saw her she lay down. Pablo fired once. She died quickly.

Sue cried, feeling she had failed me and was responsible for the jaguar's death. I held her close, telling her she had done as well as I would have under the circumstances. But I felt angry. Why hadn't I tried to instill in her the distrust of people she needed to have for this study? Why hadn't I thought to explain that when locating a jaguar, I would always point the antenna and face the wrong direction after noting the true direction of the strongest signal? I knew people watched us constantly and were beginning to understand just what we were doing.

"How do you do this?" she asked me. "How do you put up with all this and still keep going?" In a week and a half, she had gotten an inkling of the difficulty of this work.

Sue had grown even closer to the Indians while I was gone. The women in particular thought her very brave for staying alone in Cockscomb and tracking the jaguars. The first two nights, Adriana sent her children over to sleep with Sue, not wanting her to be alone. The first night they appeared at the door just after dark; they hadn't eaten yet, so Sue fed them.

Before going to sleep they all took off their dresses, held them by the hem, and slapped them against the bed several times. Then they laid them neatly in a corner. Each child had very few clothes, often handed down from the next oldest child. Since each item might be worn by several children, it was important to keep them as neat as possible. When they all finally went to bed, Juana lay down on the floor, and Agapita and Prudencia wrapped themselves in the blanket, their bodies and heads completely covered, and snuggled on the bed against Sue's back.

In the dark, Juana talked more freely than she ever had before. She told Sue how the people at the neighboring village of Maya Center just went to church to see the pretty dresses that everyone else was wearing and how the preacher there, Mr. Sho, had a fat belly and talked too much. She said that some Americans wanted to come to Cockscomb and build a church like they had built at Maya Center.

The next morning Agapita awoke as cheerful as ever. As Sue

was cooking a big breakfast for everyone, she noticed Juana and Agapita whispering in the corner. Agapita approached Sue. "Juana got shit!" she said to Sue. Sue was taken aback; they were the first English words Agapita had ever said to her. She wondered why they hadn't just gone outside like they did at home when she realized they were waiting in the bathroom. They wanted to try the toilet. Juana had been too embarrassed to let Sue know what was on her mind.

Sue showed them how to sit on the toilet and to pour a bucket of water down the bowl to flush it. It was the first time they'd ever used one and they loved it. After Juana finished, Agapita approached Sue again. "Me gotta pee-pee, man," she said. Sue quickly learned that Agapita knew more English than she admitted to. After that the three of them spent most of the day trying to "pee-pee" so that they could use the toilet and watch the water flush down the bowl.

I got Ixchel's skull and radio collar from Pablo. I was not surprised to find that the loss of her upper right canine was due to an old bullet wound through the maxilla bone of the skull. But in addition, there were new bullet wounds in the skull that could only have come from the gun of Pablo's neighbor the night Sue heard the shot. Pablo had not shot the jaguar in the head. The wounds looked severe enough to indicate that the jaguar probably would have died soon anyway. Sue felt vindicated. That night she helped me compile the data from Ixchel.

During the time she was tracked in the vicinity of the cattle pasture, Ixchel traveled within a ten-square-mile area, including both the cattle pasture and a section of forest. When in the forest, her activity pattern was similar to that of all the adult males we had tracked thus far. After a cattle kill, her activity became more diurnal, and she traveled most between 9:30 A.M. and 12:30 P.M. Overall, she was active 60 percent of the time.

I was annoyed with Cirillo for not helping Sue, so I continued using Pablo. I couldn't blame him for killing Ixchel. Cirillo was

not pleased and I learned that Pablo was ostracized by the Indians in both Maya Center and Cockscomb. I was told he was
"bad," though no one explained to me what "bad" meant. I later
found out that what the Indians were upset about was that Pablo
grew a small patch of marijuana in the forest behind his house.
In a good year he harvested about sixty plants, each yielding
approximately a pound of drug per plant. He could sell it to a
local dealer for Bze$70 per pound, or Bze$4,200 for a maximum
crop, a sizable income for a Maya.

Fecal analysis still indicated that small prey—armadillos, anteaters, pacas, agoutis—was the jaguar's major food source. This
seemed scant fare for an animal whose principal food in other
areas included capybaras, caimans, and peccaries. I suspected
that jaguars were opportunists, taking different species depending on availability and ease of capture. However, to prove this,
I needed to ascertain what was available to them in the forest
and see if it tied together with what they were eating and their
behavior patterns. The Indians were opportunistic hunters, killing anything they considered edible. Why should the jaguars be
different?

I decided to conduct surveys to assess the densities of different
prey species in the basin. The basin was covered primarily by
homogeneous lowland forest whose thick vegetation made visual surveys all but impossible. Instead, I could do what I was
doing with the jaguars—watch for sign, primarily by looking
for tracks of different species. With some animals, other kinds
of sign could be used. Armadillos could also be identified by
their digging behavior and den sites, while agoutis and pacas
could be identified by chew marks on nuts from the cohune
palms. Termite nests that had been ripped apart meant anteaters. The number of individuals of each species could be deduced
by track measurements, the direction of travel, the freshness of
sign, and the proximity of sign to one another, though this was
difficult. Arboreal species, such as the kinkajou, or semiarboreal
species, such as the coati, were virtually impossible to estimate
by this method.

Random trails, about half a mile long, were cut into the forest within the ranges of the various jaguars. I decided that our first survey for prey availability would be done in the range of Ah Puch. As Pablo and I drove back into his area, we came around a bend and almost drove into the largest jaguar I'd seen in Cockscomb. He crossed the road and stopped at the forest edge to look at us. I motioned to Pablo to remain still. It was probably the uncollared male, but I wouldn't know until I saw his tracks. He looked larger than old Itzamna and was apparently occupying at least part of the same range. He paused no more than a few seconds before disappearing into the forest.

I got out of the truck and examined his tracks. There it was, the slightly crooked toe of the jaguar who had escaped my trap. I could smell his strong, musky odor. He was a mysterious cat, and I didn't think I'd catch him in my trap again. Shortly after his escape, he had returned to the trap and ripped away the cohune leaves trying to get at the pig from the back. He didn't go near the door and never came near the trap after the second attempt.

At least the tracks of this big male were always easy to distinguish from those of other jaguars. By recording where they occurred, I hoped to at least get some movement data on this jaguar. I felt he deserved a name, so I started calling him Ah Kin, short for Ah Kinchil, the powerful sun god, thought to be immediately below Itzamna in prominence.

During our survey that day, Pablo discovered an occupied paca den inside a hollow log. It contained a female with two large young.

"I've never seen one of these animals up close before," I told Pablo.

He immediately went to work to capture one to show me. There were three entrances into the den. He plugged up the largest and told me to jam a stick into a second opening. When the pacas became frightened and tried to escape from the last exit, Pablo grabbed one of the young animals. But the female, who must have weighed about thirty-five pounds, was right behind and clamped down on his hand. He screamed and pulled his hand away, still holding one of the young pacas. He held it proudly to show me. "See it here, Alan."

All I could see was a nearly severed finger and blood pouring onto the ground.

"Let it go," I ordered, rushing up and grabbing his hand. He was bitten through to the bone yet showed pain only when I squeezed the wound shut. He packed some dirt on it to stanch the flow of blood and wanted to continue with the survey. I wondered what his pain threshold was. We immediately returned to camp, where I poured alcohol onto the wound, closed it with a few stitches, and applied Betadine ointment and a bandage. Then, at Pablo's insistence, we returned and finished the survey.

The tracks of a new female jaguar appeared on the entrance road within Chac's range, where the other female had been killed. I was still having no luck trapping the female in Ah Puch's range, so I decided to close that trap and shift it to the entrance road. Maybe I'd have better luck trapping this new female there.

The second trap we still kept open within Ah Kin's range. So far track data, sightings, and radio tracking indicated that Chac, Ah Puch, and Ah Kin were occupying separate but overlapping ranges, the extent of which I still didn't know. There was at least one female known to be within the range of Ah Puch and one within the range of Chac.

As we drove out to move one of the traps, I thought again how the roads in Cockscomb were deteriorating faster than I could repair them. After twice digging the truck out of ruts with a machete, I now carried pick, shovel, and wooden planks as standard road gear. I'd been lucky so far that none of the bridges had collapsed or had been washed away.

One day Sue and I went to Santa Rosa to buy another pig for the traps. The town's residents had heard about this white woman in Cockscomb who could speak Maya and was helping me catch tigers. When they saw her with me, they gathered around to test her Maya. They asked her her name. She answered them in Maya, but when they tried to repeat it, they merged her first name and her last name together. She tried to simplify it for them by dropping the last name.

"No, no, it's just Sue," she told them. Now they understood. From then on, her name in the village and eventually in the surrounding areas became Just Sue, the tiger woman.

The gringo pig, realizing he had the run of the camp, had begun to travel farther and farther from the house. Sometimes he'd stay away overnight. Whenever we'd start to worry about him, Sue would just go outside and yell "PIG," and he'd come running in from the nearby jungle. When he didn't return for a week, and Sue's calling produced no results, I thought he might have become a meal for Chac or Ah Puch. I actually missed his snorting and begging at the door.

One morning, I came out and found the gringo pig dead under the house, where he usually slept. There were no obvious injuries. It could have been a number of things that had killed him, but whatever it was, he had come home to die.

I decided to hang the pig's body from a tree where Ah Puch had been traveling the last few days. I had been told that jaguars would eat only meat they themselves killed, while others said a hungry jaguar would eat anything. I tended to believe the latter. By the second night, the head of the gringo pig was cleanly severed from the body. The body had been raked by claws, but no other part of the carcass was taken. Ah Puch's tracks led from the site into the forest. I left the body hanging for a week before I threw it into the bush.

Suddenly, Pablo went crazy because his wife left him, taking the children to her parents' hut nearby. He said that it was because he refused to become a Baptist. She had told him that if he didn't allow himself to be baptized, he'd be forever damned and would damn her with him.

Pablo's first reaction was to decide it was time for a younger woman anyway. He had seen a pretty, single, young girl in

Maya Center who he thought might make a nice new wife. He asked me to write a letter to her from him. He dictated:

Dear Rosita,
   I see you in village and I think I like you. I think you the prettiest girl in the village, except for all the other girls. My wife, you know, she left me. I need new wife. Tell your cousin Margarito if you like me. Then I come see your family. I wait.
   Pablo

She never responded to Pablo's overtures. He sat in his hut sulking, and talked of running off to Guatemala. Though he continued to work for me, he soon became unreliable and starting blaming me for his troubles, making up stories about why I was in Cockscomb. His wife eventually returned and he calmed down, but, by that time, I had stopped asking him to work for me.

During this entire time Cirillo continued coming over to my house regularly and told me several times that, when I finished with Pablo, he'd work with me again. I think he missed our times in the jungle together. He came by one afternoon after several days of heavy rains that kept me from driving very far on the timber roads into the basin. He'd been out hunting in the jungle that morning about six miles west of camp. He said there was no longer any road into the area where I had put the trap to catch Ah Kin.

We went back together. I drove the truck as far as possible, then we walked the rest of the way. He was right. A large portion of the road leading down into and across South Stann Creek had collapsed, leaving a sheer fifteen-foot drop to the water. The trap was on the other side only ten feet from the water line. The river was swollen, so I had to get the trap out of there before it was swept away. The next day, Jorge, Cirillo, and I floated the trap across the river, lifted it up the vertical mud wall, and dragged it nearly a quarter of a mile uphill to where the truck was parked.

From then on, Cirillo worked with me again. He and I continued the prey surveys, and our first time back out, he tried to lose me in the jungle again. I realized how much I had missed him. I was becoming more adept at following his trail until a near-calamity shook me up once again. Sue had come into the field with us that day, and we decided to do a prey survey near camp. After cutting into the jungle no more than a hundred yards from the timber road, Cirillo noticed an armadillo hole and went over to see if it was fresh. I saw him bend over, then leap back.

"What's wrong, Cirillo?" I asked.

The next thing I heard was Cirillo saying, "Tanks God, I never go in de bush again." I rushed over to see what brought such a strange statement from Cirillo's mouth.

When he had stuck his hand near the armadillo hole, Cirillo found himself looking into the eyes of a large fer-de-lance, coiled up and shaking its tail. As soon as I saw it, I helped him cut a long pole with a forked end. Cirillo crept back and pinned the snake behind its head.

"Alan, kill de snake wit de machete. Chop it up, but no chop it tru," he instructed me.

"Why not, Cirillo?" Sue asked, as I started cutting the snake. Cirillo didn't answer.

"No chop it tru! No chop it tru!" he kept repeating adamantly.

I kept on wounding its flailing body, but the snake showed no sign of dying. After more than fifteen cuts I became impatient and chopped the body cleanly through about eight inches behind the head.

The head and body segment promptly took off, the entrails hanging out. Cirillo fell against me, and I watched with horror as the head turned and started coming toward us, the jaws open. I couldn't believe what I was seeing. We all ran in different directions as the head disappeared somewhere in the underbrush at our feet.

"I tell you no chop it tru!" Cirillo yelled at me. "I see dis happen before."

"But you never told me why I shouldn't chop it through!" I yelled back.

Cirillo smiled. Then he pointed at the head moving slowly in the underbrush. I grabbed the pole and bashed it in. Cirillo wouldn't go near the head or body, but insisted it would be better if we hung the body from a tree. I collected the head.

We continued with the survey. Sue reminded me that one of the snake doctor's words of wisdom was that where there is one tommy-goff, there is always a second one. I laughed. After chopping ahead another ten yards Cirillo stopped abruptly, machete in midair. "De next one here," he whispered. "I hear it."

I didn't hear anything, but I knew better than to question Cirillo. We all froze, examining the brush around our feet. Two feet from where Cirillo had stopped was a second fer-de-lance, about the same size as the last one, directly on the path we were moving along. Its gray mottled coloration blended perfectly into the surroundings. We killed it.

"Dat de she tommy-goff," Cirillo told me. "De oder de he tommy-goff."

"Let's go back to camp," I said. I had had enough excitement for the day.

The Indians' belief in fate allows them to continue to function in a relatively hostile environment with little fear. Yet throughout the range of the fer-de-lance, they consider it one of the true dangers of the jungle. During his travels in the Amazon, the contemporary writer Peter Matthiessen asked people what they felt were the most dangerous creatures in the area. Tied for first place—the bushmaster and the fer-de-lance.

Back at camp, I placed the fer-de-lance head in alcohol, after photographing it with its jaws open and fangs extended. My house was becoming a jungle version of a believe-it-or-not museum. The Indians knew less than ever what to make of me. The feeling was mutual.

On one of my trips into Dangriga, I received a letter from the Belize Audubon Society warning me that two Indians from Cockscomb, Margarito Bolong and Martin Chun, had gone to the lands commissioner in Belmopan and applied for title to two hundred acres of land per family, or a total of two thousand acres in Cockscomb. I was surprised that they knew how to go about such a procedure and would make a special trip to the capital on their own. Then I remembered the Baptist missionaries who had been in Cockscomb the week before.

My first encounter with the missionaries had been two months earlier. I had met a group of charismatic Southern Baptists building a concrete church with a zinc roof at Maya Center, nestled among the thatched huts. As I pulled the truck over to talk with them, I saw several of their children trying to kill birds with slingshots.

"I'm studying the jaguars in this area," I told them. "We might even try and have the area designated a preserve. Would you please ask your children to stop trying to kill the birds."

"We save souls," one of them replied. The rest just looked at me. That was all. I turned and left after telling the children I'd come after them if they killed any more birds.

They visited the Cockscomb Indians shortly after and showed them a movie depicting sinners burning in hell. They told the Maya to repent. I became angry at their methods and self-righteous behavior and tried to bar them from Cockscomb, telling them it was a restricted study area. They turned my anger against me. I was used as an example to the Indians of how the devil works through people to prevent the saving of souls. Though most of the Indians in the area liked and trusted me, some of the more fervently religious ones became frightened of and even angry with me.

The missionaries promised the Cockscomb Indians a new church similar to the one they were building at Maya Center if they could obtain legal ownership of the land. They instructed Margarito, Cockscomb's Baptist preacher, how to go about this. It was soon after this that I learned that the lands commissioner was receptive to the idea of giving them title to some land in the basin. If that happened now, there was no way the area could be made a jaguar preserve.

I realized I had to spend more time in Belmopan. Cockscomb

was presently designated "crown land," meaning it was in the hands of the Lands Department and could be sold or deeded to anyone. I needed to get it redesignated "forest lands" under the control of the Forestry Department. Then I could work on getting it protected.

If we succeeded in getting Cockscomb designated a forest reserve, the Maya would be forced to leave. Did I want this? Despite our misunderstandings and conflicts, I was starting to feel accepted by the community. Women came by my house while I was in the field and quietly left tortillas or meat stew from their meager supplies. Some of the men wandered over to work out with my weights or to sit with me in the evening. Children stopped by to play and talk with Sue. Agapita would come running over to borrow something for her mother. She'd try to ask for it in English, and when we'd pretend not to understand her, she'd crinkle her eyes and laugh, cupping her hands over her mouth. I loved these people. But the Maya could move, and the jaguars could not.

Jaguars still thrived only in relatively untouched pockets, such as Cockscomb, having been pushed out from much of their range. I knew that when the last wild jaguar died, few would mourn its passing, but the world would never be the same. On the disappearance of jaguars from the United States, Aldo Leopold, a respected zoologist and author, wrote that "freedom from fear has arrived, but a glory has departed from the green lagoons."

The Indians were not wrong in what they wanted. Nor was I. There was no good or evil in this situation. Yet our interests were diametrically opposed and someone would have to lose. The jaguars had always lost before. This time I wanted to help them win.

Sue and I had not been getting on so well since my return from the United States. It was mainly my fault. The project had taken me over. I just wasn't willing to put time or energy into anything else. I started withdrawing deeper into myself and I could see Sue feeling that she was losing me. I could see the hurt in her face. But I'd do anything to complete the project and protect these jaguars.

The foreman from a nearby cattle ranch, known to have killed several jaguars in the area, drove into Cockscomb one day with a truckload of armed ranch workers. I was told they wanted to picnic and hunt as they had always done in previous years. I told them the situation was different now. Though legally I couldn't keep anyone out of Cockscomb, a hunting permit was required by law. Without such a permit, they could go into Cockscomb only if they left their guns with me. The foreman became irate.

"I hunt here for years," he said to me arrogantly. "You new here. No one ever stop me before."

The day had begun badly. Sue and I had argued that morning. I was prepared to do battle on this one. He saw I wouldn't give way and asked if we could talk privately.

"You have hand in de tiger mout," he said, telling me I was in a dangerous situation. "Dere talk in Kendall to get rid of you," he said threateningly.

"You hear such talk, Menchu, or you start it yourself?" I asked, knowing he was probably just trying to scare me. "Remember, fish get ketch by de mout," I told him, using a Creole warning against loose talk.

"Me, nooo," he quickly replied. "I your friend, I warn you about de bad people."

"I know you shoot plenty tigers, Menchu," I said, smiling and patting him on the back for the people in the truck to see. "You're not going to do that in here anymore. Now, take your people and get the hell out of here or I'll go to the police about you next time I'm in Dangriga."

"I see you again, soon," he said with a scowl.

"Yes, you will," I replied.

14 OBEAH MAN

I sat up quickly, still groggy from sleep. My sheet and pillow were drenched with sweat. Was it a bad dream? I couldn't remember. I slid out of bed to check my watch on the shelf: 3 A.M. I looked over to see Sue sleeping soundly, no sign of the tears and anger that had surfaced again that evening. We had argued over something trivial, but our words and feelings had quickly gotten out of hand in the hot, confined quarters of the house.

A scraping sound on the wall made me grab a flashlight. It was another scorpion, no more than a foot above my head, crawling down toward the pillow. Was that why I awoke, or was it another of those dreams I'd been having about jaguars stalking me in the forest? I grabbed the scorpion by the tail with a tweezer and dropped it into my collection jar. That made seventeen caught in the house so far. I wondered if I could collect fifty before the study ended. Then I heard it.

A jaguar was calling from the forest near the camp. Its low hoarse coughing sounds seemed out of place in the silence of the early-morning hours. I now knew what had awakened me. I listened closely and heard the grunts repeated five times before there was silence again. I waited ten minutes but heard nothing more. What was going on out there? It was the first time I'd heard a jaguar calling in Cockscomb. I was fascinated, but at the same time I was frightened. With large cats, calling was thought to be a method of letting one's presence be known, either to keep males away or to attract females.

I got out of bed, went into the front room, and plugged in the mast antenna to the receiver. Chac's signal was blasting. He was moving around camp. It was probably him I had heard. I went outside to see if I could hear his signal with a small antenna. It would indicate how close he was to camp and whether I should try and pinpoint his location. The jungle was completely silent now, but it was a deceiving silence. If I had not heard that grunting or the radio signal, I wouldn't have known that a jaguar was silently moving through the forest within a hundred yards of camp.

I got into the truck and drove a mile west of camp, where I picked up another reading on Chac. I changed frequencies and I could hear Ah Puch from the direction of the Outlier. He was too far away to have been a cause of Chac's vocalizations.

I was fully awake by this time, so I drove farther into the basin and got a location on Ah Puch. Two miles up the road I suddenly smelled the strong unmistakable musky odor of peccary. I stopped the truck and got out, scanning the area to make sure they were not in my immediate vicinity. As I reached a creek, less than twenty feet from the truck, a mass of tracks in the wet sand showed that not long before a herd of these wild pigs had walked along the creek bisecting the timber road. I looked closer, trying to estimate the size of the group, and suddenly spotted a different imprint. There in the sand beside the hoofprints were jaguar tracks, moving in the same direction as the herd. They looked like Ah Puch's. Had he found his evening meal?

The Indians told me that behind every herd of peccary there was a jaguar waiting to pick off stragglers. Although considered favorite prey, peccaries were not easy for a jaguar to catch. There are two species in Belize, the collared peccary and the white-lipped peccary. These tracks were of the collared peccary, a highly social animal, known to travel in herds of more than thirty. Within the herds there exists a hierarchy system to reduce aggression among the animals. When threatened, they chatter their teeth, a sound that sends even the bravest soul looking for a tree to climb.

There were reports of jaguars being torn apart by the knife-like tusks of an infuriated herd of peccaries. So fearsome is the power of these herds that the Amazon Indians told Humboldt that jaguars stayed in trees because they dreaded being surrounded in the forest by peccaries. Theodore Roosevelt, the president of the United States and an avid explorer, naturalist, and writer, gave a similar explanation for the reason jaguars climbed trees. But whether or not jaguars truly fear peccaries, they still often feed upon them, and I regularly found peccary remnants in jaguar feces.

I returned to camp and stayed up the rest of the night, writing by kerosene lantern and recording the cat's activities at fifteen-minute intervals. Ah Puch became inactive and rested until sunrise; Chac stayed active until 7 A.M. I wondered if Ah Puch had gotten one of the peccaries and was now satiated. I closed my eyes and pictured him resting peacefully beneath a large tree, after having matted the underbrush and scraped the ground to make a bed.

It was at times like this that I thought my research was much more exciting and challenging than if I actually observed the jaguar making his kill and going about his life. It was a huge jigsaw puzzle for me, and I had to make a major effort each time I tried to fit a piece into place. The work was often frustrating, but when the pieces began to fit together and a picture started to emerge, it was extremely gratifying.

Agapita, Prudencia, and Juana wandered over shortly after sunrise to watch us cook breakfast and to talk with Sue. Soon Julian came by for his 7 A.M. weight-lifting session. Finally Cirillo wandered over at 7:30 A.M. to go with me and Sue to move a trap. I was already tired from the night's activities, and the day's work hadn't yet begun.

There was a steep portion of road we had to drive over to get to the trap. I hadn't realized how much the road was undercut recently from water washing down a gulley beneath it. As the truck climbed the steep, muddy embankment, the tires lost their grip and the truck slid sideways. Suddenly part of the roadway gave way. It all happened quickly, and the truck came to rest over a fifteen-foot-deep trench, tipping up on its side while balancing on its front axle. Sue was on the side hanging over the trench, and she had to carefully slide over to the driver's side before we could pull her out the door. We had to walk seven miles back to camp, and I added another area on my list of places in the basin where I could no longer drive.

The truck remained there for two days, until Tino and Nari got one of the abandoned skidders operating again. To get to the truck, they blazed a new road through the forest, perpendicular to where it was stuck. The skidder's blades slid under the axle and lifted the truck out of the trench as if it were a toy.

As I sat inside the metal cage of the skidder with Nari, ten feet above the ground, I sensed for the first time the enormous power of these machines. These jungle-eating beasts knocked down forest as easily as cutting through grass. Sadly, I had to give the human mind credit for building a machine that could set back thousands of years of evolution in seconds.

While driving back to camp, I slowed down the truck to ford the creek when I heard Sue gasp. I looked ahead and saw Ah Puch standing about twenty feet on the far side of the creek. This was the same creek where I had seen his tracks following the peccary herd. He watched us as we slowly crossed the creek and approached him, then lowered himself to a half crouch. It was the first time I'd seen Ah Puch since his capture, five months before. He looked wet and was covered with mud. He turned and walked up the road. I inched the truck along behind him, trying to assess his condition. Finally, he disappeared into the forest. I jumped out of the truck with my camera. His musky odor hung in the air. I went to the place where he had just entered the jungle, and stood there, emitting jaguar-like grunts. I wanted to see him, try and get a picture, maybe even get an answering grunt. He was nearby, I could feel it. But there was only silence within the sea of green.

I'd been trying to keep the traps out of areas frequented by Ah Puch because I didn't need or want him recaptured yet. But now he was within Ah Kin's area, close to where another trap was set. I decided to leave the trap a few more days, then move it farther west, out of Ah Puch's known range. But I never got the chance. Two days later Ah Puch was recaptured.

I decided to sedate Ah Puch and use the opportunity to check his weight and condition. As I approached him, I spotted blood frothing around his mouth. There was trouble.

He wouldn't let me close to the trap, so while Sue distracted him, I moved in quickly and jabbed him with the syringe. As soon as I made contact, he swerved, breaking the needle and knocking the pole from my hands. I fell back just as he reached through the bars and swiped upward toward my face. Like old Itzamna had done, Ah Puch tried to fight the effects of the drug.

When he was nearly sedated, Sue held the trap's door open while I grabbed Ah Puch by the collar and pulled him out. I yelled for Sue to inject him with Valium while I held his head toward the ground and kept away from his flailing claws. Finally, he slept.

When I opened his mouth to find the source of bleeding, I moaned in anguish. Ah Puch had broken both his upper canines at the gumline. The breaks looked fresh, and I could only guess it happened while he pulled at the bars, trying to get out of the trap. Nerve endings were hanging from the stubs. When I touched them, his body recoiled reflexively. The cat was in agony. As I turned to get more Valium, Ah Puch suddenly jumped to his feet and, stumbling, headed toward the forest.

I couldn't let him get away in that condition. Feeling a surge of adrenaline flow through me, I dropped the syringe and rushed over, grabbing him by the scruff of his neck. I turned his head around and started walking him back toward the trap. I immediately realized what a foolish thing I was doing, but I had to see it to its finish. I got him back in the trap and closed the door, then sat on the ground to calm myself. Sue stood pressed against a tree, eyes wide in fear.

I injected Ah Puch with additional Valium and followed it with a heavy dose of penicillin to prevent infection of the wounds. There was nothing more I could do with the equipment I had. I spotted one of his canines lying in the mud near the front of the trap. I put it in my pocket, and we left Ah Puch to wake up on his own.

I blamed myself for what had happened. My original reasons for using these large box traps instead of other equipment, such as cable snares or leghold traps, was to lessen the chance of major injury to the cats. I had failed. When Sue tried to assuage my grief, I lashed out at her. I was sick inside, thinking of the agony Ah Puch was going through because of me. I didn't even know if he would live, but even if he did, that magnificent wild jaguar that Bader and I had first captured would never be the same.

Once again the hand of man had interfered with nature's art, albeit with good intentions, and had caused irreparable damage. Again I had to question whether it was worth it. Was I any less to blame than the hunter killing for a skin or a trophy? Was it just a matter of degree? I had to force such doubts aside and persevere. I loved my work and I could rationalize my misdeeds by looking at the larger picture, the greater good, the species. I could tell myself my actions were justified despite the pain they might cause to a few individuals. In truth, I almost believed this, but not quite. The individuals mattered too. I wasn't there to sacrifice a few for the good of many. I wanted to save them all.

The day of Ah Puch's recapture, November 19, was Settlement Day, the major Carib holiday in Belize. Sue and I were expected by friends for a big celebration at Hopkins, one of the rural Carib settlements. I didn't feel much like celebrating just then, so I sent Sue off with Jorge.

The Black Caribs originated on St. Vincent Island, West Indies, where West African slaves brought to the New World intermixed with the aboriginal Indians called Red Caribs. When they rebelled against British rule, they were deported to the Bay Islands off the coast of Honduras in 1795. From there they settled along the mainland coast of Central America, reaching as far north as Stann Creek or Dangriga. Settlement Day celebrates their arrival in Belize.

An early report I had read described the Caribs as "exceedingly friendly, reliable, and honest people, addicted to polygamy and obeah superstitions." These coastal people have created a pattern of life greatly contrasting with the Spanish and Creole cultures. Few live outside their main settlements, where fishing and small-scale agriculture is practiced at subsistence levels. They speak their own language, Garifuna, still containing many elements of their original African and Indian languages.

I had been warned that Black Caribs are considered inferior by the predominant ethnic group in Belize, the Creoles. Creoles often told me that Carib men are lazy, making women do all the work, and that Caribs constantly smell of fish and are "rough-living." Eventually I became very close friends with some of them, particularly several individuals at Hopkins.

The women are incredibly hard-working, often more than the men. The men often have to find work elsewhere, in Belize City or even the United States, because there are few jobs available in the towns. The women provide the stabilizing core and central influence of the household, and they tend the agricultural plot.

The Carib people seemed to me ambitious and intelligent, as well as the most trusting and hospitable people I met in Belize. The majority of teachers in rural villages throughout Belize were Carib. Yet I quickly learned that few Caribs ever spent time in the jungle, just as the forest-dwelling Maya rarely visited the coast.

My closest Carib friend, Miss Eunice, was the midwife for Hopkins. Her grandfather founded the village, and she was the most dynamic individual I'd yet met in Belize. She was looking forward to our visit on Settlement Day, having prepared a special Carib dish: fish boil-up, a mixture of fish, yams, cassavas, plantains, bananas, and onions.

By midafternoon, I decided that wallowing in self-pity was not the solution, so I hopped on the motorcycle and joined Sue and Jorge in Hopkins. It would have been a wonderful day had Ah Puch not been on my mind. It was hard to celebrate anything thinking of how much pain he was probably in.

I tried to forget by drinking rum and coconut milk with Jorge. Of course, it turned into a contest—who could climb the coconut trees the fastest. In the meantime, Sue and Miss Eunice became immediate friends, drinking anise liqueur out of calabash cups and discussing the delivery of babies.

After several hours of drinking, Miss Eunice gave us cups of chicory coffee to wash down each drink "to make we not have *goma* [hangover]." As darkness descended, the rhythmic beat of Garifuna music, played on drums of mahogany and deerskin, could be heard throughout the village. Even the smallest children were encouraged to play the drums and dance. I closed my eyes and thought how easily I could let myself be absorbed into this world. But I had other thoughts on my mind. I left shortly after dark, leaving Sue and Jorge, who remained there late into the night.

The next morning Jorge came by the house very upset. Sue was still passed out. She would have *goma* despite the coffee.

"I know der obeah for true now," he said to me emphatically.

"Why you say that, Jorge?" I asked him.

"Dem Carib boys, I see dey do sumting to Sue. Make she want dance funny and go off wit dey."

I wanted to laugh but Jorge was too serious. "It a good ting I dere," he continued. "I push de Carib boy away, make Sue cum back to Cockscomb. Dey try for do obeah on she for sure. I never goin back dere."

I tried to picture the scene in my mind.

Sue finally woke toward midafternoon, but she remembered little of the previous night. She had been dancing to the beat of the drums when Jorge created a scene among the Carib men, she said. She felt sick now. I knew the only obeah that was done on her had been in the form of too much alcohol.

I couldn't find Ah Puch for a week after he broke his canines. An aerial search pinpointed him within the southern part of Itzamna's former range. We flew low over the treetops and his signal went active. I was relieved. Please don't die, I said to myself.

Though I'd seen similar injuries in captive jaguars, Cockscomb was the real world. Examination of these jaguars showed me they carried no excess fat on their muscular bodies. Their average weights were lower than those recorded by Aldo Leopold in Mexico and even those reported in other parts of Belize. The jaguars in Cockscomb walked a fine line between survival and death.

Slowly I came to the realization that, despite their solitary nature, jaguars were finely tuned to the whereabouts of all their neighbors. Whenever Ah Puch was away from the Guam Bank area, Chac would soon find his way to their area of overlap. When they were widely separated, fecal deposits were not as common along the roads as when they were in close proximity to each other. Evidence of the females along the road was much less frequent than that of males, particularly when the males were in the area.

One morning I awoke at 5 A.M. and went outside to watch the sun rise and enjoy the silence. I loved this time of the day. A fine mist hung over the camp, giving the area a mystical quality. Then my eyes noticed something out of place. A short old Indian man, a stranger to Cockscomb, was standing by the Smith house looking in my direction. As I stood watching him, he turned and walked toward the Indian village. For a brief moment, gazing through the mist, I thought I was having a strange vision.

Later I asked Nari if he knew anything about this man. Nari didn't want to answer me at first. When I pressed him, he told me that the man was a well-known obeah practitioner from the Maya village of San Romaine. He was related to a new family that had just moved into Cockscomb a month earlier.

The new family had come from a more progressive Maya village to the south and was not well accepted by the Cockscomb Indians. I never understood why they had moved back into the forest, but during my first encounters with them, I detected an immediate hostility. They seemed jealous of me and thought I should give them whatever they asked for. Soon I stopped acting friendly toward them and did not invite them to my house. I found out that many of the other Indians were reacting toward them the same way as I was. Anyone not accepted by the Indian community was virtually ostracized and didn't last long. They were no exception and left after several months. While they stayed in Cocksomb, however, they stirred up trouble in camp.

Nari said I shouldn't eat or drink anything the Indians gave me while the stranger was here. I asked jokingly if he was after me, and Nari spoke quietly. "Some Indians vexed with you I hear. They say you greedy."

"Who say that?" I asked, knowing immediately it was the new family.

"I don't know nutting," he said.

That day the house was left open, as it always was, while Sue and I went into the field. I hadn't thought any more of the obeah man until early the next morning, when I woke up before sunrise and began to dress. The last thing I always put on before walking out the door every morning was my baseball cap, which hung on a nail on the wall. This particular morning, as I lifted the hat to my head, a small snake, about eighteen inches long, fell out and bit me on the face. I jumped back and screamed for Sue. She came running over as I wiped the blood from above my eye.

She pinned the snake on the floor and we knelt to examine it. Relief! It was only a small boa constrictor, called *wowla* by the natives. This snake is highly regarded by the Indians, thought not only to be poisonous, but able to sting with its tail. It is also considered the mother of all snakes, bearing different species in its litter. Fortunately, none of these beliefs are true.

The bite above my eye was minor, but the damage to my psyche was not. I tried to find an explanation. The house was raised above the ground and completely screened. I had never had a snake in the house before, and I couldn't come up with any reasonable explanation as to how the snake could have gotten into my hat by itself. Though I had no proof, I felt it was all tied in with the presence of that strange little man.

I was interested in learning more about obeah and in seeing this man work, though not on me. Cirillo would have nothing to do with him, and I learned that most of the families disapproved and were more than a little frightened of his presence in the basin. As converted Baptists, they could not accept obeah as part of their theology. Yet, as I was to observe repeatedly, magic and certain other spiritual beliefs were still held in high regard by these Maya. I didn't want to approach the man myself, feeling strangely uncomfortable whenever I saw him, and Nari finally agreed to talk with him for me.

That night Nari came by, very nervous, and said the obeah man was waiting for me near the big cottonwood tree up the road. Nari didn't want any part of this exchange, so he returned to his shack while I went to talk to the man alone.

I walked up the road.

"Turn off de light," whispered a voice a short distance ahead. I switched off my flashlight and walked the rest of the way in darkness toward the outline of the little man, only about four and a half feet tall.

As I stood next to him, he spoke again. "If anyone cum, we stop talk." I had to lean over to hear him. "Plenty people, dey after me."

"I find *wowla* in my hat today." I couldn't see his face. "It bit me plenty, but it no hurt me. See the bite." I leaned over putting my face near his to show him the wound.

"Oooo . . ." He made a noise almost like a moaning sound. "You no get sick?"

"No sick at all," I lied. "I feel good."

"Dey say you talk wit tiger. Maybe you have strong spirit." He never admitted he had anything to do with the snake. I never asked directly.

We walked along the road in the moonlight.

"Why you here?" I asked. "What make you come all the way into Cockscomb?"

"My brudder daughter [niece] here," he said. "She ask me for visit."

"So you leave soon?" I asked.

"Many people 'fraid of me. Dey say I talk wit devil and bad spirits."

"That true?" I asked.

"You talk wit tiger. Maybe you bad."

We started getting close to camp. An Indian dog was barking.

"I know you do obeah," I said. "I want you to work for me. I pay you good."

"What you want?" He looked at me suspiciously.

"Can you make tiger come to my trap?" I asked.

He was silent for a minute. "Oooo . . ." He made that strange noise again. "Everyting have owner," he said. "I need talk to owner, ask him send tiger. Maybe he do dat. Maybe he no want do dat."

I was intrigued and a little frightened. I wanted to learn how he worked, and I wanted him on my side, like the snake doctor was. He told me I must drive him back to his village to pick up things he needed in order to talk to the owner. I agreed.

The next morning we left Cockscomb together. After thirty minutes of silence he started talking freely. His name was Miguel Ith, a Kekchi Indian in his sixties. He had grown up in the southern Toledo District of Belize, but learned obeah in Guatemala while still a boy. He told me that someone wanting to learn obeah should do it before they had a woman. If you had a woman first, the obeah might turn on you and make you kill yourself. A good obeah man should never have a wife.

He told me he could do anything for me. He could make a *puchinga*, a black doll, and bury it near the house of someone I wanted to harm. He could make any woman come to me, make snakes stay away from me, and many other things. His enthusiasm started getting me nervous and I told him I would be content with his bringing a tiger into my trap. When I tried to question him further on that, he insisted again that he couldn't talk to the tiger directly, just the owner, and that the owner might send the tiger.

Later I learned that the Kekchi Indians believed in an earth deity named Tzultacah. He was the principal guardian of animals, their protector and owner. He was lord of the forest. Stories were told of Indians taken to him because they injured too many animals without killing them.

Though he was not always called by this name, the belief in a guardian of the forest still seemed to linger in the minds of some Indians, such as Miguel. But the belief was dying. Some felt that the degree to which the Indians held on to the beliefs was directly related to how much forest remained in its primal state. As powerful animals, like jaguars and tapirs, became scarce, the spirits of the forest were thought to retreat.

As we pulled into his village, Miguel stopped talking and became very serious. "Stop dere," he commanded, pointing near a patch of forest that would hide my view of most of the village.

"Can I come with you?" I asked.

"No! I soon cum." He got out and disappeared among the huts.

I got out of the truck to stretch my legs. Some Indians had come to the roadside to look at me. I started walking toward them as Miguel came running over carrying a little satchel. "We go now," he commanded.

During the trip back, my attempts at conversation were met with a tense silence. I was becoming more frightened of this little man and I wanted this whole bizarre episode to be over as quickly as possible.

15 CHICLEROS

I didn't see Miguel again for two days. Then on the night of the second day, Sue and I had just finished dinner when we heard a soft tapping at the door. Before I reached the door, Miguel slipped inside, looking over his shoulder to make sure no one had seen him. He immediately asked for a little table or bucket, a candle, and a dish. Then he looked at Sue, uncertainly. I said she knew all about what we were doing and I wanted her to stay. He nodded.

He placed the candle and dish on the overturned bucket, then pulled out a large chunk of copal wrapped in a dried corn husk. He handled the copal as if it were a gem, and I thought again about how sacred this hardened resin had once been to the ancient Maya. At the time of the Spanish conquest, plantations of copal trees were cultivated by the Maya and used as a valuable bartering item and in religious ceremonies. Copal embedded with jade beads had been found in the sacred well at the major Maya ceremonial site of Chichen Itza in Yucatán.

He placed the bucket so that we felt it was facing toward the east, then put the copal in the dish. We extinguished all the lamps as he lit the candle and set the copal ablaze. Then he started mumbling in a barely audible singsong voice. Occasionally, he'd stop talking and contort his face, as if straining to listen.

Then suddenly he turned and looked through me. "What is your name?" he whispered.

"Alan," I whispered back.

"No, what is your name?" he asked again, louder.

"Alan," I repeated.

"WHAT IS YOUR NAME?" he yelled at me.

"ALAN!" I yelled back. I was getting nervous.

He turned toward the candle, his face hidden by copal smoke, and started mumbling again, occasionally saying my name. He told me afterward that he needed to confirm my name to the owner.

The ritual lasted fifteen minutes. The room was filled with the pungent smell of copal smoke. Miguel stood, looking a bit drained. "De tiger cum close to you in tree days," he said to me quietly.

"But will it come into my trap?"

"I tell you what de owner say—he say tiger cum close in tree days."

"But do you think it will come into the trap when it comes close?" I wanted to pin him down.

"What you got in de trap?"

"A live pig."

He looked thoughtful for a few moments. "If tiger hungry, he cum in de trap," he said seriously.

I paid him, and he asked for a drink, explaining that talking to the spirit world was a stressful task. I realized just how stressful it had been when during the next hour he finished the rest of my rum and started on my tequila. Sue and I wondered if he'd ever leave. I wasn't going to throw him out, not as long as he had black dolls to bury.

Two hours later, as he babbled incoherently, I steered him out the door. I watched as he stumbled a zigzag pattern across the open field, the moon casting a strange light on his little body. He left Cockscomb the next day and I never saw him again.

I seldom saw the Maya drink, another result of their newly acquired Christian beliefs. The exceptions were usually older men, such as old Mr. Bolong and Juan Tyul, or younger men caught between two worlds, such as Pablo and Porfilio. When the old men drank, it was serious business, with them ending up as falling-down drunks. This, like some of the spiritual beliefs, may have been a holdover from the old Maya festivals.

Before the white man brought sugar cane and rum to the New World, the Maya men drank balche, brewed from fermented maize, the bark of the balche tree, honey, and water. Its intoxicating properties were said to be well suited to bringing them closer to the gods. Even in the first half of this century, observers of the Maya in Belize, such as Frederick A. Mitchell-Hedges and J. Eric S. Thompson, commented on their heavy drinking, which often resulted in fighting and wildness.

In the beginning of my stay in Cockscomb, I tried to convince the Maya that the old ways were not wrong, just different. After a while, however, I stopped trying to influence their newly found religious beliefs. It saddened me to watch the young Maya girls embarrassed by nudity, which was both innocent and practical, and to hear the boys laugh at some of the old traditional stories that were now told as fairy tales. Yet the very real power of the forest wouldn't let them completely lose hold of their heritage.

Thompson wrote that although the church had tried to eliminate what remained of the old Maya religion, the blending of paganism and Christianity resulted in a form of polytheism.

There was a good example of this in Margarito Bolong, the preacher and the most zealous Baptist in Cockscomb. Every Sunday he'd stand at his pulpit in the thatched church and give hellfire and brimstone sermons to the villagers. But when certain events needed explanation, he resorted to jungle lore.

One day Cirillo told me that Margarito's one-year-old son was dead. I was shocked. I hadn't even known he was sick. No one had come by, as they usually did, for help or medication. Margarito had placed his faith elsewhere. I learned that an evil spirit in the form of a little man was believed to have started coming out of the forest by Margarito's house and giving his child convulsive fits. Margarito said they could hear the little man running a stick along the outside of their hut at night. When the spirit continued his visits, the family simply packed up and abandoned the hut, thinking that the spirit would not follow. He built a new hut next to his brother-in-law Gregorio in the middle of the village, farther away from the forest.

When the convulsions became more frequent and violent, Margarito brought the child to the church and prayed over him. One morning he found his son dead. I listened to Cirillo relate the symptoms: headache, vomiting, sleepiness, and convulsions. It sounded like the child might have had meningitis or cerebral malaria, serious but not incurable maladies. Whatever it had been, if they had told me in time, I could have at least gotten the child to the hospital and given it a chance to live.

I drove Margarito into Kendall the day after the child's death and would never have known about it had not Cirillo told me later. I saw no grief, no hint of anything different in his behavior.

I had heard that death is viewed among the Maya with complete indifference. This is not true. They simply accept death as the result of forces beyond their control. Mourning is foolish and accomplishes nothing. The past is not dwelled upon; it is only today that matters. The powers of the forest spirits are unquestionable but do not alter any feelings regarding the sanctity of the church. In their minds, as Thompson had observed, it all fits together. No matter how much I thought I was becoming a part of their world, I knew that I'd always be a world apart.

The third day after the obeah ritual was performed, Sue and I drove out to check the trap, as we did every morning. I was half asleep, spilling most of my coffee in my lap. I had almost forgotten about Miguel until I realized the trap was closed. Inside, a jaguar lay quietly, almost as if waiting for us. Sue and I looked at each other thinking similar thoughts but neither of us wanting to express them. We'd both been taught that such things had rational explanations.

I thought I had finally captured Ah Kin. Grabbing the drugging equipment, I approached the trap. As soon as I got within six feet, I saw the jaguar had a collar. It was Ah Puch, still alive but thinner and strangely subdued. Why would you walk back in? I asked myself. What agony have you gone through since I saw you ten days ago?

When I jabbed him with the needle, he put up no resistance and was soon asleep. Though his weight had dropped five pounds, the nerve endings from his canines were gone and the stubs were already discolored. There was no smell of infection. I started to have hopes that he might live. After giving him another large dose of penicillin, I put him back in the trap.

Cirillo was waiting at the house when we returned.

"Cirillo, you're not going to believe this," I said excitedly. "It's the third day and we had Ah Puch back in the trap."

"Yes," he said as if I just asked him if he wanted a glass of water. "Obeah man say tiger cum in tree days, so tiger in trap."

It all made perfect sense to Cirillo. He would have been more surprised had there been no jaguar in the trap. Why Ah Puch again? I kept asking myself. Was there really something to the obeah ritual?

The next week I decided it had been too long since I'd spoken to any government officials. I felt it was time to pay a visit to the Ministry of Natural Resources again and make sure Cockscomb

stayed on their minds. I had learned that several high government officials were opposed to any change in the status of Cockscomb, while others were in favor of the idea. I needed to explain
the realities of the situation to these officials while maintaining
a low profile. I was still a gringo, an outsider.

I had formed a close friendship with the president of the
Belize Audubon Society, Jim Waight. This gray-haired, distin-
guished-looking seventy-nine-year-old Creole man had spent
much of his youth surveying the jungles of Belize. He was well
respected by the government and understood the need to preserve areas like Cockscomb for future generations.

The government didn't want to hear the word "park." To
them, a park implied locking up resources and preventing economic development. Right now, the only thing I wanted was a
little time to come up with a firm proposal and some data to back
it up. With the help of the Audubon Society, we convinced
several members of the cabinet to temporarily withhold approval of all requests for the acquisition of land in Cockscomb
until the situation was studied in greater depth. It would give
me time to collect more data while we talked at greater length
about the future needs of the area.

After several trips by Jim Waight and myself, the government
agreed to delay action. We had moved a small step forward. I
also knew I had just pushed the Indians a step back and that
didn't please me. Was I doing the right thing? In my heart, I felt
I was.

There were other incidents that helped convince me as well.
I returned from the field one afternoon to find a modern version
of the great white hunter waiting for me. He stood a little under
six and a half feet tall, with a belt of bullets around his waist,
holding up a .357 magnum pistol. He introduced himself in the
manner of a man whose name should mean something to people.
It meant nothing to me. I was later to discover he was from one
of the wealthiest families in the United States, and was indeed
well known.

"I'm here to get a jaguar," he said to me immediately.

"Sorry, but jaguar hunting is illegal in Belize."

"Well, I know that, but I'm sort of a special case." He produced a paper that showed me I could still be surprised by Belize.

The document stated that this man was given permission to hunt for one week and kill one jaguar. It was signed by Prime Minister Price. I was flabbergasted.

"Why of all the places in Belize did you pick Cockscomb to hunt jaguars?" I asked.

"Several of the government people told me you were doing a great job catching jaguars," he replied matter-of-factly. "Everyone thinks they must be pretty plentiful here."

"So you felt this would be the best place to kill one," I finished the thought for him.

"Fact is, I only have three days in the country. I'd like a trophy pretty badly. I kinda hoped you might be able to get me one in a trap I could shoot. Might be some money in it for you."

The man's audacity was so outrageous, I laughed. Glad to see me agreeable, he pressed the point. "Think we might try and get one today?" he asked.

He was the one with a .357 magnum, but I glared at him. "Let me tell you something, buddy. I don't care who you are. You'll have to bring the prime minister himself in here if you want to hunt in Cockscomb. And even then, I'd never catch one in a trap for you. I'm trying to save these animals, not give people like you a better chance to kill them."

He seemed surprised at my outburst and left Cockscomb in a huff. I heard that he never got his trophy before leaving the country. For that I was glad, but the circumstances that led him to me made me realize it was going to be an uphill battle with the government.

Apart from the recapture of Ah Puch, I was having no luck catching new jaguars. The two females and Ah Kin were not even going near the traps. I needed to get into new areas no longer accessible by truck. The problem was that the traps were

heavy and cumbersome. On my next trip to Dangriga, I went
to see a welder, and we drew up plans for a jaguar trap that
could be built in pieces. I could carry it into the jungle and
assemble it at the trap site.

While in town, I made a long-overdue visit to a shop owner
named Gungara I had heard about from Pablo. He sold vegeta-
bles above the counter and bought cat skins below the counter.
His current rates were a pitiful Bze$50 for jaguar skins and
Bze$30 for ocelot skins. Of course, he had already heard of me
and was actually delighted I had finally come by. He was sure
we could make a deal that could be profitable to us both. I played
along.

"Dis year been no good. I got 'bout fifty tiger and fifty tiger-
cat. I like plenty more. You got?" he asked.

"Maybe I got some," I said. "But I gotta be careful. The skins
gotta leave town quick. How I know you get rid of these skins
quick?"

"I get ridda dey plenty quick." He leaned his face close to
mine. His breath stank. "Dis man, Rosada, he cum down from
Mexico City, two, sometime tree, time a year. He buy everything. He want more."

"That sound good," I said. "But I gotta think 'bout it."

I went directly to a phone and called the Forestry Department
in Belmopan. Yes, they knew of this man, they told me. But
there was not much they could do about it. They'd have to catch
him with the skins. I knew there was little chance of that. I hung
up, frustrated, knowing it was fruitless to press the point.

While waiting for the new trap to be built, I decided to examine
some other jaguar habitat in the country. Although I had plenty
of work in Cockscomb, I wanted to find an assistant for the
second year of the project so that I could do additional jaguar
research in a second study area. I decided to revisit an area that
my survey showed had the highest density of jaguar sign in the
country, the Gallon Jug-Hill Bank area in northwestern Belize.
This flat, swampy, heavily forested area was rejected as a pri-

mary study site because it was on good agricultural land and was under the ownership of the Belize Estates and Produce Company. This company was the largest private timber concern in Belize and as late as 1966 owned nearly 20 percent of all the land in the country.

The Gallon Jug-Hill Bank area had been one of the richest hardwood forests in Belize but was heavily and irresponsibly exploited first with oxen, then railroad, now trucks and bulldozers. It was never systematically reforested and now was mostly secondary forest. I knew that it would eventually be cleared for agriculture. Bader hunted here and he knew the area well. I talked with him by phone, explaining my plans. We arranged an expedition for the following week.

It was Sue's first trip in Belize to any area other than Cockscomb. I was hoping it might ease some of the tension that had been building between us and provide a break from the rigors of life in Cockscomb. She got along well with Bader.

I realized what I had been missing most in Cockscomb as soon as I awoke the first morning in the Gallon Jug area: the sound of howler monkeys, called baboons by the locals. At first, the calls seemed distant, sounding like a prolonged, almost mournful wail. Then, as others chimed in and the howling rose in intensity, the sounds became aggressive, staccato. If I hadn't known what it was, I would have been frightened. During his travels through Belize, Ivan Sanderson wrote, "Once you have lived under the sound of the howler's roar the echoes of the slumbering, silent jungle will have entered your soul." Fritz W. Up de Graff, another Amazon explorer, wrote of the howlers: "The first time I heard it, it seemed that all the jaguars on the Amazon were engaged in a death-struggle." Such vocalizations are believed to be territorial displays for the monkeys, as well as a means of communication within a group.

There had been a troop of howlers at Guam Bank until the timber operation disturbed the jungle and the Indians shot some of them. I was never to see one in the basin, though they may have lived far back in the rugged areas to the west that I never penetrated. Cirillo had killed one years before but said he'd never kill another because its death screams and facial expressions were too much like those of a person.

In the Amazon, Alfred Wallace was told that jaguars have the power to mesmerize howler monkeys. He was told of an instance where a jaguar looked up into a tree at a howler and made it come lower and lower, until finally it fell at the jaguar's feet.

I had an encounter of a different sort with the howlers. While I was looking up into a tree, trying to get some pictures of a small troop of five monkeys, a large male came out onto a branch above my head and started jumping up and down, screaming at me in defiance. When I persisted, he started to defecate and then urinate on me. His aim was incredibly accurate and I never got the pictures.

After two days of searching in the Gallon Jug area we found no jaguar sign. I had found abundant sign there the previous year. Though Bader was surprised, I was not. Numerous abandoned hunting camps gave part of the explanation. Finally we found fresh tracks of an adult male and followed them until we came on a two- or three-day-old peccary kill. It was picked clean and the skeleton was disarticulated, but there was no doubt as to the cause of death. The skull lay a short distance from the rest of the skeleton. When I examined it, I saw that the top of the cranium was missing, like a piece of a puzzle. Only one animal in this part of the world had the power to do that.

As I had seen repeatedly, the killing power of a jaguar was awesome. The remains of skeletal fragments and body parts from their prey, such as bones, hooves, claws, and teeth, found in their feces showed how easily they crunched bones. With larger prey, particularly livestock, I saw repeated evidence of how they punctured through the skulls or vertebrae. Never had I seen the cranial cap lifted off as it was here. I tried to imagine how it happened.

Maybe the jaguar had been following a herd of peccaries for

hours. Finally, one inexperienced young peccary drops back, pausing to browse on a particularly tasty plant. The jaguar sees it separated from the pack and flattens himself on the ground, inching up through the bush, his head slightly lifted and his eyes never leaving the prey. Suddenly, a leap by those powerful hind limbs as the jaguar bursts through the vegetation, closing the distance between him and the peccary within a blink of an eye. In an instant, the canines clamp the skull, and the large front paws grab and twist the neck sideways at an impossible angle. The peccary is dead before it hits the ground, its skull pulled apart by the motion of the jaguar's jaws.

On our last evening, as we were looking for a place to camp, we came upon a working chiclero camp. Though I'd met several of these hardened jungle men by this time, I wasn't quite prepared for Kaniko, a sixty-four-year-old wiry Mexican. He, his son, and another chiclero, a Creole, Mr. Balum, were settling in for the evening as we arrived. Bader and Kaniko knew each other, so we decided to set up an adjacent camp and share our supplies for an evening meal.

While there was still daylight, I walked around their camp examining the leather receptacles filled with the thick, milky chicle collected from the sapodilla tree and used to make chewing gum. This tree grew wild in the forest and had an interesting history.

The tree itself had been valued by the ancient Maya, its hardwood used extensively for lintels and utensils. Later, the chicle sap became a product important to the economy of Belize. At the beginning of the twentieth century, Belize was exporting two million tons of chicle per year. After World War II, the demand for chicle declined sharply as a result of competition from synthetics and other varieties of gum. The working of chicle had virtually died out in Belize, until recently, when a small resurgence in demand made it profitable for a few hardy people, such as Kaniko.

I walked over and watched Mr. Balum, his lean, hard, black

body pouring sweat, as he stirred a large cauldron filled with steaming, bubbling chicle. This process removed all the moisture so the chicle could be made into a hard brown block for transport. He said they were presently getting about Bze$250 per pound for the chicle. Kaniko explained that all of them working together from sunrise to sunset could bring in a hundred pounds in a week and a half. During a five- or six-month season, relatively good money could be made.

But their life was not easy and sometimes took a heavy toll. A chiclero I later met in the Chiquebul Forest, west of Cockscomb, showed severe facial disfiguration and scarring, signs of leishmaniasis, which is so common among them that it's called chiclero's disease. Few of them will leave the forest for treatment. One of the biggest problems for chicleros, as Bader explained it, was that after six months in the jungle, much of it spent alone, they would take their earnings and become crazy drunk in the nearest town. Then they quickly spent the rest of their money or were easy targets for robbers. After that they'd have to go right back into the forest.

Kaniko's contribution to the dinner that night was the largest flour tortillas I had ever seen, each about eighteen inches in diameter. I thought one of them could satisfy the hardiest of appetites. Kaniko ate five of them. Like many bushmen, Kaniko was an excellent storyteller and during the meal entertained us with tales of his exploits in the jungle.

He acted out a story about one of his encounters with a jaguar, leaping around the fire and gesturing wildly with his hands, telling how he came within a hair's breadth of being eaten by the animal. Of course, he killed the jaguar before it killed him. This was the typical ending to such stories. While talking, he never took his eyes off Sue. I knew that he was enamored of her and was trying to impress her with the story. Upon their first meeting, Kaniko's face had lit up as he asked, "What is dis sweet-looking angel doing back here?"

After dinner, Kaniko gestured Bader aside and I heard them

arguing and laughing. Later that night in our tent, Bader told us of the conversation.

"I no see woman in five mont," he had said to Bader. "She look nice, I want she." He was referring to Sue.

"She with the gringo," Bader explained to him.

"Dat no matter. I want she. You take de gringo back in de bush and lose he. Den I have a lil fun."

Bader had laughed at the idea, but Kaniko seemed serious. When Bader refused, Kaniko handed him a drinking cup. "Bring·dis to de woman," he said. "Tell she to pee in it, only 'bout half full. If I no can eat de meat, I want drink de juice."

The chicleros, like the Indians, had a devastating effect on the wildlife wherever they went. They feared jaguars and pumas and would go out of their way to hunt and kill them. Kaniko told us how he had killed a puma several weeks earlier and how a neighboring chiclero had shot a jaguar just the night before. The animal had escaped but left a lot of blood behind. The old wounds in the skulls of problem jaguars flashed through my mind.

I asked Bader how often jaguars got shot and ran off wounded. He said that such incidents were relatively common and that over half of all the jaguars he'd killed had former wounds in the skull. I made a mental note to get more data on this.

We woke up the next morning at sunrise. Kaniko's camp was empty—everyone was already in the forest gathering chicle. After a quick breakfast, I followed Bader's Land Rover out to the Northern Highway, where Sue and I said good-bye to Bader and started back for Cockscomb.

We stopped at a restaurant near Orange Walk, where Sue and I were approached by a drunk Spanish man. In a mixture of Spanish and English he told me he had the four hundred pounds of marijuana waiting for me outside in a truck. I was taken aback at first, but played along, thinking it was a joke on a gringo.

"Is the stuff good?" I asked him. He seemed offended. I went on, "It better be good or my boss in the States get very mad."

"We get this done quick," he said looking around him, his

expression suddenly becoming very serious. "We go in back."

It was no joke. It dawned on me that he had mistaken me for someone else. I became nervous at the thought of what he might do once he realized his mistake. I played along a little while longer, insisting we drink more beer. Finally he went to the bathroom. Sue and I quickly made our exit.

16 EYES OF XAMAN EK— BLOOD OF AH PUCH

Throughout much of the jaguar's range there exist stories of unprovoked jaguar attacks on man. Some are about children who had wandered off from villages and been later found with "hardly anything but the gnawed, bloody bones and scraps of cartilage being left." Some are about jaguars attacking men as they return from the bush. There are even stories about jaguars entering huts and snatching them from their hammocks. Roosevelt documented two cases of unprovoked man-eating, in one of which the jaguar sank his canines into a man's skull.

Yet most natives consider the jaguar nonaggressive, even cowardly. And anyone who has spent any time in the jungle knows how slim the chances are of coming across one of these animals. Ivan Sanderson never saw one, even after weeks in the forests of Belize. He wrote: ". . . despite all you may have heard to the contrary, meeting one of the large cats is more than exceptional in most tropical forest countries which are known to be infested with these creatures."

Encounters usually consist of a brief glimpse of this powerful predator before it disappears into the forest. Wallace told of such an encounter in the Amazon: "In the middle of the road he turned his head, and for an instant paused and gazed at me, but having, I suppose, other business of his own to attend to, walked steadily on, and disappeared in the thicket."

Humboldt wrote of an interesting story in which the innocent worlds of two Indian children and a young jaguar merged momentarily, until each realized its proper place:

Two Indian children, a boy and a girl, about eight and nine years of age were seated on the grass. . . . At two o'clock in the afternoon, a jaguar issued forth from the forest, and approached the children, bounding around them; sometimes he hid himself in the high grass, sometimes he sprang forward, his back bent, his head hung down, in the manner of our cats. The little boy, ignorant of his danger, seemed to be sensible of it only when the jaguar with one of his paws gave him some blows on the head . . . the claws of the jaguar wounded the child, and the blood flowed with violence. The little girl then took a branch of a tree, struck the animal, and it fled from her. The Indians ran up at the cries of the children, and saw the jaguar, which retired bounding, without making the least show of resistance.

Of all the great cats—tigers, lions, jaguars, and leopards—the jaguar is the least known to attack man unprovoked and is virtually undocumented as a man-eater. I always sensed while I was in the forest that jaguars knew of my presence long before I came upon evidence of them. Why did they never attack me? Why wasn't I viewed as potential prey? No one has been able to answer these questions satisfactorily. Most researchers have encountered few documented cases of jaguar attacks on human beings. Yet the natives greatly fear this cat wherever it is found, mainly because of its strength and potential ability to harm man, if provoked. In all my encounters in Cockscomb, the jaguar wanted only to disappear into the forest.

The explanation for such behavior may have something to do with the ability of both man and jaguars to avoid each other throughout much of their habitats. Johann R. Rengger, documenting the wildlife of Paraguay in the early nineteenth century, thought that jaguars were shy and retiring in more uninhabited regions but bold and sometimes aggressive where they were used to the presence of man. In the Brazilian Pantanal, Tony Almeida, a well-known jaguar hunter, wrote that there were no man-eaters because man was the scarcest animal around.

In other parts of the world, where man-eating is more common among the other large cats, much of the cats' habitat has been destroyed and man has been present in greater numbers and for a far longer time than in areas inhabited by jaguars. Jim Corbett, the famous hunter of man-eating tigers, said that tigers didn't normally regard humans as prey. It was only those who were overstressed that adopted such an alien diet.

It is believed that many man-eaters become cattle killers first. Such may be the situation with jaguars when their ranges are cut down or invaded, people start to live in close proximity to them, and their food resources become nonexistent. Where this has already happened, jaguars are killed before things get out of hand or before they become accustomed to the presence of man. I wondered how used to my presence the cats in Cockscomb were getting, as I traveled through their area every day.

A short time after we left the Gallon Jug area, Bader came down to Cockscomb and dropped off his young female margay, Kashka, for a month while he and Mary Ann went away. Though I didn't approve of wild animals as pets, I owed Bader more than I could repay. I agreed to the arrangement, knowing that this margay had recently been taken from the wild and might give me some new insights into the species' behavior.

Kashka was a terror from the very beginning. For the first few days she stayed in the shack demonstrating her acrobatic skills. I was extremely impressed with the agility of this little five-pound ball of fur. She could jump from one end of the shack to another in almost one leap, and demonstrated this repeatedly when anything moved across the floor and struck her fancy, like our toes. She would sink her little canines in, as if crushing her prey, and quickly draw blood.

She exhibited a voracious appetite for her size. Bader had told us to feed her only raw meat and, while she ate, no one could approach within two feet of her. Usually, she'd drag the meat out of her bowl and hide under the bed. Any eye contact was met with a low, rumbling growl and hissing.

When she was not eating or scurrying after something, she'd stay above ground level. She had picked one particularly high shelf in the corner of the front room, where she would sit with her back to the wall and watch the world. Her arboreal instinct was definitely at work.

Most of the Indians stopped coming into my house while she was there. Tame or not, she was still a tiger-cat, and nothing I could say or do would dissuade them from fearing her. Within several days, Kashka started ripping at the screen door and crying, indicating she wanted to venture into the outside world. It was time to cut the apron strings, and I was only too glad to get her out of the house for a while. Bader had not housebroken her, and on top of all the other smells in our place, her feces stank worse than the jaguars'.

When we first let her out the door she bounded into the front yard, felt the earth under her little paws, and hesitated. She stayed near the house for ten minutes, then took off into the adjacent forest. It was like going home.

She'd often stay away two or three days at a time, even during heavy rains. Just when I'd start to think she was lying dead somewhere in the forest, we'd hear her crying at the door. There she was, bedraggled, a bit thinner, and perhaps a little wiser, realizing that she didn't quite have the hang of this hunting game. There was a little more to it than catching toes.

Yet she kept on proving to me that she was cleverer than I thought. On one occasion she returned in the middle of the night and got no response to her scratching at the front door. She then came to the rear of the house, leaped about five feet into the air onto the screen over the window by my head, and screeched loudly. Sue and I both jumped up. I thought the master jaguar had finally come to claim me. On those occasions when Kashka granted us a few nights of her company in the house, she insisted on sleeping on the bed curled up between Sue's face and mine.

Just as everyone was getting used to Kashka running around camp, she decided to start paying regular visits to the Indian village. This immediately worried me. One afternoon, as I was walking over to find Cirillo, I heard screams of terror from the creek where the women bathe and do their laundry. As I ran over, two children carrying buckets of water were standing at the top of the hill pointing toward the creek. Standing naked in the middle of the creek was Rosa, one of the new Maya women in camp, sixteen years old, and expecting her third child. She was clutching her two-year-old baby to her breasts and wailing loudly. Halfway down the path stood little Kashka, calmly watching the woman scream. When I called to her, Kashka bounded up the path and followed me home.

That was only the beginning. Soon after, Martin's wife came to the door very upset. Kashka had walked into the village and killed two chickens. I agreed to pay for the damage, but I knew that wouldn't solve the problem. Kashka had learned where to obtain easy food. The Indians would now categorize her as a chicken killer, and it would not sit well with them to allow a cat to kill their chickens even if I continued to pay for them.

We went to the village to get Kashka. When she was chased away from the chickens by one of Martin's sons, she had dashed into one of the huts and all the Indians had run out. She was angry. I went in and found her standing on one of the shelves, her haunches raised. As I reached up for her, she hissed angrily. Annoyed, I made a quick move to grab her. She lashed out with her claws and opened up a large gash down my arm. I walked out bleeding, without Kashka. The Indians started mumbling in Maya. Sue walked in then, soothed Kashka, charmed her into coming down from her perch, and came out carrying her. The Indians were very impressed.

The next few days we tried keeping Kashka in the house, but to no avail. She had gotten a taste of the wild and she wanted more. We had no alternative but to take her out of Cockscomb and leave her with Bader's foreman at his ranch. I was sorry to see her go, but the Indians weren't. Capturing and releasing wild jaguars was unnatural enough to them, but keeping a wild tiger-cat as a pet was crazy!

The new portable trap, consisting of seven pieces, was finally ready. It was much heavier than I had expected and required five Indians and myself to carry it any distance. I decided to assemble it back in an area of the basin where I'd recently seen the first definite puma tracks in Cockscomb and where I'd seen jaguar tracks earlier in the study. The road was no longer passable there.

Data from my survey of the tracks of fourteen pumas throughout Belize showed that the front paws averaged three inches long by almost three and a half inches wide, and the back paws, three inches by three inches. In a similar survey of the tracks of nearly seventy jaguars, the front paws averaged three and a half inches long by four inches wide, and the back paws, three and a half by three and a half inches. In areas where both cats occurred, the tracks were sometimes difficult to differentiate. However, plaster casts taken from captive jaguars and a captive puma at the Belize Zoo showed some clear distinctions.

Puma tracks are generally more elliptical in shape, while jaguar tracks are almost round. Puma toes tend to be more pointed and puma pads have better-defined lobes.

The tracks of the cat I wanted to trap were definitely a puma's. I assumed pumas were more common in Cockscomb than the frequency of their tracks along the roads suggested. Two had been killed in the basin in the three years before I arrived, and there had been at least one sighting by an Indian while I'd been in the basin.

Though pumas and jaguars are about the same size, the puma is not classified with the other great, or roaring, cats. Pumas have an ossified hyoid in their throats, enabling them to purr instead of roar. The puma's head is small, and its body, lithe and narrow. It gives the impression of being much more catlike than the short-limbed and bulky jaguar. Perhaps its physical build, allowing the puma to be relatively quick and agile, helps explain why the puma is often the victor in Indian accounts of battles between jaguars and pumas.

Yet the puma is known as a very unaggressive cat and has a reputation of being a "cowardly animal," little feared by local inhabitants. In truth, it is simply solitary and elusive, with the largest range of any native New World mammal species. It can be found from British Columbia in Canada through Patagonia in South America, and was once distributed throughout the United States. I began to realize just how elusive this cat was when I tried to catch it in a trap.

George Schaller had found that where pumas and jaguars overlapped in the Pantanal of Brazil, pumas were more abundant in drier habitats, while jaguars preferred wetter areas. During my survey of Belize, the only area where the density of pumas appeared greater than that of jaguars was in the high, drier Mountain Pine Ridge area. However, data from Cockscomb, as well as sightings by locals in other parts of Belize, indicated that pumas are present though rarely observed where jaguars are abundant. I wondered if, in the presence of jaguars, they simply remained more wary and avoided traveling the same routes.

During the first two weeks of trapping, the puma never approached the trap's front door. It came to the rear of the trap, tore away the cohune leaves, and tried to get at the pig. After several failed attempts, the puma began avoiding the portion of road where the trap stood. Tracks showed that it would go into the forest about thirty feet before reaching the trap and exit the forest on the other side of the trap.

Instead of adjusting to and ignoring the trap, the puma seemed to exhibit the opposite reaction. The longer the trap sat, the more infrequently the puma walked that section of road. Finally, I closed the trap and tied the pig outside. If he took the free meal, maybe he'd walk into the trap after a second pig. The puma wouldn't come near the pig. Frustrated, I dismantled and removed the trap and left just the pig. Over a two-week period, the puma still wouldn't touch the pig.

During this time, I was given another lesson on the role of parasites in the jungle. One afternoon, while checking on the pig, I noticed an open wound above his right eye as a result of rubbing against the tree he was tied to. I had been having problems with small wounds made by vampire bats, usually on the pig's ears. The bats came back every night and reopened the same wound for their evening meal. As long as I cleaned and treated them, the wounds presented no problems. This was a larger wound and I made a mental note to return the next day with medication.

Flash flooding kept me out of the area for three days. When I was finally able to reach the pig, I was met with a sight straight out of a horror movie. The pig's right eyeball was gone! In its place was a mass of squirming screwworm larvae emerging from the empty socket. The pig smelled of rotting flesh but was alive and hungry.

I brought the pig back to camp. After sedating him, I poured alcohol and then screwworm medication into the eye socket. He was a tough little pig and healed quickly. He had served enough time in the jungle, so I gave him to Cirillo, in whose care he grew big and fat and was eventually used for a corn harvest feast.

The screwworm fly belongs to a general category known as

blowflies. It can attack living tissue, laying its eggs in wounds or in the nostrils of its host. The larvae of these flies cause considerable damage to domestic livestock throughout its range from North through South America. If I hadn't treated the pig, it would have died from what had started as a superficial wound. Any animal can be affected by these parasites. I again realized how important it was to avoid any wounding of wild animals while working with them.

Studies of large solitary cats have shown that they rarely have physical encounters, using such techniques as marking and vocalizations to avoid one another. This seems to be the case with the jaguar. During the two years of my project my examination of the seven cats I had captured, as well as of dozens of hides throughout the country, revealed very few scars or wounds that might have been the result of physical aggression.

In an area as rugged and competitive as Cockscomb, any abnormality or temporary weakness could prove fatal to a jaguar. Numerous parasite species, whose life cycles depend on finding an appropriate microenvironment, wait for just such opportunities. In a fight between two large cats, there may be no victor.

I finally gave up on the puma. I shifted the trap to the northwest edge of the area where the timbering operation had penetrated two years earlier. We carried the parts of the trap one and a half miles uphill to a stream where the tracks of another jaguar had been seen. There I assembled it.

On December 18, five days after the trap was set, I raced up the hill ahead of Sue to find the trap's door closed. Inside, a small, uncollared jaguar was sitting calmly. A female, I thought immediately; it had to be. Its head seemed small, but it was covered with mud from the previous night's rain and I could barely see its spots.

The three males that I had captured thus far had become very aggressive when I approached the trap, but this jaguar flattened its body against the floor of the trap as if trying to hide in the nonexistent underbrush. I stood up from my crouched position and began circling the trap. The cat remained quiet, flattening its body even more, but keeping the head up. The jaguar lay like a statue, its musculature clearly defined beneath the mud. Only the eyes shifted, following my every movement.

Toward the rear of the trap I stopped, surprised. She had testicles. It was not a female after all, but a young male jaguar. Of course. Everything about its behavior indicated that I was probably the first human being he'd ever seen. He didn't know what to make of me.

I went to the front of the trap and sat down, my face no more than a foot from his. A low guttural growl rumbled from his throat as our eyes locked. Even for something undefined, I was a bit too close for this jaguar's liking. I held my ground, waiting to see if he'd do anything. The growling stopped and he continued looking at me. I understood why these cats were thought by some native people to have the power of mesmerization. I wanted to insert my hand through the bars or put my nose up to his. What are you thinking? I wondered. Do you wonder if I'm edible? I edged my face closer.

"What are you doing?" I heard a whisper behind me. "You're too close," Sue said.

The sound of another human voice broke the spell. She was right. I slowly reached for my camera and put the lens against the bars. I had to get those eyes on film. The click of the shutter brought another low growl.

After taking several pictures, I backed away. It was the closest I'd ever been to an undrugged jaguar, and the bars, though separating us, had disappeared for a few moments.

"You're the most magnificent animal I've ever seen on this planet," I said quietly before moving away.

Jabbing him with the syringe was easy. But after that first contact he was never complacent again. He lunged against the bars, his growl now a roar. Man had now been classified. He was painful, he was enemy. I felt a pang of regret yet hoped that in his next encounter with man, he might not be so fearless. Maybe he would live longer.

He felt so light as I pulled him out of the trap. Sue stood to one side taking notes:

Sex—male
Age—young adult
Total length—72 inches
Tail length—21 inches
Head circumference—20 inches
Height at shoulder—17 inches
Height at hip—17 inches
Weight—85 pounds

His neck circumference of sixteen inches was virtually the same as that of adult jaguars, but I left extra space between the collar and his neck in case of additional growth. His teeth were white and showed little wear, but I was not sure of his exact age. I felt he was transitional between subadult and a young mature adult, somewhere around three years old. I had more regrets about capturing this animal than any of the others. I hoped he'd live a long and healthy life.

After finishing with the jaguar, I placed him back in the trap, leaving the door slightly open. Sue and I were covered with mud, and the jaguar's musky odor clung to us. I knew of a beautiful stream a little over a mile from the trap where we could bathe while waiting for the jaguar to come out of sedation.

As we walked there, we were both silent, caught up in an ecstasy that had rarely come to either of us. It was not just the collaring of a new jaguar that thrilled me but the fact that I was able to experience the true wild nature of the animal, before the outside world had interfered. Sue, after seeing the injury of Ah Puch and the death of Ixchel, felt almost cleansed.

Several days earlier we had both decided that it might be best if Sue returned to the United States after the new year. Sue had started to withdraw from me in order to prevent more pain. But that afternoon in the jungle stream all our differences and tensions vanished. The raw beauty and energy of one of the greatest wild creatures on earth filled our hearts.

Surrounded by boundless jungle, we romped naked in the stream. Little fish called billums nibbled at our bodies. A colony of Montezuma oropendolas, large chestnut-colored birds with bright-yellow tails, peered out from their nests hanging high above us in the trees and cackled, their raucous calls cheering us on. We made love, slowly and tenderly, forgetting the bitterness and tears of previous days. I nibbled on her body like the billums and imitated the growl of the jaguar we had just caught. Sue laughed and laughed. I looked into her face and saw the girl I had met leaning over a microscope in my biology class in Tennessee three years earlier. We had done a lot together in those years. What could she see in my face? I wondered. Could she see the pain and the anger that had been pushing her away from me? I hoped not. Not right now. Right now we were just two children playing naked in a jungle stream.

We usually rested the day after a jaguar capture. Sue decided to spend some time with the Indian children, while Jorge and I went to Kendall to purchase supplies and to drink some beer. I had named the new jaguar Xaman Ek (pronounced Zamanek), after the god of the North Star, another benevolent deity, important to travelers and merchants.

The village of Kendall, located right outside Cockscomb, on the Southern Highway, consisted of a small wooden shack that served as a store and no more than ten dwellings, inhabited by Maya, Creole, and Spanish. Kendall was the ultimate one-horse town.

The store sold the basic necessities and had a kerosene refrigerator that, when working, stocked ice-cold beer and soft drinks. It was the liveliest place for several miles around and was where everyone gathered to tell lies and pass on information. Once I became known in the area, it was a useful stopping place to find out all the goings-on. If I treated people to enough beers, I could get them to start bragging and thus obtain information about reliable jaguar sightings and shootings in the area. If I wanted to start rumors or spread information, all I had to do was mention it here.

We stayed only two hours before returning to camp. As I pulled up to the house, Sue came running out, a strained look on her face. "Juan Tyul came over and said there's a jaguar with a collar lying dead along the path to his plantation," she said, putting a clenched fist to her mouth to keep from crying.

I could feel Jorge's eyes on me, wondering how I'd react. It must be Ah Puch. We had been picking up his signal around camp for days. One of the Indians told me that two nights earlier, while he was sleeping at his milpa, a jaguar had come around and urinated on the side of his hut. I had had a premonition for the last week that things were going very badly for Ah Puch.

"Damn!" I said and started to run toward the Indian village. "Cirillo!" I yelled, hoping he might tell me it was all a mistake. Florencia came to the door, looked at me, and rushed inside.

"Alan, wait!" Sue yelled, racing behind me. I turned to her, dazed. "Calm down, Alan."

"Go in and tell Juan I'm coming. Tell him I want him to take me to the tiger, NOW!" I yelled at her.

Rage was building inside of me, a rage with no outlet, and there was no one but myself to blame it on. I knew I had to hold it back, but I didn't know if I could. I was standing in the middle of the village and all the Indians were by their huts watching me. Somewhere to my left I heard an Indian woman whisper, "He crazy, crazy, bad."

Tyul, who was in the middle of a meal, came racing out in fluorescent-pink underwear, afraid to look at me. He ran down the trail. I caught up to him but said nothing. Seven Indian men, four boys, and Sue followed behind.

We ran down an old skidder road, then crossed South Stann Creek, the water chest-deep and roaring from the heavy rains. Then we followed a narrow trail along a milpa. Fifty yards up the trail lay the jaguar. I stopped short, six feet from him. It was worse than I had thought.

"Ah Puch," I groaned.

I didn't know this jaguar. What I saw before me was skin and bones, the ribs protruding through the muddied, dull fur. Only the white collar hanging loosely around his neck gave him away.

"Ah Puch," I cried again in anguish.

Without thinking, I ran to him, fell on my knees, and cradled his head in my lap. Something snapped inside of me. I could feel the emptiness. Something had just left me forever.

Then I noticed the shallow breathing. Ah Puch was not dead, at least not yet. I pried open his jaws and put my face to his mouth. It smelled horribly of infection and I flashed back to a story told in Bruce Lamb's *Wizard of the Upper Amazon* about a man caught in a death struggle with a jaguar: ". . . his breath was in my face and it had a hideous stink."

I looked up to see the Indians staring at me in disbelief. In that instant, Ah Puch used some of his last reserve of strength to clamp his jaws shut over one of my fingers and lash out with his paw, ripping open my shirt and gashing my shoulder. I tried pulling away, but my hand was caught in his mouth. I knew that if he had not been so close to death, he would have taken my finger right off. Instead, his incisors penetrated my nail and I could feel my warm blood mixing with his saliva. I needed to get those jaws open.

"Help me," I screamed to the Indians, tears of pain and anguish rolling down my cheeks.

No one moved. No one dared move. They thought I had lost my mind. I grabbed his nose with my free hand and pulled up hard. His jaws parted for an instant before clamping shut again. My mangled finger was free. Ah Puch lay his head back down in my lap, the last of his energy expended. He waited to die.

Standing, I lifted Ah Puch and put him over my shoulder. I felt his hot, fetid breath against my face. What I was doing was crazy, but I had lost all sense of what was sane and what was not.

I started back along the trail, tears streaming from my face. All the months of loneliness, anguish, and frustration were rising to the surface.

I was crying for Ah Puch, Itzamna, and Ixchel. I was crying for myself, for all the scar tissue forming over my emotions. The Indians stayed behind at a safe distance. Sue later told me it was the most unreal scene she had ever witnessed. During those moments, she didn't know whether she could ever return to a "normal" life in the States.

I crossed the creek, stumbling, barely aware of the water rushing against my chest. I would never let go of Ah Puch. If I fell, we'd go together. I kept talking to him through my tears, searching for explanations, trying to make him understand. "Why, Ah Puch, why did you break your teeth, why are you going to die? Why, why, why?" I cried.

As we walked, Ah Puch moaned and grunted.

"Forgive me, Ah Puch, please forgive me," I pleaded.

The Indians later spread the rumor that they watched as the jaguar and I talked to each other. I wish that had been true.

At the house I lay Ah Puch on the floor and sat beside him, the tears never letting up. The Indian men crowded into my shack. The women stood outside, looking in. There was no laughter, no smiles—just silence. I looked at them, my shirt hanging in tatters, my hand and shoulder bleeding. Having no place to direct my pain, I transformed it into anger toward the Indians. I kneeled over Ah Puch, whose breath was becoming shallower, and picked up his head.

"This is who's killing you," I cried, pointing his head at each of the Indians. "One by one, they kill you," I continued. The Indians stepped back as if physically struck.

"Stop it, Alan," Sue cried, her eyes swimming with tears. "Stop it, stop it, please."

"Get out," I screamed to her. "Get out, all of you." When they left, I lay alongside Ah Puch. I could no longer bear to see him die so slowly. I filled a syringe with a massive dose of Ketaset, wanting him to die in his sleep, hoping that in his last moments of life his dreams might be nicer than reality had been. Fifteen minutes later his breathing stopped.

I put him into the truck and brought him back into the area where we'd first captured him. I lay him in the shade, at the base of a tree, closed his eyes, and walked away. "Forgive me, Ah Puch," I kept saying. "Forgive me."

I returned to the house and sat down on the floor in the corner of the bathroom. I cried as I had never cried before in my life. I wondered if I'd ever be the same again. But then, I wasn't sure I wanted to be. I was responsible for Ah Puch's death. No one else was. I had killed him.

17 COCKSCOMB CHRISTMAS

Ah Puch's death was a turning point. His death had been my fault, yet many like him were dying all the time. I realized more than ever that I had to get Cockscomb designated a preserve, and I went at it with new fervor. I wanted to make sure that Ah Puch's death was not in vain. There was a lot more work to be done before we had all the facts, and I realized I had become far too emotionally involved with my study animals. Some of my enthusiasm had to die with Ah Puch.

It was late December and the temperature during some of the nights dropped as low as fifty-four degrees. I wore my down vest, closed the windows, and still sometimes felt as cold as if I were on a mountaintop in the Sierras. My first Cockscomb Christmas and my thirtieth birthday were rapidly approaching.

Often these days I'd look around the camp, watch the Indians, and notice how much had changed since my arrival. The forest was reclaiming most of the camp, and at least half of the road system was no longer passable. There were huge ruts and washed-out bridges everywhere. Though I had been somewhat accepted by the Indian community, I no longer hoped to achieve the closeness I had first thought possible. They knew I cared about them, and I knew that if I really needed them, they'd help. That was enough.

I'd been feeling very run down for almost two months, but my health seemed to deteriorate further after Ah Puch's death. Despite ampicillin treatments, my bitten finger wouldn't heal and the pain worsened. The rancid smell told me it was infected. On the same hand, little tunnels in the pattern of a road system were starting to form, and I had no idea what was causing them. And for nearly a month a fungal infection, tinea versicolor, had been causing little spots to develop all over my skin. My body was rotting away.

Sue and I were beset by agonizing abdominal cramps, with alternating bouts of diarrhea and constipation. It was similar to how I felt before we found the dead dog in the well. None of this was enough to make me seek medical attention until I started passing blood in my stool. I thought I might be suffering from a severe case of amoebic dysentery. My first reaction was to tell Cirillo about it.

He laughed. "Dat no problem. We shit blood plenty. Maybe you have worm. Last year my lil girl sick and a worm come out dis big when she shit," he said, holding his hands about eight inches apart.

The next day Sue and I drove to Dangriga to see a doctor. The doctor was surprised I had waited so long. He gave my finger five injections of Xylocaine, grabbed the blackened, crushed nail with tongs, and ripped it off so that the infection could drain and be treated. It was quick and painful. The blood and cramps, he agreed, were probably from amoebic dysentery.

The doctor asked if the bottoms of my feet had been itching, and I suddenly realized that they had. He told me that because

I lived with the Indians and had been feeling run down, I probably had intestinal hookworm along with everything else.

He seemed most interested in the tunnels on my hand. Commonly called creeping dermatitis, it was caused by a species of hookworm common in cats. It bores under the skin and forms tunnels that, if left untreated, can eventually spread all over the body. He gave me various topical ointments and pills to take care of all my maladies. I felt like a walking pharmacy, but my entire bill came to only Bze$15. I hated to think what the same examination and minor surgery would have cost in New York.

I was glad I had visited the doctor and thought about how the Maya persevere despite these maladies. I saw no evidence of malnutrition among the Maya, but I frequently saw chalky, anemic complexions among the adults from malaria, and swollen bellies among the children from worms. Their recurring bouts of malaria often left them weak for up to a month after. This way of life obviously took its toll on them.

A person acquires malaria only through the bite of an infective female *Anopheles* mosquito, which picks up the plasmodia—the causative agents—from someone afflicted with malaria. At one time, Belize had a reputation of being the "white man's grave" because of the high incidence of malaria and yellow fever. The mandatory spraying with DDT throughout the country has helped control the problem, but it still remains the most serious malady among the Indians. Left untreated, it leads to progressive debilitation.

One of the most pervasive elements of the Indian way of life is the prevalence of intestinal parasites, particularly hookworm. Some of the more common parasites, such as roundworm and whipworm, are passed from feces to mouth. The Indians use corncobs or their bare hands to clean themselves after defecation, so this is a fairly common mode of infection.

Hookworm infection can be one of the most damaging diseases of childhood. The hookworm eggs leave the body with the feces, then hatch in moist soil. The larvae then penetrate the skin of a person's bare feet, often causing them to itch. They then burrow their way into the blood and are carried to various parts of the body, resulting in coughing, weakness, and anemia.

The Maya in Cockscomb and surrounding areas commonly walked barefoot and didn't use latrines. They defecated in the bush around their house, believing it was more sanitary than all of them sharing a common hole in the ground. The problem was that their pigs ate and stepped in their excrement, often spreading hookworm around the living area. The Indians were continually reinfected. When reinfection persists and adequate nutrition cannot be maintained, chronic debilitation results.

There was also a high level of parasite infestation among the wild cats. Of forty-five fecal samples I analyzed, nearly 90 percent contained parasites, predominantly hookworm.

Some interesting movement patterns emerged among the jaguars after Ah Puch's death. Chac's large tracks showed that he was spending virtually all of his time within the area of overlap he had shared with Ah Puch. By the end of one month, he ceased venturing into the eastern part of his own range. Instead, he slowly penetrated deeper into the basin, starting to occupy Ah Puch's former range. At first he deposited feces regularly, but perhaps because he realized he was the only male in the area, he deposited less and less. He no longer had to mark off his area in response to the presence of another male jaguar.

The fact that Chac completely shifted his range, never to return near the cattle pasture, filled in another piece of the puzzle, providing additional evidence against the argument that all jaguars are cattle killers.

Ah Kin's crooked tracks also started to appear more regularly on the road in the western portion of Ah Puch's former range where the two cats had overlapped. Eventually, Ah Kin shifted his range slightly eastward, but never fully expanded into Ah Puch's former range the way Chac did.

Locating young Xaman Ek presented new radio-tracking problems. He traveled between the Outlier and the Cockscomb Range through some of the most rugged areas of the basin. This explained why he had never encountered people. I could pick up his radio signal only when I was atop the Outlier or during aerial tracking. When he was in the vicinity of Victoria Peak, even aerial tracking was difficult. We would fly low to locate him, and the plane would get caught in crosswinds or down-drafts. Too often for comfort, I wondered how close we were cutting it.

My skin fungus and dysentery cleared up, but I still hadn't taken the worm pills. The doctor had advised me to set aside two days for the treatment. I hadn't yet found the time. Meanwhile, one night Sue woke with a sharp cry, clutching her breast. I thought she'd had a bad dream until she told me she felt that something with sharp and pointed teeth had bitten her on the breast. I saw it immediately: a small, raised, hardened area with a little breathing hole on top. Sue had a botfly larva inside of her, and it was right on her nipple. One of Sue's worst fears had come to pass.

We had to kill the larva before trying to pull or squeeze it out. Two anal hooks held them firmly in their burrow. If they burst inside, infection could result. I had learned a quick and easy cure from the Indians. We taped a piece of moistened tobacco over the hole and left it for several hours. The nicotine soon killed the larva. When it was dead we had to squeeze it out. Sue bit down on a pillow while I squeezed her nipple hard between my fingers. Within seconds the larva popped out onto the floor, leaving Sue's breast sore for a month. She collected the tiny little larva, no more than a quarter of an inch long, and saved it in a small jar of formalin to show people back in the States. She knew it would make an interesting conversation piece at a party.

I don't remember seeing a warm-blooded animal of any sort in Cockscomb that wasn't infected with botfly larvae. I wondered how they affected the health of jaguars, especially when they seemed more prevalent in some jaguars than in others. Though I knew a well-adapted parasite never killed its host outright, these larvae can be enough of a problem to affect an animal's behavior.

One of the most interesting examples of this parasite affecting behavior involves oropendola birds. Another bird of the same family, the cowbird, lays its eggs in the nests of oropendolas, some of which eject the cowbird eggs, while others do not. Research has shown that the cowbirds hatch earlier than the oropendola young and are able to defend themselves and the oropendolas against botfly larvae, which are a major cause of death in oropendola young. In trees where these larvae are a problem, the oropendolas do not eject the cowbird eggs from the nest but proceed to incubate them and then rear the young.

I had already experienced two botfly larvae in my body, one in my head and one in my buttocks. Knowing the pain I experienced from a small larva, killed shortly after it had started chomping, I couldn't fathom how a jaguar could live with twenty of these in its body, each about one and a half inches long.

I knew this might be the last Christmas we'd all be together, so Sue, Jorge, Tino, Nari, and I planned a large fiesta. I went to Santa Rosa to buy a hundred-pound pig. When the Indians asked why we suddenly wanted such a large pig, after having bought numerous small pigs for the traps, I told them we were after the master jaguar.

When the weather looked bad for several days, I decided to take the hookworm medicine. The tunnels on my hand were spreading up my arm and I felt so run down that it was hard getting out of bed in the morning. It was a two-day treatment, consisting of the ingestion of three pills of 100 mg of mebendazole each day.

If my reaction was any indication of the severity of the infection, I must have had a thriving colony of worms inside of me. Within an hour after taking the first pills, I felt nauseous. When I urinated, the smell of a rotting carcass rose from the floor. It was worse than any smell we'd had inside the house, and Sue and I immediately thought something had died in a corner somewhere. But we found nothing.

Finally I realized the smell was coming from the toilet and that it was my own urine. The only dead or dying thing was obviously inside of me. That was only the beginning. I soon had a case of flatulence that lasted all day and through the night and smelled like the urine. Soon after that I started burping and couldn't stop. Every time I burped, I tasted something dead in my mouth. Sue said my breath smelled like I had eaten an old road kill.

During the day, Sue went to stay with the Indians and left me to my misery. But at night she had to sleep in the same bed. I was burping, farting, and running to the bathroom all night. The shack smelled like a sewer. Sue spent a nearly sleepless night with me, keeping the blanket wrapped around her face. When I'd look at her, with the blanket around her head and only her eyes peeking out, I couldn't help but laugh, and then I'd burp. She'd see that and start laughing, then smell the air and pull the blanket up again.

The second day was not as bad, but I remained inside and Sue kept everyone away from the shack. By the third day, I felt like a new person with energy I'd forgotten I had. My body must have been harboring hookworm for the last few months. Now I understood some of the reasons behind some of the Indians' lethargy.

It had been a wet muddy December and on Christmas Day there was no reprieve. The entrance road was flooded by rains, preventing people we had invited from the surrounding villages from coming to our feast. It was a small, lonely Christmas party. Nari and Tino cooked the pig over a large open fire. We cut the skin and fat into pieces and boiled it in an oil drum to make a Spanish delicacy called *chicharrón*.

Only a few Indians came by, and not many of them stayed because we were drinking rum and were cooking the pig in a way they were not accustomed to. They stewed all their meat using special hot spices, and would not easily try anything different. It was also obvious the Indians were not comfortable around the Spanish. Even Tino, Nari, and Jorge, who lived and worked with the Indians, were condescending to them.

Nari and Tino were wearing shirts purchased in a little town to the south, Mango Creek. One shirt said, "A lude'll put you in the mood," and the other read, "New York—The Big Apple." Sue, who had been depressed and uncommunicative the preceding few days, quickly drank four large glasses of rum and passed out twenty minutes after the party began. Jorge and I huddled, wet, chilly, and muddy, under a lean-to against Nari's house, drinking rum and eating plates of *chicharrón*. That was our Cockscomb Christmas party.

That night I kept one end of my body on the toilet and the other in a pigtail bucket throwing up the *chicharrón*. Sue was moaning in the next room, obviously influenced by the same obeah she had gone through at the Hopkins celebration.

The next morning Cirillo was over early, laughing at the gringo who had tried to eat too much pig skin. "You eat too much tiger meat," he said to me jokingly.

The Indians, like most of the Belizeans I'd met, would never consider eating cat meat. Yet I knew of people who claimed that, properly cooked, it was excellent.

Cirillo had come to tell me that Julian had seen a black tiger on the entrance road that morning. As I drank my morning cup of coffee, trying to forget the sick feeling in my stomach, I explained to Cirillo that there were probably no black jaguars in Belize. In fact, there were few reliable reports of black jaguars throughout Central America.

When he indicated its size, I knew he had probably seen the black phase of a jaguarundi or a tyra, a large member of the weasel family, with a black body and white head. He asked me where black tigers occurred, and I got out some maps to show him.

Black jaguars are uncommon throughout the jaguar's range. The most frequent sightings of them have been in particular areas of the Amazon. Indians told Humboldt that black jaguars were rare and never mingled with the common jaguars, while the English naturalist and explorer Henry Walter Bates on the upper Amazon found black specimens to be more common in some places than spotted. Where they occur, black jaguars are thought by Indians to be stronger and more ferocious than the spotted phase.

Theodore Roosevelt speculated that the coloration of cats plays no role in their survival; black does as well as spotted. Yet the study of captive jaguars reveals an interesting fact. The black phase of the jaguar is controlled by a dominant allele of a gene, contrary to previous belief. In leopards, the black phase is also uncommon, but it is controlled by a recessive allele. Why should a characteristic controlled by a dominant allele be rare in the wild? That question has not been satisfactorily answered. Obviously, something else is at work with the jaguars. Their coloration, possibly tied to other genetic traits, plays a role in survival, which we've not been able to establish.

Cirillo seemed truly fascinated by all of this. While I was talking, Agapita, Juana, and Prudencia had come over and were sitting quietly against the wall. I decided to entertain them as well.

"You ever hear the story of why tigers have spots?" I asked Cirillo, thinking of a story documented among the Kekchi Indians by J. Eric S. Thompson. He said he hadn't.

"This story I'm going to tell you came from the Maya in Belize, long ago," I said. "It's very old, but maybe it's true." I looked over and saw that the girls were listening.

"Once there was a jaguar cub, and his mother told him to be careful of man because he was very dangerous. The cub didn't believe her and wanted to test his strength against man's. One day, wandering through the jungle, he came to a place where a man was chopping wood.

" 'You're a man, aren't you?' the young jaguar said to him. 'I've come to test my strength against yours.' "

The girls giggled as I made my voice deep to imitate the jaguar talking. Juana interpreted for them.

"The man agreed and told the young jaguar to put his paw in a split in the tree trunk he had opened up with his axe. The jaguar did what the man said and when the man pulled out his axe, the wood came together, locking the cub's paw in its grip. Then the man beat the young jaguar with a stick and let him go. The jaguar cub's body was covered with black bruises and blood that looked like spots. Since then the jaguar's body has always had spots."

Cirillo smiled, and the girls' eyes were wide. I turned and saw that Sue was listening from the bedroom.

From my field notes, December 31, 1983:

My 30th birthday and the end of the most incredible year of my life. My intestinal hookworm is gone and much of my creeping dermatitis has dried up. Some still lingers. Sue and I finally recovered from the Christmas party but there's a distance between us. There have been good locations on Xaman Ek and Chac. I'm still following tracks of Ah Kin, the puma, and two females. Life is looking up.

Sue and I went to Dangriga to eat in a Chinese restaurant for my birthday dinner. It was another miserable rainy day, but I was determined to turn thirty with a bang. I had a bottle of some cheap unknown brand of champagne, the only kind sold in Belize City, stashed in Cockscomb. I wanted to drink it in the company of my Indian friends, even if most of them wouldn't drink any with me.

We returned to Cockscomb after dark and the Indians were all singing in church. Without a flashlight, we walked through the blackness of the moonless night, moving from hut to hut and trying to stay on the little narrow planks that they placed over the large mudholes near their huts. I was looking for the few

stragglers who always stayed away from church. It proved fruitless. Tonight, for some reason, all of them had been enticed in.

It seemed strange standing in the darkness, clutching a bottle
of champagne and listening to the out-of-tune Indian voices
singing Christian hymns in Maya. I opened the champagne
where we stood. I looked at Sue. We stood there ankle-deep in
mud, drinking champagne, and laughing. It hadn't worked out
between us, and soon we'd part, but we were still best friends.

That night, standing in the empty Maya village, half a bottle
of champagne gone, I loved my life. Despite the pain, anguish,
frustration, and terror, I was glad to be in Cockscomb, in the
jungle, surrounded by Maya and jaguars on my thirtieth birthday.

"Right now, Sue, at this instant, is there any other place on
earth you'd rather be?" I asked her.

"No." She said it without a moment's hesitation.

The cloud cover started breaking up and the stars were twin-
kling in the sky. The Maya singing seemed far away and blended
strangely into the jungle.

18 BEN

Columbus came near Belize on his last voyage, in 1502, when he touched at one of the Bay Islands in the Gulf of Honduras. Several years later Spanish navigators sailed along the coast of Belize using the Sierra de Caria (Cockscomb Range) as a marker. In 1524 Cortez traversed the Maya empire with about a hundred and forty soldiers and three thousand Indians, passing through a part of what is now Belize.

The buccaneers, or international privateers, were thought to have been the first to use the Belizean coast for rest and rendezvous. The offshore cays served as refuges for several infamous figures. In 1717 the pirate Blackbeard spent time in the waters off Belize where his bosun Israel was said to have buried a chest of treasure on one of the cays. Later, the notorious pirate Jean Lafitte was pursued by the British throughout these cays.

The first true non-Indian settlement occurred in the mid-seventeenth century, when British lumbermen arrived in the area to cut logwood trees. At the time logwood yielded one of the most effective dyes known in Europe and was a major export item. It grew prolifically in the tropical climate and required no cultivation. By the late eighteenth century, however, new methods of dyeing cloth were developed and the export of mahogany outstripped logwood in importance.

Through numerous treaties between England and Spain and, later, with the independent countries of Mexico and Central America, Belize became a British colony, called British Honduras. However, its boundaries were never clearly defined and remain in dispute to this day. As of this writing, Guatemala still does not officially recognize the right of Belize to exist and it is not delineated on many of their maps.

Sue and I were talking about all this as we drove to Belize City for a week of relaxation before she flew back to the United States. Belize City is quite a story in itself, and though I had been there on numerous occasions, I had never taken the time to walk its streets and closely examine its way of life. I hadn't liked it enough when I saw it the first time.

The city is thought to have been founded by Captain Peter Wallace, who landed in Belize in 1640. It became such an important and fashionable colonial port for a while that in 1824 the Indians of the Mosquito coast held the coronation of their new king in Belize instead of Jamaica. A British adventurer, Richard Davis, described Belize City during his travels in 1896:

> There is much to be said of Belize, for in its way it was one of the prettiest ports at which we touched, and its cleanliness and order, while they were not picturesque or foreign to us then, were in so great contrast to the ports we visited later as to make them most remarkable. . . . There was a great bustle along the wharves, where huge rafts of logwood and mahogany floated far into the water.

In 1927, Charles Lindbergh flew from Guatemala to Belize in the *Spirit of St. Louis*. It was the first time an airplane had landed in the country. However, partly as a result of its location, this city was never without its problems. Stephen Caiger, an author on the history of Belize, described it this way:

> Next to Jerusalem, Belize must be one of the most often "utterly destroyed" cities in the world. The Spanish razed it to the ground again and again. Great fires have ravaged it. Several times it has been overwhelmed by hurricanes.

When timber, the primary reason for the country's existence, began to decline in the late nineteenth century, agricultural growth and diversification were forced upon the colony. Unfortunately, Belize got a late start and attempts at diversification couldn't prevent the country's downward economic slide. By the mid-twentieth century, Belize City had fallen into an advanced state of decay. Mitchell-Hedges had a particularly snobbish, unsympathetic reaction to it. During his trip there in 1931 he wrote:

> Have you ever been to Belize? . . . If you haven't, don't go, unless you have a stomach of cast iron and no sense of smell. . . . It is historical that Belize was built on a swamp filled in with mahogany chips and empty gin bottles. I often wonder why it was built at all. Go where you will, you will find no capital like it. . . . Belize is a disgrace to the British Empire —a monumental blemish—the worst possible advertisement for British administration.

Victor W. Hagen, another author writing about the area, added his description of Belize City, calling it "an untidy, shabby, tropical port—the postern of Middle America."

Belize City's dominant ethnic group is Creole. Creoles are descendants of the early European lumbermen and the African slaves and freemen. I was told that status symbols among the

Creoles include a zinc roof on their house, a kerosene or gas stove, a bathroom, and a water vat. I would say the list should also include a television set. In fact the television is more important than the bathroom.

Belize City still has the dubious distinction of being one of the last major cities in the world to have open sewage canals. The smell of the city assaults you at least a mile out of town, and the lack of a sewage system has not prompted many to install toilets. Instead, they use "shit buckets." Every day, usually before 7 A.M. or after 7 P.M., the women and children carry out all kinds of receptacles, which they empty into the open canals or into the harbor.

By the time Sue and I arrived at the airport, our minds were already miles apart. I was thinking of the jaguars back in Cockscomb, and she, of the new direction her life would take once she was back in the States. We kissed, wished each other well, then parted.

During the week's stay in Belize City before Sue's departure, I had heard that both George Schaller and Chuck Carr were coming to Belize to see me. When Sue left, I went to Belmopan to arrange for them to meet some high government officials. On my way to the capital, I picked up a police officer hitchhiking to a neighboring village where a crime had occurred the previous day. If he had no other means of transportation, I could see why crimes outside the cities often went unpursued.

I thought back to an afternoon in Dangriga when a handbag belonging to Adriana had been snatched from the back of my truck by a young Carib boy. I had been in the store at the time when I heard Adriana yelling. I rushed out to see a small mob of Carib men pursuing the thief. Ten minutes later they were dragging him to the Dangriga police station, having recovered Adriana's bag. That was one way to keep law and order.

"Where do you live?" the police officer sitting next to me asked.

"I'm American, but I've been living down in the Cockscomb

Basin, down in the South Stann Creek District," I answered him.

He seemed unnaturally quiet.

"Do you know the area?" I asked.

"No, I don't know the area, but a good friend of mine had been down there. He was killed in Cockscomb."

I said nothing, waiting for him to continue.

"His name was Guermo. I was told by some of his relatives that he was with a gringo looking for gold. They found it. They said the gringo didn't want to share any of it, wanted it all for himself. The gringo and his friends tricked Guermo into walking somewhere where they'd seen a tommy-goff earlier. They carried Guermo out, but kept the gold for themselves."

"Do you think the story's true?" I asked.

"Everybody knows there's gold in those mountains," he said. "The gringo got greedy. Plenty of men get greedy over such a thing."

I changed the subject. I wondered if he suspected I was the gringo.

Rumors of gold in Cockscomb were widespread. I never learned how they all got started but I suspected it had something to do with the earliest expeditions to those mountains. Traces of gold in quartz and quartzite fragments were reportedly found and explorers speculated on the possibility of greater quantities there.

Then I heard a story about a prospector who had disappeared into the Cockscomb Mountains and was believed dead. One day he reappeared and refused to tell anyone where he'd been. Everyone believed he had made a rich gold strike. Such beliefs are perpetuated even in modern writings. Caiger, describing the uninhabited Maya Mountains, asks, "What minerals, what unsuspected source of wealth lies beneath that terrific mountain mass . . . ?" Now even my own project, owing to an unfortunate accident, was perpetuating this myth. My conversation with the policeman reminded me that I had heard nothing from the police in Stann Creek about the marijuana fields I'd reported. The only result had been the destruction of my airstrip. While waiting to see government officials in Belmopan, I stopped in to see the commissioner of police for Belize.

He knew all about the jaguar project and what I had been doing in Cockscomb. It was obvious he had checked me out. I was both surprised and relieved that I didn't have to explain my situation to him. He told me of the rumors that had been circulating that I was associated with the marijuana dealers in my area, hinting that the rumors had come from the police themselves. I was surprised, but started seeing the connection. I told the commissioner about the marijuana fields in Cockscomb. Now he was surprised. He had heard nothing about it despite the reports I filed.

The commissioner called in two of his assistants and asked me to repeat what I had just told him. After they left he told me to be careful whom I spoke to and what I said. "That goes for the police as well," he warned. When he asked if I would watch and report any illegal activities in the Stann Creek area, I politely refused. My interest was in the jaguars and Cockscomb. The last thing I wanted was to be caught in the middle of a drug war.

The arrival of Schaller and Carr was a refreshing change. They were worried about the hookworm that was still tunneling through my hands, but I told them I was in great shape compared to a short time ago. By the time we met with the Belize Audubon Society and the Ministry of Natural Resources, they already had a draft of the Cockscomb Management Plan that I had agreed to compile. It presented the known facts concerning the soil, hydrology, geology, and wildlife of the Cockscomb area, and outlined its economic potential.

After some discussion, we were told that the government was willing to seriously consider making Cockscomb a forest reserve, in order to keep it out of the hands of private concerns and put it under the jurisdiction of Natural Resources. The lands commissioner had been informed of this decision and for the time being would turn away all requests for land in Cockscomb. There had been an impression made after all. We were moving forward.

As soon as Schaller and Carr left, a seal broke in the front differential of the truck, causing all the fluid to drain, grinding down all the bearings. It was major damage. I needed seven new sets of bearings and four seals to fix it, and they had to be ordered from the United States. I knew it would take at least a month. We pulled out the front differential and I returned to Cockscomb without four-wheel drive. It was three months before the parts arrived and I could get the truck fixed.

When I arrived back at Cockscomb, Jorge was gone. He had found another job and couldn't wait for my return. I was sad that I didn't get to tell him good-bye. He had helped me through some hard times. I never saw him again.

I realized in the first few days back how much of the burden of menial tasks Sue had removed from me and how much the Indian women respected her. Some of the women were saying that I was evil for chasing her off. No one sympathized with me or would listen when I said it had been a mutual decision.

I was frightened of being alone again. I found myself drawn to Cirillo more than ever, and we started spending more time together. He was still capable of many surprises. When I returned from bathing in the river one evening, the truck was facing the opposite direction from the way I had parked it that afternoon. I had left the keys in the ignition, as I always did while in camp; no one else could drive the truck except Nari. Or so I thought. Nari was gone for the day, and as soon as I realized what had happened, I knew Cirillo had to be the culprit. I just didn't know how he'd done it.

Over the last few months, I had refused Cirillo's numerous requests to teach him to drive the truck. So instead, he closely watched me and picked it up on his own. Finally, after deciding he had the hang of it, he waited until I was away for a few minutes and drove the truck back and forth along the road in front of my house. He might have gotten away with it, but he had forgotten which way I had parked the truck. It was such a feat that I couldn't possibly be angry at Cirillo. When I asked him about it, he smiled. "I tell you I know for drive dat truck."

"Didn't you think I'd get vexed with you, Cirillo?"

"No, I know you no get vexed. I no smash de truck, so you no can get vexed."

After that I let him drive it occasionally while I sat nervously in the passenger seat.

While I'd been in Belize City, Adriana had given birth to a little boy, whom they named Sylvino. On the second day after my return, I went to visit her. As soon as I stepped into the hut, I could tell something was wrong. The hut lacked its usual atmosphere of noise and gaiety. My eyes fell to the hammock and I saw that the baby was lethargic and pale. It was dying. I questioned Adriana, and her only response was that her breasts were dry and there was no money for milk. All they had to feed the baby was mashed-up corn and water.

I bent over the hammock and looked into the baby's face. His eyes were sunken, and the stained cloth used for a diaper showed he had diarrhea. I pinched his skin and felt the soft spot on his head. The skin had virtually no elasticity and the soft spot was concave. The baby was dehydrated and, with its diet of corn and water, would soon be dead.

I knew the Indians well enough to know that the baby's death at four weeks of age would be culturally acceptable. But my mind would not accept that fact so easily. If I could save a human life, I should try.

I got into my truck and drove to Kendall, where I bought a case of enriched powdered milk. When I returned, I forced it on Adriana, without even talking it over with her. Then I prepared a rehydration drink of honey, salt, baking soda, and water, and showed Adriana how to administer it.

Later I began to question my sensitivity. Had my actions been more for myself than for Adriana? The case of milk lasted only two months. Adriana now had a three-month-old baby, who could not be left to die so easily. But her physical condition and economic situation had not changed, and I was not prepared to go beyond the initial act of saving a life. Now she was forced to do everything in her power, even at the expense of the other children, to care for the baby. I could walk away smugly.

Who was I to judge what was right or wrong, good or bad? Was I any different from the missionaries, whom I tended to judge so harshly? Sylvino grew to be a chubby, playful little boy, and when I watched him laugh it was hard to think I should have let him die. Yet, I still wondered.

During my next trip to Dangriga, I realized that another situation I had meddled in could have cost a life—my own. I was stopped on the street by a stranger identifying himself as a "friend" from El Salvador. I told him I didn't have any friends in El Salvador. He didn't smile.

"You talk plenty 'bout de marijuana fields, yes?" he asked in a tone that was decidedly unfriendly. I knew there was no point in lying. He was asking questions he knew the answers to.

"Yes," I answered. "I work with the tigers. I 'fraid for the tigers. I no want them walk near marijuana fields in Cockscomb."

"It not your business," he said harshly. "I tell you now, it not your business. It easy for pay some Guatemalan or Salvadoran twenty dollar. Dey need money bad. Dey walk up and shoot you in de head for twenty dollar," he said, pointing his finger at my head.

"Are you threatening me?" I asked, feeling both frightened and angry.

He smiled, showing dirty, crooked teeth. "Me? Noooo. I tell you I your friend. I tell you leave it alone and everybody happy. No one shoot tiger. No one care 'bout de tiger."

He walked away and I never saw him again. But I took his advice; I left it alone. I was there to work on jaguars and getting Cockscomb designated a protected area, nothing else.

When I finally resumed radio tracking and following the jaguars' tracks, I found that Chac had firmly established himself in a new range, encompassing and expanding Ah Puch's former range. The entrance road no longer showed his large footprints or any fecal deposits. Ah Kin's crooked tracks indicated that he was still moving farther into Ah Puch's former range and that his range now overlapped Chac's. Most of the feces were now in the area between Chac and the jaguars to his west, young Xaman Ek and uncollared Ah Kin.

We saw the tracks of the two females more frequently on the roads during times when there was no male in an area, such as after Ah Puch's death and after Chac's shift to the west. It seemed likely that the females avoided the males, coming together with them only to mate.

I felt that the time had come to open a second study area. Data collection had become routine, and the amount of time and effort that I was putting into trapping new jaguars could be better spent elsewhere. I found an assistant who could continue the work in Cockscomb. His name was Ben Nottingham, a twenty-nine-year-old graduate student at the University of Tennessee. Ben and I had done a considerable amount of caving together while I was studying bats in the Great Smoky Mountains, and I knew he'd be well suited to this way of life. He was willing to come immediately.

I also learned that Dr. Mike Konecny, a man with whom I had spoken earlier and discussed the potential for catching small cats in Cockscomb, had received a grant from the National Geographic Society to come to Cockscomb. Though I felt I was handing over the child I had weaned, I knew that additional work and a higher scientific profile was vitally important in our struggle to protect this basin.

In the days before Ben's arrival, I savored my last moments alone in Cockscomb. I looked around at my shack and thought of what had happened here: Ah Puch dying on the floor, me sitting on my new toilet the first time, me being sick with worms for two days, Cleo's first litter of puppies.

I looked closely at the decor in my shack. It could be considered strange, I thought, but it definitely reflected my way of life here. Hanging on one wall were the skins of a one-week-old jaguar, an adult jaguar, and a red brocket deer, all gifts from hunters. In one corner, there were weights and barbells on the floor, a chinning bar in the door frame, and a piece of wood hammered to the wall to hold my feet for sit-ups. Tacked on the wall in this area were five Frank Frazetta pictures depicting near-naked muscular men and women. On another wall hung my blowgun, dart rifle, and machetes. Above my bed, where I could see it every morning, was a poster of a log cabin amid snow-covered peaks in Europe, a present from Sue.

Part of one shelf was filled with an assortment of drugs and medication for my medical clinic. The rest of the shelf contained a jaguar caller made from a calabash, and three handwoven Maya baskets made by old Emano Balong. A second shelf contained jars with twenty-three scorpions, a tarantula, and two fer-de-lance heads. Next to these was an assortment of jaguar fecal samples and labeled animal parts. In my bedroom, there were two shelves with books on subjects ranging from Sartre to Taoism to Louis L'Amour. On a third shelf was my cassette player, with tapes ranging from Tchaikovsky to Eric Clapton. In addition to the wooden bed, the shack's furniture consisted of a small mahogany chair, a hardwood table, a Mexican "honeymoon hammock" bought for five dollars in Villahermosa, and three pigtail buckets, used as stools and for carrying water and storing camera equipment.

Pigtail buckets are at the heart of Belizean life. Large white circular receptacles with watertight lids, they can be seen throughout the country in the thousands. Though their initial purpose is to transport assorted pig parts or lard, it's after they are empty that their potential uses become obvious. They are used as furniture, "shit buckets," jaguar callers, drums, water and food containers, and for all sorts of other purposes.

Ben arrived in March and adapted to Cockscomb as quickly as I thought he would. His open, easygoing manner impressed the

Indians immediately. In fact, watching him and Cirillo getting along so well the first two weeks after his arrival, I felt a pang of jealousy. I was being replaced.

Ben and I went off into the jungle at night, along the same trails I had cut for the prey surveys. The daytime surveys were not telling us about arboreal, nocturnal species, such as kinkajous, known locally as nightwalkers. Though fecal samples showed the evidence of only one kinkajou eaten by a jaguar so far, I felt it was important to assess their density. I also wanted to compare the animal sign we observed during the day with what we could see at night.

The Indians had told me when I first arrived in Cockscomb that whenever they went into the bush at night they saw or heard these nightwalkers. The Indians didn't eat them, so they were rarely killed. During Ivan Sanderson's travels in Belize, he had also found kinkajous abundant, claiming they were a pest during his night hunting.

We also found this furry, fruit-eating member of the raccoon family to be relatively common. Kinkajous were easily surveyed by walking at night and shining a strong light into the trees. If there was one within sight, two piercing bright green eyes would be shining back at us. Like most nocturnal vertebrates, these animals have a reflective layer called tapetum that lies behind the retina. Light hits the visual sensors twice, once passing into the eye and once on reflection, so that they can have maximum advantage of whatever light is available.

When I could see the outlines of their round heads or bodies, I always thought they looked like little men, watching us from the treetops. Could this be where the stories of little forest men came from? Sometimes a light was not even necessary to detect their presence. Walking along, we'd hear branches rustling above our heads or their eerie vocalizations, almost like screams, piercing the night. It was a sound I could not compare to anything else I'd ever heard before, and even when I was listening for it, I was always thrown off guard. When they'd shake the branches, I'd imagine a snake was about to fall on my head, and their cries brought to mind angry Maya spirits of the forest.

The night surveys and Ben's subsequent sampling of two-and-a-half-acre jungle areas called quadrates showed there was about one kinkajou occupying every five acres in the basin. The night sampling also confirmed my original suspicions that any attempts at visual estimates of jaguar prey species, such as pacas and armadillos, would grossly underestimate their numbers.

Ben and I worked together for four weeks, until he knew the study area almost as well as I did. He decided to set up a few of the small cat traps I had brought down to Belize but never found time to use. At first we used live chickens as bait. After a week, the only animal captured besides one of the several species of opossums, was a six-foot-long boa constrictor. It had eaten the chicken and had gotten its head stuck in the grating of the trap trying to get out. Fortunately, these are mild-tempered non-poisonous snakes, and we freed it without injury.

During the second week, using sardines as bait in a trap placed along the airstrip, Ben captured his first cat, a beautiful female ocelot. She stayed relatively calm at our approach and was sedated easily. She was a pleasure to work on compared to the jaguars.

Sex—Female
Age—Young adult
Total length—48.5 inches
Tail length—14.5 inches
Head circumference—13 inches
Height at shoulder—16 inches
Height at hip—15.5 inches
Weight—25 pounds

As we examined her coat, Ben noticed that three of her teats were enlarged. I squeezed one between my fingers. She was lactating. When I palpated her, I realized she was pregnant. Her nipples were smooth and pink. It was probably her first litter. We put on one of the smaller radio collars and placed her back into the trap. I was hoping she might provide us with interesting information since she was captured within the ranges of at least one male and female jaguar.

Ben went to find Cirillo, who had never seen one of these cats up close. We took pictures of one another holding the animal. Cirillo's delight clearly showed on his face.

Ben now had his hands full. In addition to the ocelot, he had to continue following the collared and uncollared jaguars, and the puma. He also hoped to continue the day and night prey surveys and, when there was time, to begin quadrate sampling for additional density estimates of the jaguar's prey. I would be taking the jaguar traps into a new study area—the Mountain Pine Ridge. The day before leaving, I called Cirillo aside. "How you like Ben?" I asked.

"He good, but he slow. He de slowest gringo I ever see."

I laughed. Ben was deliberate and meticulous. His personality was the opposite of mine, and we could only work together when we did different tasks. What I found amusing was that this was the first time I'd ever heard a Maya think anyone was slower than he was. I knew they'd get along with Ben.

19 KUCHIL BALUM

The Mountain Pine Ridge, an area of approximately four hundred and fifty square miles, is considered by many to be the most scenic place in Belize. Its rolling grassy uplands, interspersed with native pines, are in stark contrast to the low wet forests and savannas that dominate the remainder of the country. The excellent natural regeneration of pine and its suitability as salable timber have made this area an important economic resource to the country and forced the government to designate it a forest reserve.

During my survey, the Pine Ridge and the Chiquebul, an adjacent lowland rain forest to the south, also part of the reserve, showed abundant puma and jaguar sign. This fact, along with the extensive road system throughout the area, its protected status, and the fact that it adjoins Cockscomb in the east, made the Pine Ridge an ideal site for my comparative jaguar study. Or so I thought.

I was soon to learn that the Pine Ridge was ideal for many other operations as well. Approximately two hundred chicleros had started working in the Chiquebul during the rainy season. In the short time I was there, I was told of several jaguar killings and the capture of two jaguar kittens in the preceding months. A timber concession in the area was operating three logging trucks on a twenty-four-hour rotation during the dry season through the Chiquebul.

The Belize Forestry Department maintained a base of operations and had built a little village, Augustine, in the heart of the Pine Ridge, where forestry officials were in charge of regulating the selective burning and cutting of pine stands. Then there was Blancaneaux Lodge, a tourist facility whose staff bragged of shooting any endangered ocellated turkeys and big cats that appeared in the vicinity of the lodge.

I sought out areas that isolated me from all of this, but there was one thing I couldn't hide from. The British army was using the Pine Ridge and the Chiquebul for war games, working out of two outposts set up in the reserve. They were firing live ammunition and setting off plastic explosives here and there throughout the forest. I had already come across the skeleton of a tapir they had killed because it had gotten in the way of a Land Rover.

During one of my trips into the forest, I stumbled upon one of their outposts. An officer warned me that the area I was going into that day was off limits because they were detonating explosives there. No one appeared concerned that I wouldn't have known anything about it had I not chanced upon their base of operations.

I returned to my camp and packed up. I had come to do research in a reserve and found myself in a mock war zone. After six weeks of traversing the area, I decided that if I collared any animals, I'd never know if their movements and activities were natural or in response to exploding bombs. Another problem was that I was too visible in this area, and everyone knew what I was doing. The restriction on guns was virtually ignored, and some of the forest officers themselves hunted illegally. I was afraid that my trapping might put some of the animals in jeopardy. It was clear that the government of Belize took a very liberal view of the meaning of forest reserve. I missed the wildness and beauty of Cockscomb.

The only positive outcome of this episode was that I became close friends with a Creole woman, Maggie, who lived in one of the outlying villages. I had met her while investigating a problem jaguar in the area. She had been fascinated by my work from the outset and was one of the few Belizeans who seemed to appreciate the wild beauty of her own country.

She took me to meet her family the first night we met. It was good to forget about jaguars for a few hours as we sat on the porch of her house and she told me stories of Belize that she had heard as a child.

During my last weeks in the Pine Ridge, I tried to see Maggie as often as possible, and when I finally decided to leave the area, I asked her if she'd return with me to Cockscomb. She was hesitant at first but then agreed to give it a try. She told me I could expect her in Dangriga in two weeks.

Returning to Cockscomb was like coming home. The porch thermometer read a little over a hundred degrees, and Ben was getting his first taste of the dry season. As we sat in the sweltering heat of the house, Ben couldn't stop talking. I smiled, realizing what I must have sounded like the day the British soldiers landed in the helicopter.

There was some good news. There was a new jaguar, probably an adult male, walking on the entrance road in Chac's former range. The tracks, with new fecal deposits, started showing up right after I left. Then Ben explained how the female ocelot had been ranging in an area of one and a half square miles in the vicinity of the airstrip. He'd been getting good data when, for no apparent reason, he lost the radio signal and hadn't picked it up since. Then he smiled and related his first encounter with the Maya sense of humor.

While driving to Kendall one afternoon with Julian, Pedro, and Cirillo in the back of the truck, Ben happened to glance back and see that Pedro was gone. Julian and Cirillo were laughing. When Ben stopped the truck and asked where Pedro was, Cirillo said that half a mile back he had fallen off the truck, landing on his head. Ben panicked and rushed back, thinking Pedro might be badly hurt. Instead, he found Pedro standing in the road, rubbing his head and laughing. Everyone was laughing except Ben. When he asked Cirillo and Julian if they had planned to tell him that Pedro had fallen out, Cirillo just kept on laughing and said, "Yeeees, maybe on de way back." He and Julian thought it would have been funny if Pedro had had to walk back.

The constant turmoil of Cockscomb hadn't changed. The evening of my arrival, Ignacio ran up to the shack with a very bloody Cleo in his arms. I had missed that scrawny little white dog that Sue had taught to do tricks. When first Sue and then I had left Cockscomb, Cleo started spending more time at Adriana's house, where she'd been born. Ignacio told us that she had always been too gentle to be a good hunting dog, and then when Sue began spoiling her, she didn't want to do anything but be with Sue. After our departure, Ignacio tried to make her a working dog again by taking her with him to his plantation every day.

On this particular day, on the way back from the milpa, Cleo took off into the forest on the scent of an animal. Soon after, Ignacio heard a high-pitched scream. As he ran into the forest, Cleo came stumbling toward him covered in blood, her head hanging to one side. She had run right into a sleeping jaguar, probably the new male in that area. Fortunately, the jaguar was as surprised as Cleo. It lashed out with its claws before disappearing into the jungle.

I looked at Cleo and didn't think she would live. The muscles on either side of her neck were ripped through to the windpipe, and she had several puncture wounds on her body. As she gazed at me with those sad, pitiful eyes I knew so well, I felt I had to try something.

We lay Cleo down on some empty corn sacks while Ben lit two kerosene lanterns on either side of her. The shadows cast by the lanterns on Cleo's bloody body made the scene look more like a satanic ritual than an operation to save an animal's life. It was 7 P.M. and I'd been back in Cockscomb only three hours.

After sedating her heavily, I cleansed the wounds and poured alcohol and then iodine into the gaping holes. Using suture material and a sewing needle, I carefully sewed the muscles together, hoping I was making the right connections. Finally, I closed the wound and poured more iodine along the suture. Then I applied Betadine ointment and bandaged the neck.

Infection was the greatest potential danger, so I gave Cleo a large dose of penicillin. I knew she'd tear the bandages and rip open the sutures as soon as she woke up, so I drugged her again to keep her asleep for the next twenty-four hours.

I sat that night watching Cleo, thinking again how difficult life in the forest was, how quickly it aged living things. In one year Cleo had gone from a skinny young female to a scarred weary mother. I thought of the similarities to the life of a Maya girl.

Twenty minutes after she awoke, Cleo removed all the bandages. By the second day her neck swelled to the size of a grapefruit, and the pain in her eyes was almost too much for me to bear. I fed her liquids every morning and ampicillin tablets three times a day. Each day I expected to find the wound infected. Had it been any other dog, I would have let nature take its course.

It took months for Cleo to recover. But by the end of the study, she had regained full movement of her neck, although she retained just a slight tilt to her head. I could hardly tell anything

had ever happened to her. The Indians were amazed by my
medical skills. I knew that I hadn't done much. The real reason
for her survival was a toughness and tenacity that animals must
possess in order to survive for any length of time in the jungle.

Despite daily attempts to locate her, we never picked up radio
signals from the ocelot again. I was convinced that the collar had
failed after only two months. A sighting of the cat later proved
this to be true. She was now probably a mother, and had shown
limited movement during the time Ben followed her. The data
indicated that the ocelot had been most active from sunset, 6
P.M., until 3:30 A.M. Overall, she was active 35 percent of the time.
Of the ten fecal deposits attributed to her, eight contained the
remains of unidentified small rodents and a four-eyed opossum.
The rest showed evidence of paca, Virginia opossum, and armadillo.

We also found a single jaguarundi fecal deposit within her
area. I had seen these sleek little black cats running in the vicinity of camp on several occasions. At least two of them were
killing and eating the Indians' chickens. No matter how often
the Indians sat and waited to shoot these cats, they were too
quick and clever. The deposit had been covered with dirt and
was surrounded by several scrapes, the longest being ten inches.
The cat's track was nearby, measuring a little over one inch in
length and one inch in width. The feces contained the remains
of a four-eyed opossum.

The conclusions that I had drawn earlier from the jaguar feces
remained consistent throughout the study. In over two hundred
fecal samples, we identified seventeen different species of prey.
Armadillo made up over half of all the identified remains, followed by paca, anteater, brocket deer, and peccary. These five
species accounted for more than 80 percent of the prey we identified in the feces. The rest of the evidence showed that jaguars
also ate agoutis, Virginia opossums, iguanas, coatis, river turtles,
small rodents, four-eyed opossums, skunks, kinkajous, snakes,
and birds. In addition to animal remains, nearly a third of the

fecal deposits contained grass. On several occasions, vomit containing only grass had been found along the roads.

The fact that the armadillo was a dominant prey species for the jaguars was not unique to Cockscomb. On an average, over half of the fecal deposits and kills documented outside Cockscomb during the first survey also consisted of armadillo. The Swedish scientist Claes Olrog, working in South America, regarded jaguars as one of the principal predators of these animals, finding numerous armadillo carcasses along jaguar trails.

These food habits posed an interesting question. If the jaguar, as the dominant predator, was feeding primarily on small prey, to what degree was there overlap in food habits between the five different cat species in the area? There could exist an interesting competitive situation.

Three puma fecal deposits collected while following the puma's tracks contained the remains of small rodents and four-eyed opossums, both of which are rare in jaguar feces. Yet pumas are capable of killing and feeding on the same prey as jaguars. In parts of North America where pumas are the dominant predator, they kill such animals as elk, deer, horses, and cows. In areas of South America, such as Paraguay and Brazil, they feed on brocket deer, peccaries, anteaters, agoutis, rheas, monkeys, and pacas.

My studies in Belize indicated that pumas might be avoiding areas where they overlapped with jaguars and where jaguars were relatively abundant. It seems possible that in these same areas they were selecting among types of prey that they fed upon in order to reduce competition. Similar partitioning was observed by John Seidensticker, a scientist in Nepal, where tigers and leopards overlapped. If this were the case in Cockscomb, then the pumas might be competing for food more with the smaller cats—ocelots, margays, and jaguarundis—than with jaguars.

I often wondered how aware the smaller cats were of the presence of jaguars and pumas in the area. I thought it might be particularly important with the ocelot, one of the larger of the terrestrial small cats. In instances when Chac was located close to the collared female ocelot, we'd often find ocelot and, occasionally, jaguar feces along a trail through the area.

A story told to me by a hunter made me speculate even further on this possibility. He said that one night while hunting he heard a jaguar grunting in the bush and crept over to investigate. He came upon an ocelot up in a tree hissing down at a jaguar, which was standing, paws against the trunk of the tree, growling up at the ocelot. He shot and killed the jaguar, so I never found out what the conclusion to such an encounter might have been.

Though aggression among cats, both within and between species, seems to be rare, it is not undocumented. A Venezuelan scientist, Edgardo Mondolfi, reported sighting a jaguar carrying an ocelot in its mouth that it had killed. He also reported evidence of a probable encounter between a jaguar and a puma where all that remained of the puma were the feet, the rest presumably having been eaten by the jaguar.

The new jaguar that Ben had been following along the entrance road was now spending increasing amounts of time traveling near the camp and depositing its feces whenever it was near the border of Chac's new area. By now I was more convinced than ever that fecal deposition had to do, at least partly, with marking or testing the boundaries of the cats' areas. The new jaguar started spending three to four days every second week in Cockscomb. I was very curious about where it was the rest of the time.

Before trying to trap this new jaguar, I tied a fifteen-pound pig on the road as a free meal for him. Within two days, the pig was gone, only the intestines and stomach remaining to tell the tale. Of four pigs I had allowed jaguars to kill, twice the viscera had been left while the rest of the pig was gone, presumably dragged off and eaten. Similar behavior was occasionally observed by George Schaller studying jaguars killing capybaras, the largest rodent in the world.

Chac started showing extraordinary movement patterns, traveling into areas he'd not been tracked in before. Most of these movements were along large waterways. During one week he was located along the Sittee River, outside the basin, and far from his previous areas of travel. We were now in the middle of the dry season, and I realized that Chac's movements might be related to those of his prey.

During the dry season I noticed a slight increase in the frequency of peccary and paca remains found in the feces. Many of the smaller creeks and streams dried up in Cockscomb at this time of year. It seemed that the prey might be more likely to be found near water sources. This would be a mixed blessing for the jaguars. The cats might now be able to feed more easily upon species that were normally difficult to catch. However, the prey would be less uniformly distributed over wide areas, and a jaguar might have to travel farther to feed regularly.

Ben and I decided to move into one of the larger houses in camp in preparation for Maggie's arrival. The small house was barely large enough for one person and all the project's equipment, but three people in this shack was unthinkable. We took over an adjacent house that had belonged to Don Smith's brother, who had helped set up and run the original operation. Its best attribute was a large screened porch, which would serve as the living and dining area. A single large room in the back would be the bedroom, with a small bathroom off to the side. It already had a toilet.

Three days after we moved in, I went to pick up Maggie at the Dangriga bus terminal. As soon as I saw her I knew I wanted her with me, yet I knew too that there was no permanent place for her in my life. A warning signal was going off inside of me, but I chose to ignore it.

Though I knew Maggie was a bit nervous about living in Cockscomb, I was still surprised when she unpacked a .38 snub-nosed pistol and insisted upon sleeping with it. Until we broke her of that habit, Ben and I made a lot of noise whenever we came back from the field at night. The Indians took to Maggie immediately, but wanted to know why I had replaced Sue. I tried explaining again to them that I hadn't replaced Sue, that Sue was special and we were still friends, but that our feelings had changed. It made no sense to them.

Shortly after Maggie's arrival, I decided to visit a doctor in Belize City who specialized in skin disorders. My creeping hookworm had never completely healed and was becoming worse again. It was oozing and starting to smell badly. With Ben now in Cockscomb, continuing the fieldwork and watching over the place, I felt much better about leaving the area when I wanted.

The doctor told me of an unorthodox way of getting rid of the hookworms. He didn't have the necessary chemical on hand, but I did, back in Cockscomb. I decided I'd do it myself. Inserting a one-and-half-inch-long needle into the head of each tunnel where the parasite was located, I injected a small amount of concentrated formalin, the chemical used to preserve dead animals. I had to be careful not to puncture too far beneath the skin, which would end up preserving my own tissue. It worked immediately, and within a few days the tunnels started drying up. After a month my hands were healed and all that was left were several white patches of skin that had been destroyed by the formalin.

Our vehicles were breaking down, like my body. The motorcycle broke down for the seventh time, and I stopped counting with the truck. This was rough country for machines, and it was even rougher to get tools or parts to fix them. I quickly learned how people make do with what's available. They taught me that nearly anything can be held together with a coat hanger.

The truck, however, was a different story. Even a simple malfunction often became a major problem when there were no parts to be had. The truck was only thirteen months old, and I looked at my journal to see what had already gone wrong or been replaced. So far it had taken two sets of front-end bearings, two sets of brake linings, a set of strut rubbers, four universal joints, an oil seal, and two new sets of tires. Also in that time all the seals and bearings in the front end had gone bad and had still not been replaced; there was a short circuit in the electrical wiring, so there were no panel or brake lights; I'd had six flat tires; and the passenger side door had been smashed in by a skidder tire.

On one occasion, though, the truck's malfunction proved to be fortuitous. Cirillo and I were looking for an overgrown skidder road we'd never been on before. I was listening for young Xaman Ek and looking for puma sign when a grinding under the cab told me I was losing another universal joint. I didn't feel like pushing our luck and walking back nine miles to camp.

I parked the truck on a level area of the timber road and decided we'd walk the rest of the way. Cirillo started cutting through the bush over to the skidder road. Suddenly I saw a hill rising up from a flat area. It seemed out of place in this terrain, but it looked like a good high spot to listen for Xaman Ek. I pointed, and Cirillo started chopping toward it.

When I caught up with Cirillo, I found him staring at the mound in a strange way. It couldn't be. I chopped quickly over to the base of the hill. My heart quickened when I saw the cut stones protruding from the dirt in a regular pattern around the base. I looked up. The mound, rising at least fifty feet into the air, clearly had three levels. I could make out a platform with two terraces above it, their square-cut stones protruding through the earth at each level. It was an ancient Maya ruin, a temple deep in the basin.

I climbed to the top and looked around. Cirillo was following slowly. I knew that many of the Indians were afraid of these old places. To the north, I could see the main timber road through the trees, no more than fifty feet away. How often had I passed this temple? How many times had I looked directly at it, seeing nothing but a dense wall of green vegetation? To the south, the terrain sloped steeply down to a large stream. Using a different route, I had often crossed that stream, which eventually joined other tributaries to form South Stann Creek. Had it been used for travel?

I cut a path to the timber road and walked back and forth along the road, examining it with a new eye. Cirillo hadn't spoken a word since we found the temple, and I didn't press him. I knew his thoughts were probably on a different plane than mine. A careful scrutiny of the road and the discovery of little chips of cut stone confirmed my suspicions. The timber operation had cut their road through the ruin, and the rise over which I had driven so often in the past was probably part of the base platform for the site.

Often, the ancient Maya elevated their temples and palaces by building them on platforms. Trees and underbrush were cleared and the land leveled to permit the construction of foundations. Tons of stone had to be quarried and transported by hand or on log rollers before it could be cut, shaped, and set into place by masons.

I looked around me, denuding the forest in my mind's eye and picturing the site as it must have once been. The steep cliffs of the Outlier were not far off. Could that have been their source of building material? I looked at Cirillo, standing by the forest edge, and I mentally dressed him in a jaguar headdress and skins. You belong here, Cirillo, I thought. You've always belonged here.

I knew that this was the site Jorge had told me of. But there was much more to it than I had imagined. There had probably been a thriving cultural center back here, I realized. How incredibly exciting! We needed to fully explore the site, but I wanted someone experienced with me.

I called Cirillo over. "You no tell nobody where this place is, Cirillo," I said. "You and me the only ones that know this place now. We come back soon."

Cirillo didn't say anything, but I knew he'd do as I asked. We returned to camp.

As soon as I was able to get to a phone, I contacted Logan McNatt, a Peace Corps volunteer and resident field archaeologist for the Archaeology Department in Belize. We had become friends during my first trip to Belize, so, despite a heavy work load, he agreed to make Cockscomb a priority and come down within a month.

He was later to tell me that he had expected to find just another series of small house mounds, so common throughout the country. Many people often mistook them for something more, and these mounds made up the majority of reported finds. He was not prepared for the temple mound I took him to. I could tell by his excitement that we had found something of significance. He called it a minor ceremonial site.

Radiating from the temple mound, we cut new trails and found two smaller mounds west of it. Then we heard a cry from Cirillo. He had found a circular stone, almost five feet in diameter and a foot thick. It lay between the temple and the other mounds. The surface was pitted, but there were no carvings or inscriptions. Logan said it was an altar stone. A shallow hole to one side was undoubtedly the work of Jorge, who had thought he'd be returning to dig beneath it.

Then we crossed the road, passing over fresh jaguar tracks, to where the plaza continued. We found another mound, and then we saw, nearly hidden by a fallen tree, an odd-looking pair of oblong stones, each about two feet high and five feet long, situated a little over three feet apart. Logan had not seen anything like them before, but thought they probably had some ceremonial significance.

They had not timbered this side of the road yet, and I was sure that no one knew about this part of the ruin. While the others continued the search for mounds, I lingered by these oblong stones. As I gently rubbed my hand over one of the stones, a sense of timelessness overwhelmed me. I sat down between the stones, blocking out the forest.

Here I was, sitting in the rain forest of Central America, at an uncharted Maya ruin, with jaguars and pumas still roaming the forest. It was possible that the last human beings to be at these strange oblong stones were the ancient Maya themselves, the creators of one of the world's greatest civilizations.

During the return to camp, Logan told me I'd probably get to officially name the site for the record book. It should be something appropriate, he said. But the name of the site was already etched in my mind. It would forever be known to me as Kuchil Balum, the Mopan Maya words for "Place of the Jaguar."

20 EK CHUAH

The untouched Maya ruin occupied my thoughts for weeks. As I watched the Indians in Cockscomb go about their daily lives and attend regular church services, I could easily imagine them building and worshiping at these ancient temples. Anthropologists had told me that cultural continuity between the bearers of ancient cultures and their modern descendants is not uncommon. This was easy for me to see now, as I re-ordered the world in my mind.

The artifacts that the Cockscomb Indians had found in the vicinity of the camp were primarily tools. It seemed likely that the Maya of Cockscomb were part of a self-sufficient group that formed what the prominent Maya archaeologist James Gifford called the village homeland. These small rural population centers were supposedly associated with minor ceremonial sites that could be serviced by a rotating system of priests coming from some of the major sites. The discovery of Kuchil Balum and the tool artifacts uncovered in the areas of milpa cultivation fit well into this picture.

Archaeological evidence indicates that throughout the lowland jungles there existed a vast expanse of contiguous tribal homelands, always interacting and possessing numerous ceremonial centers of various sizes. Each tribal unit had a slightly different culture. The majority of the population of the Maya empire probably lived in these rural agricultural settlements.

In the vicinity of Cockscomb, several Maya ruins had already been uncovered. There was Pomona on North Stann Creek, Kendall on Sittee River, and Pierce Ruins on South Stann Creek. They were all small centers, with only a single major pyramid, as at Kuchil Balum. Today, there are small communities of Maya settled in these same areas in villages like Cockscomb, Maya Center, Kendall, and Santa Rosa. Though each village is separate and self-sufficient, they interact with the others. It seemed no different from what might have been in A.D. 500 except that the Maya priests have been replaced by numerous non-indigenous religious groups, trying to destroy any remnants of old ways.

A bizarre incident soon took my mind off the Maya. For a week I decided to direct all my efforts on obtaining data on young Xaman Ek while waiting for the new jaguar to return to Cockscomb. There was one particularly high knoll still accessible by truck that overlooked Xaman Ek's known range. After searching for jaguars during the day, I returned every evening to this place and concentrated on documenting Xaman Ek's activities.

It was a lonely, peaceful place. Between radio-tracking intervals, I lay on the hood of the truck, watching the sky and feeling the energy of the jungle pulsating around me. I knew now that there was more here than just plants and animals striving to keep their hold on life within this complex ecosystem. Here the ancient Maya lived and prayed to the gods of the forest and the sky. When they looked up, they saw the same stars as I watched now.

On the fourth night I went out as usual to the hill. It was a particularly dark night because rain clouds hid the moon and stars. I put on the headphones and scanned the darkness for Xaman Ek's signal, moving the antenna in a full circle. There was no signal, but there was something else. I sensed something was wrong. Even wearing the headphones, I could feel a stillness in the forest around me. A chill ran down my back, and for an inexplicable reason, I felt frightened, unsure of the darkness.

Countless times I had tracked at night but never had I felt this way. I continued listening for the jaguar over the next half hour, but the feeling that something was wrong wouldn't leave. I decided to return to camp.

The truck was facing the forest. As I turned on my headlights and swung the truck around toward the timber road, a strange sight flashed before my right headlight. Standing at the edge of the forest, I had a brief glance at what looked like a little man, about three feet tall, holding his left hand up, palm out as if signaling me to stop.

My first reaction was terror. I had heard too many stories of the *duendes* of the forest. I raced down the road before deciding my imagination was getting the better of me. After driving two miles, I turned around and went back to the site. Maybe the obeah man had returned to Cockscomb and was out looking for me, I thought, trying to rationalize what I had seen. But I knew there was little chance of that. When I returned to the spot, there was only a bush where I thought I'd seen the little man. Yet, an uneasy feeling, a tingling sensation came back to me stronger than ever. I didn't linger.

The next morning I told my story to Ben, Cirillo, and Maggie. Only Ben was skeptical.

"I'm not saying that anything was *really* out there," I said, trying to convince myself more than anyone else. "But I thought I saw a little man."

"You see a *duende*," Cirillo said emphatically. Maggie nodded in agreement.

"Nah. You've just heard too many *duende* stories," Ben said. "That jungle is scary at night. You could imagine you were seeing anything."

I wanted to agree with Ben, but a little nagging doubt remained in the back of my mind. Then Cirillo said something that surprised me. "You know *duende* close when you feel like it cold."

"That's just what I felt, Cirillo," I said, no longer so sure it had been my imagination.

"The *duende* was close. Even when you went back. You must have surprised it the first time, but it was hiding when you returned," Maggie explained.

"He have hand like dis?" Cirillo asked, holding up just four fingers of his hand.

"I didn't stay around to count them," I said.

Cirillo laughed. "I tink you 'fraid of nutting."

"I plenty 'fraid of *duende*," I replied.

It surprised me to learn how prevalent the belief in these little men was among most people I spoke with. Ivan Sanderson wrote about sightings by many educated people throughout Belize:

But men educated as well as uneducated who had lived and worked in the jungle areas not only believed in but had evidence of the existence of dwendis. I have talked to dozens who said they had seen these little people, and my informants have included forestry department workers who received their training in Europe or the United States. . . . A junior forestry officer in British Honduras told me he had on several occasions noticed two of them watching him at the edge of the forest reserve near the Maya Mountains. . . . Who are we to say just what is and what is not in the jungles?

I returned to that site several times but never had that strange feeling or saw the little man again. Unfortunately, after that incident, the hill lost its appeal for me. I could never again lie comfortably atop my truck there at night and let the world drift by.

The Indians started their annual cycle of cutting and burning forest, and I rarely saw Cirillo during this time. Again I watched lush forest turn to ashes and was reminded how much rain forest I'd seen denuded throughout Belize in just a year. I knew this was what the future held for Cockscomb if it were not protected. I had to keep after the government so they didn't forget me.

I left the project in Ben's hands and drove to Belize City, dropping Maggie off at her family's place along the way. The bearings and seals for the front differential had finally arrived. However, when I took the parts to a mechanic and tried to have them installed, we discovered that after driving the truck with a hollow front differential for so long the chassis had bent. Once again, working on Belize time, what should have been a two-day layover turned into a week.

I got around Belize City using taxis. I had always thought being in a New York taxi was one of life's more thrilling experiences. That has since been replaced by Belize taxis. They careen at high speeds through little alleys and side streets, past crowds, two to three people deep, occupying at least a third of the road space. The taxis often pass within a hair's breadth of these people without slowing, and the people never break stride.

But the adventure is incomplete unless a slow-moving bicycle or cart suddenly appears in the middle of the road. This doesn't phase the Belizean taxi driver. He presses his horn and careens past the cart just as it moves out of striking distance. The synchronization is incredible and I watched it happen not once but dozens of times. Never did I see an angry encounter arise from these acts of daring. In fact, more often than not, the driver knew or was related to the man he nearly hit, and greetings were exchanged as the cab whizzed by. The exchange—"Ya boss." "Okay."—had to take place in the split second of the encounter.

After nearly sixteen months in Belize, there were several people with whom I had developed a close relationship and whom I could count on to help me through hard times. My home and office away from Cockscomb was the Mopan Hotel in Belize City, owned by Tom and Jean Shaw. Tom, a hardened ex-veteran of the British army, appeared on the surface to be a gruff, hard-drinking loner. If he didn't like something about you, he'd turn you away from the hotel or refuse to serve you at his bar. Depending on his mood, he might even refuse to serve those he liked. But the gruff exterior hid a soft heart, and if he considered you a friend, there were no limits to his kindness.

His Belizean wife, Jean, I considered my Belizean mother. She kept people away from me when I needed privacy, and she used her contacts to set up appointments with government officials who were putting me off. The Shaws made me feel at home in Belize City, especially when I needed to be with people who cared but didn't intrude.

Thirty miles west of Belize City was the home of a wildlife photographer, Richard Foster. A talented cameraman from England who had filmed such TV nature classics as *Amate—The Fig Tree* and *Silva Verde,* he isolated himself back in the pine savanna amid an assortment of Belizean animals he used for his films. We had become good friends during my survey and I had used his house as my contact point. We spent many nights talking about how our different backgrounds but similar desires had brought us together. Whenever he had the time, Richard took still photographs of jaguars to help me with my work.

His assistant at the time was Sharon Matola. It was she who had sent the British army in to drag my body out of Cockscomb when she hadn't heard from me in over a month. A hard-working, independent-minded woman, Sharon had turned Richard's compound into the Belize Zoo, the first zoo in the country. She was also a major force in the endeavor to establish a conservation education program in Belize.

Among the menagerie of the Belize Zoo were two jaguars, a male and female, and a female puma, all taken from the wild when young and kept in large forested enclosures. These were the first large cats I saw when I arrived in Belize and were an important source of information for the project. Plaster casts of their tracks helped me to distinguish sex differences in the field. I also spent many hours watching the behavior of these cats so that I'd be able to interpret my own observations in the field and to verify information provided to me by natives. Though they had been reared in a similar setting, the male jaguar, Pinto, and the female jaguar, Maya, were still aggressive and could not be approached. The female puma, Inca, on the other hand, could be handled, and especially liked to have her ears rubbed.

Five miles up the road from Richard was J.B.'s, a bar and restaurant situated halfway between Belize City and Belmopan. J.B. (I never learned his full name) was an American expatriate who had been in Belize longer than he cared to remember. His place, always stocked with beer (cold when the generator was working) and good food, was an oasis in the desert. J.B.'s served as a communication center. It was always my first stop coming out from Cockscomb on my way to Belize City.

While I was waiting for the truck to be fixed, I spent some time watching the jaguars at the Belize Zoo. During one particularly productive afternoon, I watched the jaguars copulate. Maya just lay there as Pinto penetrated her repeatedly for about half a minute. When he began ejaculating he roared and bit her on the neck. Finally she pulled away, then rolled in the grass for about fifteen seconds. Pinto had worn himself out and lay down to rest no more than five feet from where we were watching him. Maya looked at him and then at us, as if uncertain whether to lie so close. Then she lay beside him, head up, watching everything around her while he slept. Richard joined me and took some pictures.

The remainder of the time away from Cockscomb I spent at the government offices. Despite their initial enthusiasm over my reports and the productive meeting with New York Zoological Society officials, I still felt I was being put off. Everyone smiled at me, but did little when I left them. They insisted I do more to help them with their livestock problems, but they would never follow any of my recommendations. From their answers to my questions, I could tell they had never read the management plan. Any solution to their problems involved, at the very least, the time and energy of government forestry officers. But when I suggested this, I was always met with the same answer: "There's no money for that now."

While I was staying at Richard's house, someone drove up and told us that a jaguar had been hit by a car a mile down the road. It was still alive. I borrowed Richard's car and rushed over. A crowd had gathered around the large male jaguar, mortally wounded but still alive and trying with its last strength to crawl off into the bush. I was reminded of spectators at a Roman arena, thirsting for blood.

The man who had hit the jaguar was the police chief of Orange Walk and he proudly claimed the kill. "That tiger nearly got by me," I heard him explaining to the crowd. "I had to swerve quickly to knock him down. When I looked back, he was still alive and starting to get up. So I quickly backed up over him again."

There were murmurs of praise among some of the onlookers.

I stood there wanting to smash the self-indulgent grin from the police chief's face as I watched the jaguar's muscles quiver in his death spasms. If I had had a gun or club, I would have ended its misery. But if I'd had a gun, I might also have wanted to use it on the crowd in front of me, watching and talking gaily as if they were at a soccer match.

Finally, its breathing stopped and I went over to examine the jaguar. The police chief grabbed my shoulder. "Leave that tiger alone. It's mine!" he said to me aggressively.

I informed him curtly that I had a permit to handle these animals and that he had broken the law by admitting to have intentionally killed the jaguar. He laughed at my brazen attitude. "Are you telling me about the law? That tiger's mine," he repeated.

I held my ground, but realized there was little I could do. "I don't want the tiger," I said. "I just want to get it somewhere where I can measure and examine it. I have that authorization. If you don't let me do that, then you'll have some explaining to do in Belmopan."

He seemed uncertain of his position for the first time. "Okay," he conceded. "But I'm following you, and when you're finished, I take the skin."

I turned my back to him and loaded the jaguar into the truck. We returned to Richard's house, where I went through the normal protocol in Richard's driveway:

Sex—male
Age—mature adult
Total length—72 inches
Tail length—24 inches
Head circumference—22 inches
Height at shoulder—18 inches
Height at hip—22 inches
Weight—137 pounds

He was heavier than any of the Cockscomb jaguars I had captured. His upper right canine was missing, and his dentition showed he was a mature adult. His coat was filled with botfly larvae.

Within two hours of his death, all the botfly larvae started to emerge simultaneously from the cold, stiffening body. It was a chilling sight to watch these one-and-a-half-inch maggots emerging from every location on the cat's body and dropping to the ground, their bloated little bodies squirming on the concrete. They obviously needed a warm, living host.

When the truck was finally ready, I was only too glad to escape the civilization of northern Belize. I picked Maggie up at her home and returned to Cockscomb, pleased to have visited with my friends but disappointed that I had accomplished little with the government. I was pleased that Maggie was anxious to get back as well. She had come to love the wildness of Cockscomb.

While driving on the entrance road, I stopped alongside a long-haired man walking toward our camp. He was a forty-four-year-old hippie from the United States who had heard about "the tiger man" and was coming to see me. Calling himself only Fire, he had recently been thrown out of Cuba and was traveling through Central America trying to organize the Indians to stand up for their rights. He described himself as part Alaskan fisherman and part antiestablishment politician. He told me he was coming into Cockscomb to "groove on a jaguar." He was a friendly man who had seen much of the world, and we enjoyed his company. I let him groove in my shack for a couple of days before asking him to leave.

Another visitor followed shortly afterward. Joe McFarlane was an amateur video photographer traveling throughout Belize filming third world life. He and Ben had similar easygoing personalities and got along well, so we let him stay in camp and help in the field while shooting footage of the project.

The first taste Joe had of fieldwork was helping us fix the roads. The ruts had become so bad from the rainy season that they threatened to stop our work completely if we didn't repair them before the new rains set in. The Indians had little time to work for us now, as they were working on their own plantations, so Joe, Ben, Maggie, and I did it ourselves. We'd spend hours loading rocks into the back of the truck, then use them to fill in holes and build supporting walls for collapsing road edges.

In addition to the day and night prey surveys along trails, Ben had started his quadrate surveys. This involved more work than any of us had anticipated. Within each quadrate, we cut trails dividing it into three equal sections. On these trails Ben put down sand for track pads (areas where tracks of animals walking the path could be easily identified) and placed small and medium-sized mammal box traps to see if he could capture any animals. We were hoping to use this technique as another way of determining the diversity and density of the jaguar's prey species. With Joe's help, Ben had an easier time of it. One night all of us decided to help Ben in one of his quadrates so that he could finish early. Gregorio was the only Indian who could find time to work for us. We split up into two groups: Gregorio and I for one half of the quadrate and Ben and Joe for the other. I disliked working with Gregorio because he feared the jungle at night even more than I did. Tonight he insisted I walk in front of him, something he'd never done before. Later I wondered if he had had a premonition.

I was going through the normal routine of shining the flashlight into the canopy looking for the eye shine of kinkajous when I heard a rustling at my feet. I directed the light toward the noise and saw a medium-sized fer-de-lance stretched out beside the trail. By now my fear of this snake was so great that I could not think rationally in its presence. I screamed, "Tommy-goff!" and jumped back without looking where I was going. A large root caught my ankle and threw me flat on my back, right alongside the snake. As I landed, I thought my luck had run out. Its tail was a foot from my face.

Fortunately, it was as frightened as I was and disappeared into the undergrowth. As soon as it was off the trail, it stopped moving. I couldn't pinpoint where it was. Gregorio had run ten feet back along the trail and had stopped, refusing to budge. He would go no farther and I couldn't blame him. I was becoming fed up with this snake. When we joined up with Ben and Joe, we told them what had happened. They were disappointed that they hadn't gotten to see the snake. I looked at them as if they were crazy. I hoped I'd never see another fer-de-lance again.

In the next few days, tracks of the new uncollared male jaguar were all along the entrance road again. During this time, Ben and I were stopped at Maya Center and told that two Indian children walking along the creek that parallels the entrance road had seen a large jaguar up in a tree. They took us to the tree and pointed at a large branch not twenty feet above the ground. The tree leaned over the water at a forty-five-degree angle and had the cat's claw marks five feet up on the trunk. We knew this was the jaguar we were after. I decided not to wait any longer to try and catch it.

We set a trap where he had eaten the pig. Four days later we had the jaguar.

Sex—male
Age—mature adult
Total length—8o inches
Tail length—24 inches
Head circumference—24 inches
Height to shoulder—23 inches
Height to hip—24 inches
Weight—125 pounds

His teeth were in good condition but showed some wear. He looked to be a middle-aged mature adult male, probably about seven years old. I was most impressed with his coat, which despite the botfly larvae holes, was thick and glossy. He was a beautiful jaguar but I felt sorry for him when I noticed three large botfly larvae peeking out of holes in his scrotum. I couldn't fathom how he could live with that pain.

Sedation went smoothly, and Joe, Maggie, and Ben all came out to help. Maggie later said it was the most thrilling moment of her life. Then she and Ben returned to camp, and Joe and I stayed with the jaguar. Joe wanted to film its recovery, so we set up the video equipment about thirty feet from the trap's entrance. I assured him the jaguar would stumble out of the trap directly into the forest. Joe believed me.

After an hour, I wondered if something was wrong. The cat's breathing was steady and deep, but he exhibited no movement to indicate he was recovering from sedation. It never entered my mind that he might already be recovered and had simply chosen to rest where he was. I decided to prod him and initiate some movement.

I cut a large pole and stuck it between the bars, jabbing his hindquarters. His eyes opened and I saw a clear-eyed jaguar looking directly at me. Fortunately, I was to the side of the trap. He jumped to his feet and was out instantly as I dropped the pole and charged for the truck. Joe dropped his camera and ran.

As soon as I began running, I knew that keeping my back to the animal was the worst thing I could do. I'd never make it to the truck in time if the jaguar really wanted to pursue us. I decided to act against my body's instincts.

I stopped running and turned to face him, screaming, "NO!" with the loudest voice I could muster. The jaguar stopped, staring directly at me. I was relieved to see him still a bit unsteady on his feet. I remembered that Alfred Wallace had been told by the Indians in the Amazon that a jaguar might spring to within a few feet of you, but will only attack if you turn your back. I hoped that that was true as I stood there facing the jaguar. He turned and walked off into the forest. I exhaled, realizing I'd been holding my breath. I turned and looked at Joe. "Did you get that on film?" I asked.

"All your captures this exciting?" His camera had fallen.

I named this beautiful jaguar Ek Chuah, after the black war captain, sometimes hostile to man, sometimes friendly.

Three days later I lost the signal on young Xaman Ek and never found him again despite intensive air and ground searches. I thought of the closeness I had felt to this jaguar when I looked into its eyes that first time. It seemed whenever I captured a new jaguar, something would happen to one of my old ones. First old Itzamna, then Ixchel, then Ah Puch, and now Xaman Ek.

21 CRASH

After collaring Ek Chuah, we followed him closely and began to understand why he had started to move into Cockscomb. Whenever he left Chac's former range, he traveled north through a narrow forest strip surrounded on both sides by cattle pasture and citrus groves. Large areas of what might have once been his range were already cleared, and the remaining areas were heavily disturbed. In an effort to stay in a forest environment and hunt his natural prey, he was shifting into the adjacent Cockscomb area. What might he have done had Chac not moved? I wondered.

The movement patterns of the various jaguars I'd observed throughout the study pointed to the same conclusion. Though the adult male jaguars showed a lot of range overlap with other jaguars, a dynamic equilibrium existed. Males were maintaining specific home areas and delineating these areas or advertising their presence in part by depositing feces and leaving scrapes. Only a certain number of adult jaguars would be tolerated within a specific area, though in the case of Cockscomb, the density of jaguars seemed relatively high.

I was not surprised that Chac immediately shifted into Ah Puch's former range as soon as he had a chance. Chac's range, between Maya Center and Guam Bank, now occupied by the newest collared jaguar, Ek Chuah, was the most traveled and hunted portion of the basin. Ek Chuah now seemed to be testing out areas as far west into the basin as he could go before being restricted by the presence of Chac. And tenure among jaguars seemed based upon a "first come" system.

Tracks from the two females continued to show up in the same areas as before, despite the shifts in the movements of the males. Though I couldn't fully determine their movements without radio-tracking them, their tracks observed in the forest and along the road indicated they were traveling within an area of a minimum of four square miles within the ranges of the males. The females still would not walk near my traps, continuing to show a more secretive, wary nature than the male jaguars.

Joe was enjoying Cockscomb immensely. He was constantly in the field with Ben, filming everything he saw. He had been with us almost two weeks and was waiting to fly with me over Cockscomb before leaving. I needed to fly soon anyway, so I called John and scheduled an aerial survey in two days. I was still hoping I'd hear Xaman Ek again. Instead, that night I heard my own name called.

Ben and Joe were out on a survey for kinkajou, and Maggie was cleaning up in the kitchen. I was working in the bedroom, looking at my maps of Cockscomb for the hundredth time and translating radio beeps into behavioral patterns. Just as I marked a location for Chac on the map, I heard my first name called twice from the darkness outside the house.

It seemed late for the Indians to be awake, but I thought someone might be sick, so I grabbed the lantern and rushed outside. Nobody was there and I was in no mood for jokes. I walked around the house expecting to see an Indian hiding there, waiting to jump out to scare me, but I didn't see anything. I suddenly realized that it wasn't even an Indian's voice I had heard. I blew out the lantern and stood listening in the darkness. I could feel that no one was around.

"Who is it?" Maggie called from the kitchen. She had heard the voice as well.

"There's no one out here," I told her. She didn't say anything.

I would have let the incident pass, filing it away as another little quirk of Cockscomb, but the next day it happened again. I had just returned from the field; Maggie was in the house reading. It was midafternoon. As I started unpacking my equipment, my first name was called twice, from outside the house.

I saw Maggie's body tense. I didn't need to go outside this time to know that no one was near the house. The whole thing seemed strange, but no stranger than many things I had experienced in Cockscomb. I did the only thing I could—I let it pass. I didn't even want to know what Maggie was thinking.

John flew in the next day. It was typically overcast, with several minor squalls blowing in from the sea, but we hoped they'd move around us or pass over us quickly. If not, we could always fly around them. Ben had left for the day, and Maggie was doing laundry by the creek.

A radio location on Ek Chuah, outside the basin and eight miles northeast of camp, worried me. The farther away he moved from Cockscomb, the greater his chances of being killed. Chac was only three miles northwest of camp. Both cats were inactive until we buzzed low over the canopy. Then their signals turned active and I imagined them looking up at the plane.

Clouds had moved in over the basin and hung over Victoria Peak. The ceiling was about fifteen hundred feet, and Xaman Ek's area was too close to the Cockscomb Range to permit safe flying. We tried circling the area once, but after encountering two rain squalls, I signaled John to head back for camp.

Another dark mass of clouds started moving in over the basin.

We could see heavy rains rapidly coming our way. As we dropped to five hundred feet and aligned ourselves with the airstrip, the first strong winds preceding the rainstorm caught us unexpectedly and started bouncing the plane. I expected John to abort the landing and circle high above the rains until it passed. We had followed that procedure many times before.

But this time, John continued on course, dropping the plane lower and slowing our speed. As we lined up with the runway for a landing, the stall buzzer went off. I hated that sound. Suddenly, a tail wind caught the plane and hurled us like a slingshot. Within a couple of seconds, we had lost most of the runway space we needed to land safely.

The trees at the end of the strip looked very close but I thought we could still make it, or at the worst, land in the trees slowly. I looked at John and saw the unmistakable signs of panic in his eyes.

While no more than six feet off the ground, the stall buzzer blasting in our ears, John opened up the throttle and tried lifting the nose to abort the landing. I couldn't believe it. One of the hills bordering Cockscomb loomed directly in front of us. That hill was the reason planes never took off in this direction in the first place. I was terrified. What did John think he was doing?

The plane started gaining altitude, but the trees were closing in fast and their crowns were still above us. We had to bank to the left, away from the hill, while trying to climb above the trees at the same time. The end of the runway was coming up fast and we were still only about fifty feet off the ground.

"We'll make it! We'll make it!" John yelled.

I knew we weren't going to make it. There was no more runway, only trees, and just as we rose above the forest, the bottom of the plane scraped against the treetops. Not now, not here, please, I thought.

One large tree loomed directly in front of us. In the next instant, it tore off our left wing and the plane plunged straight down like a rock.

We all screamed. We seemed frozen in time for one or two

seconds before impacting with the ground. I clearly remembered afterward the two thoughts I had in those two seconds. First, I was a kid again back on the big roller coaster in Coney Island, coming down the big drop. All the kids were screaming except me. It was only a ride. My second thought was that I was really going to die this time. I hoped they'd find my body.

Then there was darkness.

I blacked out for no more than a few minutes. The first thing I saw when I opened my eyes was the ground, eighteen inches from my face. My seat had broken off on impact and I was hanging upside down, half in, half out of the windshield. My head had smashed through it.

I was still alive. I wiped the stickiness from my eyes, not realizing it was my own blood, and unhooked the seat belt still attaching me to the seat. Then I pulled myself back into the plane and saw John. He seemed unhurt and was struggling with his seat belt.

We were drenched in gasoline from the tanks in the collapsed wing and all I could think of was the possibility of the plane bursting into flames. I kicked out more of the windshield and rolled out onto the ground, with John following closely behind. When I had gotten away from the plane, I heard Joe yelling, still inside, "Alan, I can't move. Help me!"

We rushed back, pried him loose, and carried him away from the site. There were no external wounds, but he complained of severe pain in his back and no feeling below his waist. I thought he had broken his back.

My head felt like it would explode and I saw that my shirt was covered with blood. At first I thought I had cut my stomach on the windshield, then I realized that the blood was dripping from my face. I could feel at least one large gash that would probably need stitches, and my nose felt flattened. Later I learned that in addition to the surface wounds, my nose was broken and my septum crushed, and I had a subdural hematoma inside my head.

We propped Joe against a tree about thirty feet from the

wreckage, then took stock of our situation. I was impressed with how calm Joe was, considering he couldn't walk. John, on the other hand, was near panic, and I felt a growing anger toward him.

Despite having flown over these forests for years, John carried no emergency equipment on the plane. All he had was a pistol. We were no more than a mile from the airstrip, but I had no idea in what direction it lay. If we went in the wrong direction, we could be faced with miles of hills and jungle. We were in sneakers and had no machetes to cut or mark a trail. Thinking of the omnipresent fer-de-lance, I was not going to walk through the forest if there was any alternative.

John, on the other hand, was ready to go off in the direction he thought the airstrip lay.

"If you go, you go alone," I told him.

He decided to follow my lead. I looked around us and thought of our alternatives, trying to fight off the pounding in my head, the blurry vision, and an almost overwhelming desire to lie down and sleep. No one could be aware that we had crashed, and it would probably be almost dark before Ben returned from the field and wondered about us.

Then I heard it: the sound of running water. There was a creek no more than twenty yards from where we had crashed, but the dense undergrowth had obscured it. I knew this creek, I thought, or at least I had traveled along the stream into which it flowed. If we followed it downstream, it should lead toward camp and eventually come out near one of the Indians' huts. That was our way out.

I explained the plan to Joe and told John with more confidence than I felt that we would soon be out. We had to leave Joe at the site, so we placed him in a comfortable position and cleared the area around him of any ground litter that could harbor snakes, or ants or other insects. I told him we'd be back soon with help.

Joe later told me that he thought he might have to crawl back into the plane and spend the night there. He said I was deathly pale when we left and looked like I might pass out at any time. John was acting so strangely that Joe expected him to run off into the forest and get lost. I was glad he kept his feelings to himself. I was having my own doubts about whether I'd be able make it very far. All I wanted to do was lie down and make the pain in my head disappear.

I looked at my watch. It was 2 P.M. We had three or four hours before dusk; if only I could hold out and keep my head from exploding. I made John stay close behind me as we walked in the knee-deep water of the creek. I was not going to walk along the dense growth of the bank without a machete. Occasionally we'd see a clearing on a hill and think it was the road into the basin or an Indian's plantation. We'd make our way through the forest only to find a gap made by a fallen tree. John kept wanting to fire the gun into the air, hoping someone would hear us. I kept insisting we wait. I didn't want to waste the bullets, knowing that even if someone heard the shot, they'd just think it was someone out hunting.

I don't need this, I kept thinking. I'm going to quit. I should be back in the United States, teaching classes and going to faculty meetings. On weekends my most complex task would be reading the Sunday newspaper or organizing backyard barbecues. I've seen enough of the reality that I thought was so important to experience. What the hell am I doing here, my face bleeding, trying to find my way out of the jungle in Central America? How many people care about jaguars anyway? I don't want to die, please God, I don't want to die.

After one and a half hours of following the creek, we saw another clearing on the hill. Running up the embankment, expecting another false alarm, we stepped out of the forest into a burnt milpa. There, in the middle of the field, stood Gregorio.

"Gregorio, Gregorio, help us," I yelled.

Gregorio swung around, axe in hand. He looked at us and with a grunt of fear dropped it and started backing away quickly.

"It's me, Alan. We've been in a plane crash. I need your help,"

I said and then realized my mistake. I might have laughed except for the pain in my head.

I suddenly remembered the stories about the evil forest spirits that the Indians believed in. Some of the spirits emerge from the forest and take the form of someone you know so that you'll come when they call you. Then they lead you to your death. There I was, standing covered in blood, calling Gregorio to come to me.

I didn't waste another moment. I had to make sure Gregorio didn't run away, so I sprinted the distance between us and grabbed him. The expression on his face was one of sure expectation of death. We struggled for a few moments while I talked to him and wiped the blood from my face. Finally he realized who it was and that I was real, with ever more blood showing. His expression quickly changed to one of concern. After hearing what had happened, he rushed us through the forest back to camp.

Gregorio rounded up some Indians to get Joe, while I ran into my house to see Maggie and bandage my face. When Maggie saw me, she screamed. I looked in a mirror and didn't recognize myself. The right side of my face was swollen, and my nose looked flattened and crooked. I realized immediately why Gregorio thought I was an evil spirit. While closing two of the gashes with butterfly bandages, I explained to Maggie what had happened.

I changed my bloodied, wet clothes and ran outside to find nearly all the male Indians of Cockscomb waiting to help me, having just returned from their milpas. Their expressions showed pain and sympathy. They really do care about me, I thought. Then we went back and carried Joe out.

Joe and I needed medical attention, so after returning to camp, we left a note of explanation for Ben and left for Dangriga. Maggie insisted on coming with us. While I drove, Maggie wiped the blood from my head. Joe sat in pain, grunting with every bump and wondering how badly his back was damaged. John was in the rear of the truck. I didn't want to see or talk to him. His only concern was for his plane, for which he had no insurance. I felt angry and cheated that his foolish decision to take off again after we were nearly on the ground had caused the accident and that he was unhurt.

The doctor in Dangriga wouldn't examine us. He insisted on getting an airplane to carry us to Belize City Hospital.

We sat in the emergency room of the hospital for more than an hour before the doctor examined us. John had returned home. Joe never complained or voiced any fear, despite his uncertainty about his injury. When he was finally sent off to the X-ray room, I desperately hoped he'd be all right. Then I was sent into an operating room for examination and stitches to my head.

The doctor seemed unconcerned about my headaches, telling me simply that they'd eventually disappear. He never mentioned a possible concussion or skull fracture, though I told him I had gone through the windshield of the plane. I had the distinct impression that, with a line of people behind me, he simply wanted to sew me up and get me out of there.

Lying on the operating table, a bright light shining in my face, I wondered about the nurse who had asked why I hadn't taken Guermo to a snake doctor. Fortunately, the nurse who now hovered over me was a different one. She prepared a local anesthetic to numb part of my face before stitching and held it out to the doctor. He told her to put it away. "We don't need that. He's a man; he can take it."

I looked at the nurse. She shrugged and smiled. I lay back and wondered if anyone ever died from stitches. What the hell, I thought. The pain from the stitches couldn't be any worse than the pain in my head right now. I was wrong. It was a toss-up.

He stitched up a gash between my eyes and one in the corner of my right eye, telling me how lucky I'd been that I hadn't been blinded.

I laughed. "You didn't see the plane crash, Doctor. I'm lucky to be alive."

He laughed and jabbed me again with the needle.

"Doctor," I said, trying to take my mind off the pain, "please don't make me look like Frankenstein".

"Franken who?" he asked. I dropped the subject.

Joe was lucky too. His back was not broken, just wrenched inside. I thought, though, that they'd want to at least keep him overnight for observation. Our injuries weren't bad enough, they said.

"Rest and stay still for five days," the doctor said to Joe. "If anything tingles or goes numb, come back." Great advice, I thought. As we waited for a taxi to take us to the Mopan Hotel, I heard a woman screaming in a nearby ward. I realized I didn't want to see what "bad enough" meant.

We were a big hit that night at the hotel. I walked in, bandages around my face, one eye swollen shut, pushing Joe in a wheelchair. Tom started laughing. Stories about that night were to become part of the legend of that hotel.

The next day Jean arranged a flight for Joe to the United States. He needed specialized care. I didn't think my injuries were any more than a broken nose, which I could straighten myself, gashes requiring some stitches, and possibly a mild concussion. I'd rest a few days, to see if any problems developed, before returning to Cockscomb. I could always check with a doctor in Dangriga.

That night I lay cradled in Maggie's arms, wondering if I could really go back. I had already passed through one breaking point with the death of Ah Puch, but this incident had taken a much greater toll. This time I had come face to face with death. Now, instead of happiness, I felt an intense weariness sweep over me. I had to accept life again.

Could I keep this up? If not, could I ever return to New York and immerse myself in a culture of which I had never felt an integral part? What could I become instead of what I was—a teacher, a banker, a lawyer, a medical doctor? I knew the answer. Why torture myself with the questions? For me, there was only more of what I'd already begun. I hated, feared, and loved Cockscomb. And I knew I would return.

Maggie stroked my head as I lay in her arms and told me it would be all right. It'll never be all right, Maggie, I thought. The greedy people, the innocent animals, the Indians wanting nothing more than to live a simple life. It has never been all right. The world continues along the same path, and only the actors and scenes change. A plane crash, even my death, would make little difference. I would just no longer be one of the actors.

"Do you remember my name being called, Maggie?" I asked through the fog starting to cloud my mind.

"Sleep, Alan," she said. "It'll be all right, tomorrow. It'll all be all right."

"Will it, Maggie?" I mumbled. I fell asleep in her arms.

22 KUKULCAN

I was an invalid back in Cockscomb. My headaches continued with no sign of abating. I returned to the plane wreckage several times to take pictures and salvage whatever equipment I could. Most of the radio-tracking gear and Joe's video equipment were destroyed. Strangely, the videotape itself was undamaged and showed the frightening moments before impact.

Joe later told me that he kept filming until the plane dove into the ground. He said, before the tree took the wing, as long as he was looking through the camera, the danger didn't seem real.

Although Ben had planned to leave the project in July, he now agreed to stay on. My continual headaches made it obvious that my injuries were more severe than I'd thought, so I decided to return to New York for a full examination. We also needed another set of radiotelemetry gear because we were now using our backup equipment. Maggie decided to stay with her family while I was gone.

Everyone at the New York Zoological Society was extremely concerned about my health. A neurological examination showed no obvious nerve damage, but a CAT scan indicated a small hematoma from a concussion. The stitches were taken out, the swelling went down, and I was pleased to see a nearly normal face in the mirror again. I was told that my nose was more damaged than originally believed and I'd need surgery to clear the passageways through my crushed septum. The doctor felt it might be contributing to my headaches. I decided to hold off on the operation.

The headaches wouldn't let up. The doctors warned that time and rest were the only cures, the two things I had the least of. I was told that the first six weeks after the crash were the most crucial. I shouldn't physically exert myself and should be near someone at all times. This was after I had already spent the first two weeks after the crash in Cockscomb. If I went easy on myself, I was told that the headaches might go away in one or two years. If I refused to rest, they might never go away completely. Neither alternative pleased me.

I remained in New York for four more weeks, trying to do nothing but eat and sleep, but my heart and mind were elsewhere. I was still in the jungles of Cockscomb. I tried finding Sue and learned she had finally made it to Alaska. I called her, but the phone connection was bad and her voice sounded distant. I groped for something from the past to bridge the gap, if for only a few minutes.

"Remember that time . . ." I said, trying to bring back some of the good times in Cockscomb.

No, she was trying to forget those times for now. Maybe later, when some of the hurt had left.

I went to visit some of the places I remembered as a child: the house I used to live in, an abandoned lot where I used to hide from the world, a playground where I remembered laughing.

But I found it hard to make the connection now. I drove to Coney Island, now a dismal, run-down shell of what it once had been.

There was the roller coaster. Of all the different things from my past, why had I flashed back to that in the moments before the plane crash? I walked toward it and suddenly had a vivid picture of the young, self-conscious boy getting on this ride. I remembered now how it had taken me weeks to work up the courage to ride that roller coaster. Some of my friends, whose faces and names I've long since forgotten, dared me to ride alone in the front car. They rode behind. As we came down the big drop I could hear them all screaming in back of me, but I wouldn't let myself scream. Afterward, I had acted as if the whole ride was no big deal. But I had been scared. That was the scene I had flashed back to.

The Zoological Society and the doctors told me I shouldn't return to the project. I ignored their advice. It was not a decision I made lightly, nor was it motivated by a desire for heroism or martyrdom. I was concerned about my long-term health, but there was over a year of hard work invested in Cockscomb and important work still remained. Ben could continue the ongoing fieldwork but could not suddenly take over the administration of the project. And I would not shut the project down, not yet. I wanted to keep the promises I had made to myself after Ah Puch's death. I wanted more than just scientific data from this project. I wanted a home for the jaguars.

I returned to Belize, promising the doctors I'd relax and just oversee the project. I even believed that myself when I landed back in Belize City in June 1984. Maggie was waiting for me at the Mopan Hotel. I hadn't thought of her much in the last few weeks, but that first night back I realized how much I had missed her.

Our emotional involvement had gone beyond what we'd expected. But I was entering the last phase of the project and soon I'd leave her world and go on to something new. There were no lingering doubts in my mind. I wasn't quite sure where my life was taking me, but I knew it'd be somewhere else. And I knew I was going there alone. There was so much of the world to see, so much more that needed to be done. We talked about it that night but decided to put off making any decisions a little while longer.

I sent word to Ben that I was back in the country and would soon return to Cockscomb. Then I settled in at the Mopan to rest for several days and work on my field data. The rest never came.

The morning of my second day in Belize, I called Bader after receiving a message that he was trying to contact me. He hadn't known about the plane crash and had been waiting several weeks to hear from me. There was another cattle-killing jaguar on the rampage. He had held off going after it as long as he could, hoping I'd get in touch. The ranchers were now pleading with him, so he was going after it. Did I want it? I packed my bags, asked Maggie to wait for me, and left for Orange Walk.

By the evening of my fourth day in Belize, I was on my way back to Cockscomb with a young male jaguar caged in the back of the truck. Rest is relative, I told myself, trying to dispel the guilty feelings I had about working so intensely so soon. At least I wasn't out climbing mountains.

This was one angry jaguar. It was a small subadult male, and when shot from the tree, the tranquilizer dart aimed at his rump was deflected by a branch and hit him in the scrotum. He was sedated quickly, but was not at all pleased during the trip to Cockscomb. I stopped for gasoline only when I had to because his thrashing in the cage terrified everyone, causing a small furor at the pump. No gas attendants would approach the truck.

By dark I reached Cockscomb. When I pulled up in front of the shack with a jaguar, Ben didn't even appear surprised. He had been in Cockscomb long enough to realize how quickly and unexpectedly things happen, especially with me. We sedated the jaguar for the second time, carried him into the house, and went through our procedure.

Sex—Male
Age—Subadult
Total length—68 inches
Tail length—20 inches
Head circumference—19 inches
Height at shoulder—20 inches
Height at hip—20 inches
Weight—80 pounds

His dentition was fully developed, very white, and showed virtually no wear. His stomach was distended from having killed and eaten a calf the day before. We placed him back in the cage, hoping he'd sleep through the night. I planned to release him just before sunrise.

That night Ben filled me in on the events taking place in Cockscomb. The new scientist, Dr. Mike Konecny, had arrived and was living in my old shack. Ben had been accumulating additional location, movement, and activity data on the newest jaguar, Ek Chuah, and on Chac while following the tracks of all the uncollared cats. More scrapes and feces had been found, virtually all in areas of known overlap between at least two adult male jaguars. There was still no radio signal from young Xaman Ek, despite attempts by Ben to locate him from the Outlier.

I was certain we had lost Xaman Ek forever and I'd never know what happened to him. His collar might have failed prematurely, or he could have been killed and the radio destroyed by someone who knew about what I was doing. That included everyone in Kendall, Maya Center, and the surrounding villages. Though we still watched for Xaman Ek's tracks, he was the one cat who least used the monitored roads, traveling mainly in the vicinity of the high peaks. If we didn't find his tracks, it didn't necessarily mean he wasn't still around.

I decided to release the young male in the former range of Itzamna. Although Ah Kin and Chac were using part of this area, there was still no jaguar sign in the southern part of old Itzamna's range since his death. I thought that the best chance for a new subadult male to be accepted in the area would be if he were released where there were no other resident adult males. It was worth a try.

At 5 A.M. the next morning I drove down an old rutted road that branched south from the main logging road. Dr. Konecny followed behind in his truck to take pictures of the release. He got more than he expected.

The morning light was starting to peek through the trees as we reached the end of the road. Julian had come along to help lift the cage to the ground. The jaguar, fully awake, thrashed back and forth.

I crouched on top of the cage ready to lift up the front door as Mike and Julian got back into the trucks. I sensed the anger emanating from the jaguar and felt a momentary sensation of fear. Of the six previous jaguars released, never had I seen one so angry. This was also the first jaguar that was completely recovered from the tranquilizer before its release. Still, I expected him to run into the forest as soon as the door opened. I hadn't learned my lesson from Ek Chuah.

"Are you ready?" I yelled to Mike, hoping he'd get some good pictures. "It's going to happen quickly."

What happened next caught me completely by surprise. The jaguar lost no time coming out of the cage; ten feet from the door he stopped and turned his head. As our eyes met, I knew I was in danger. Suddenly, he swerved and came at me. Reacting instinctively, I leaped into the rear of the truck. Don't turn your back, I told myself, remembering the incident with Ek Chuah. As I jumped, the jaguar reacted like a predator closing in on its prey and jumped too. I screamed, feeling for an instant what the weaker animal must feel before it's killed.

It might have been the overzealousness of a young animal or a flicker of indecision, but the jaguar's jump fell short. His head, with mouth agape, and his paws landed on the edge of the truck bed, while his body swung beneath the truck, hitting the bumper and knocking him onto his back. I thought it was only a momentary reprieve, for I hadn't had time to get inside the truck.

I waited for the next jump, which would easily bring him within striking distance. The crushed skulls of jaguar prey flashed through my mind. But the next leap never occurred. He stood up, looked at me, then turned and walked slowly into the forest.

I watched as he disappeared from sight, staring at the spot where the forest had absorbed him. I was shaking uncontrollably and my head was pounding. What an animal, I thought. Even in the aftermath of abject terror, I couldn't help but feel admiration for that jaguar. I named him Kukulcan, after the king who ruled over the last great centers of the Maya Indians before their final collapse.

The pounding in my head lasted two days after that incident. As I tossed and turned that night, unable to sleep from the headaches, I knew I had to get away from Cockscomb for a while. It was impossible to rest here. Ben could maintain the project.

I decided to visit Tikal, in the Petén region of Guatemala, the greatest excavated Maya center in the world. I wanted to learn more about the ancient Maya, whose descendants had become an important part of my life and the jaguar project. Since finding Kuchil Balum, I also wanted to take a closer look at the architecture of these sites and learn more about how the jaguar fit into the consciousness of these people.

Though it's known that the jaguar played an important role in the ancient Maya civilization, that role has not been clearly defined. Jaguars themselves were never considered true gods, but pictorial representations of the gods often had jaguar features. Royalty wore jaguar skins, and jaguar thrones were known from major ceremonial sites. The Olmec, whose civilization overlapped that of the Maya and who probably had contact with them, depicted figures that were half man, half jaguar.

Some Indian tribes in South and Central America still use jaguar parts and symbolism in dealing with everyday life. Jaguar costumes are used in ceremonies; teeth and claws are worn as powerful ornaments; and even jaguar blood is still sometimes drunk or used to anoint newborns to impart certain qualities. The highland Maya incorporate the jaguar into their intricate woven designs, though many of them have never seen the animal. Even in areas where they are no longer common, jaguars continue to exert a powerful effect on the world of man.

Where did jaguars fit in? They were not considered gods, nor were they thought to be simply powerful animals that shared the earth with man. It seemed as though, to the ancient Maya, they were living symbols of the gods and their power. They were creatures of the night, and allied with the underworld. They were of man's world, yet not of man's world. They were real, yet not real. They were definable by the senses, yet they represented all that was unknown and mysterious in the jungle. How to categorize their role? Perhaps they were less understood by the people than the gods themselves. We shall never know.

No one knows for certain why the more grandiose elements of the Maya civilization disappeared from the lowland region in the ninth century. Construction of ceremonial centers halted, inscriptions ceased to be made, and a decline in population left large areas virtually deserted. What happened? That question has long haunted archaeologists.

Before leaving for Tikal, I checked with the American consulate in Belize about the safety of the Guatemalan lowlands. It was safe for the time being, they told me. I soon learned that safety, like all else, is relative in this world.

I had taken the truck and left Ben with the motorcycle, stopping at Maggie's village along the way to pick her up. It never occurred to me to take out all the various field supplies that I always left under the seats of the truck. We had no problem crossing the border into Guatemala. No more than an hour later, however, we were stopped at an army outpost, manned by a group of soldiers ironically known as El Tigre, the jaguar. Many of the soldiers looked no more than boys carrying man-sized rifles. Was it a game to them, or were they just forced to grow up early? I wondered. Had any of them ever killed some-one or watched a human being die?

We were roughly searched, then they checked our bags and looked through the truck. Suddenly I heard someone yell. I looked over and saw a young soldier holding up my U.S. army surplus jungle boots that I always wore in Cockscomb. All hell broke loose.

I was thrown against the truck and a semiautomatic was jabbed in my ribs. They yelled questions at me in Spanish. Maggie stood to one side, stunned and silent. Fortunately, they didn't touch her.

I couldn't understand a word they were saying. Grabbing my Spanish dictionary, I tried to explain that I was a *científico*, a scientist, and that the boots were for *culebra*, snakes. The boots were brought over to the commander. The talk went back and forth, with occasional stares in my direction. I couldn't under-stand their conversation, but I knew they were trying to decide what to do with me.

After an hour we had made no progress and they still wouldn't let me move. Images of torture rooms that had been described in detail to me by Nari and Tino flashed through my mind. Then I remembered something.

By chance, I had brought my briefcase containing all my papers, and in it I hoped I still had a letter brought down from New York. The letter was signed by William Conway, general director of the New York Zoological Society, and guaranteed me safe-conduct. It had been prepared for my drive through Mexico when I first came down to set up the project. Written in Spanish and stamped with a gold seal, the letter meant little, but was designed to look impressive and intimidating. I had brought it down with me specifically for situations like this.

I found the letter and shoved it at the commander. He read it and showed it to one of his subordinates, who nodded sagely.

It worked, though they seemed a bit uncertain. Within minutes I was motioned by the commander to get back in my truck and leave.

They had not given me back my boots and I wanted them. I decided to see how far I could go. I demanded my *bota* as I smacked the letter several times. The commander looked annoyed, but I refused to get in my truck. *"El Presidente,"* I said, pointing to William Conway's signature, as if it were that of Ronald Reagan. Finally, he signaled a soldier to hand me the boots. I got into the truck, slammed the door, and drove off quickly. Maggie looked at me and smiled.

"What do you think about our vacation so far?" I asked her.

She had a question too. "Alan, how far would you have gone for those boots?"

23 CATTLE KILLERS

As I walked among the ruins of Tikal for the first time, I began to feel and understand more of the mystique that distinguished the Maya from other early cultures. Standing in the central plaza, dwarfed by the temple-pyramids around me, I could feel the power of the place. I tried to imagine the plaza filled with worshipers, as Gifford had described it, telling how "masses of people once gathered to watch their priest-rulers clothed in jade, plumes of the quetzal and jaguar skins."

The Great Plaza was part of a complex covering about six square miles. Yet exploration showed that there were about as many structures two to three miles out from the Great Plaza as in the city's center.

In centers like Tikal, the Maya intellectual elite developed a numerical system that included the zero; devised a written language; and had a knowledge of astronomy. In the process, they became obsessed with time, its ongoing, unending nature, and its accurate calculation. It was said they virtually worshiped time, using the obsession to dominate the masses. Places like Tikal were major ceremonial centers, with a permanent population of priests whose duty was to ensure the future of the civilization.

But still it collapsed, possibly because the religious and intellectual elite could no longer control or fool the masses. Perhaps because belief became disbelief, and the elite, who consumed but did not produce, was no longer tolerated. Gifford speculated:

> The two settlement dimensions of the Old Empire may have grown apart—the homeland rural setting where the village and slash and burn or milpa agriculture were the basic elements, and the ceremonial center where pageantry and full time specialization of human effort with an all powerful religious overview were the basic elements of focus. Corn to one, jade to the other, symbols of that which pleases and brings comfort.

But even after the majestic symbols of the ancient Maya civilization crumbled, the small rural centers, places like Cockscomb, persisted. They were all that was left to maintain the essence of the empire.

The ruins of Tikal were first encountered by the Spanish priest Father Avendaño in 1695. Not until the 1950s, when the University of Pennsylvania undertook the task of excavation, did its true grandeur come to be recognized. Already occupied by the Early Classic Period (A.D. 300–600), the city thrived for several hundred years, until its decline in the Late Classic Period (A.D. 600–900).

Despite the blazing sun and an increased intensity in my headaches, Maggie and I climbed to the top of the temples, the highest at two hundred and twenty feet. We walked among the ball courts and examined the dozens of stelae and altars. We had the place to ourselves. The tourist trade had declined sharply after the start of intense political conflicts in Guatemala. If visitors received the reception I did after I'd entered the country, I could understand why it wasn't highly recommended.

We explored for two days and I couldn't get enough. Though I had visited Maya sites in Belize, such as Altun Ha, Lubaantun, Xunantunich, and Nim Li Punit, none of them had given me the feeling I had here. Tikal, with its geographic location and immensity, was one of the great centers of the ancient Maya empire.

I strained to listen to the voices of the past, imagining thousands of laborers spending their lives felling trees with stone axes for the lime kilns and then cutting, dressing, and finishing the stones for structure after structure. Where had the knowledge gone? The intellectual elite scattered; then the Spanish came, burning their writings and crushing the spirit of the people. But what happened to the seeds of intellect that could lie dormant until ready to sprout once again? Had they been scattered too widely?

Tikal made me realize that many of modern man's efforts, thought so advanced, pale in comparison to what some ancient civilizations had done. Yet, when we "rediscover" these civilizations, we often wonder how such a "primitive" people could have accomplished so much with so little. How could they have already known the answers to mysteries that we only recently thought we had unlocked?

After the discovery of the achievements of the ancient Maya, some sixteenth-century Spanish historians, pondering these same questions, concluded that the Maya were descendants of the Lost Tribes of Israel, who had sailed across the Atlantic about 721 B.C. Others said they were survivors of the lost continents of Atlantis, Lemuria, or Mu, long since submerged beneath the sea. The Spanish destroyed most of the writings that might have uncovered the knowledge of these people. Then they sought explanations that could fit into their own rationalizations. Weren't we doing the same thing with species like the jaguar?

We sit by and allow massive destruction of the jaguar's habitat, forcing it into situations where death is the inevitable conclusion. Yet even as we are destroying it, we admire the animal —in zoos, on television, in books—and we wonder how it lives, what it eats, not even stopping to think it might soon no longer be living or eating at all. Then when the jaguar's gone from the wild, we'll carve its image in stone and speculate about how magnificent it must have been. Is there hope for animals like the jaguar? In our greed and fear we are destroying them, as the ancient Maya were subjugated and destroyed.

Though remnants of the spirit of both the jaguar and the old Maya still survive in isolated pockets, how long can they last? In half a century, will the only live jaguars be in zoos? These animals who can walk miles at night through the jungle stalking a peccary herd want nothing more than to be left alone. When the jaguar no longer walks the forests, there will never be anything on earth like it again.

Tikal made me anxious to return to Cockscomb. I had seen the grandeur of a destroyed civilization after living with their descendants who maintained only remnants of this past. I felt certain that the days were numbered for what was left of the Maya culture throughout the lowland forests. Perhaps they were numbered for the jaguars as well, but there was still a chance. The fight was far from over.

When I tried to get back to camp, there was severe flooding from the heaviest rains the Indians said they'd ever seen in Cockscomb. After waiting several hours for the water to go down over the Sittee River bridge, I decided to take the truck across. It was now only about a foot and a half above the bridge.

I paid two Indians to walk on either side of the truck and make sure that I stayed on the wooden planking. Halfway across the bridge, in the middle of the rapidly flowing water, the truck's engine stalled. My heart started beating faster. I rolled down my window, making sure there was an escape route. Fortunately, the engine started again with little trouble and we just got across before it stalled again. Getting the truck running a second time was not so easy, but at least we were across. Just coming back into Cockscomb was exciting.

I thought the previous June and July had given me a taste for the worst rains this area had to offer, but I didn't know rain could fall with the intensity I saw now. The Indians' plantations along the rivers and creeks were wiped out and I saw concern on their faces for the first time as they wondered where their supply of corn would come from. Ben, Maggie, and I were confined to the shack together for days. I worried about losing track of Kukulcan. If he left the area, I wouldn't know where to start looking for him.

During the first week after his release, Kukulcan stayed within a one-mile radius of his release site. Fresh feces alongside his tracks on the road showed he was eating armadillos. Obviously this cat could catch wild game if he had too. Maybe he would remain in Cockscomb.

Finally, the rains ended and life went back into a rejuvenation phase. The Indians salvaged what they could from their plantations, none of them ever bemoaning their fate. I contacted a new pilot and decided to go up again. Flying in small planes was part of my work and I now knew more than ever that my work was my life.

My first flight after the accident was not under the best conditions. After only twenty minutes in the air, we were caught in a rain squall and experienced heavy turbulence. There was no choice but to ride it out. We were flying low and the cloud cover was multilayered, so there was no point in trying to get above it. I tried to stay calm, but I was nervous. After hitting several downdrafts, sweat started pouring down my face and I found myself shaking. Images of the roller-coaster dive into the jungle kept on flashing through my mind.

"Let's go back," I said to the pilot.

He looked at me. "It's real rough today. You gonna be okay?"

"I'll be okay. Just take me in. I'm not ready for this yet."

For a week after the rains, we couldn't find Kukulcan. Ben did the aerial searches. I was waiting for the weather to improve before trying to go up in a plane again. Then Ben found him during the second aerial search.

After nearly two weeks in the area of his release, something was triggered inside him and he started back north in the direction from which he had been taken. Just as the translocated female, Ixchel, had done, he traveled north skirting the high peaks of the Cockscomb Range. But then he kept on going, crossing the Sittee River and continuing north into some of the most rugged regions of the Maya Mountains. There was obviously a homing instinct involved in his behavior. I was disappointed. When I thought about his movements and those of Ixchel, my hopes of using translocation as a management tool were greatly diminished.

Ben continued the quadrate surveys and night walks, working long hours in the field. I noticed that Cockscomb was taking its toll on him. He looked drawn and haggard and spoke Creole more often than English. I really started to worry when I walked into the house one evening and found him chopping up a recently captured scorpion with Cirillo. Recently Ben's hands had become covered with warts and Cirillo had told him of a Maya remedy using the scorpion's stinger.

"Ben, you're not really going to try that, are you?" I asked.

"It work good," Cirillo interjected, smiling, making me trust him even less.

Ben went ahead and tried the procedure by pricking his warts with the scorpion's stinger. Minutes later he began to feel lightheaded and faint. I watched in trepidation, ready to rush Ben to the Dangriga hospital if he passed out.

Cirillo continued smiling. "He stick it in too far," he said.

Ben eventually recovered, but the warts never went away. He agreed with Cirillo that he had probably stuck the stinger in too far and decided to catch another scorpion and try again. I convinced Ben to take two weeks off from Cockscomb.

For a while, my headaches worsened and spread to my neck and eyes. The pain and the lack of exercise was making me irritable and difficult to be around. Part of the problem was the strain of simply being in Cockscomb, but I had made that choice and had no regrets.

Not long after returning from the United States I resumed my medical duties at full pace. The prolonged intensity of the rainy season hit the Indians hard. In addition to the usual bouts with malaria, Adriana at one point was close to death from hepatitis, and Juana contracted dengue fever, a viral infection transmitted by the *Aedes* mosquito.

One afternoon, after I had swallowed my sixth aspirin of the day, Nari came running toward the house screaming my name. I ran outside to see what new calamity had occurred. Nari was holding up his left hand, now a bloody mess with empty spaces where three of his fingers should have been.

I grabbed his wrist to steady him and swallowed hard to keep from getting sick. It was a gruesome sight. One finger was completely gone, while two others were taken off at the top and middle joints. Bone and cartilage were visible where the fingers had been. Blood was flowing freely, and Nari was very pale, breaking out into a cold sweat. He was showing signs of shock.

I pulled him inside the house and tried to calm him down while applying compression bandages to the stumps. He told me he'd been fixing an old motorbike when the engine started up unexpectedly. His hand got caught between the drive sprocket and the chain, which together acted like a chainsaw.

Mike Konecny rushed over and agreed to take Nari to the hospital. Nari was just starting to feel the agonizing pain of the wound, so I gave him a large dose of codeine, and handed Mike some more for the trip. My head was pounding again. I thought how nice it was to have someone else around to share the hardships of this place.

After Mike and Nari left, I walked to the shed where the accident occurred and saw the bike lying on its side. As I got closer, I turned away in disgust. One of the Indians' pigs was eating Nari's finger, while the remaining joints were covered with ants trying to carry them off. No food sits untouched for long in the tropical forest.

That night I lay in bed alarmed by the day's events and again unable to sleep because of headaches. As I put him in the truck, Nari had cried, "I'll never be the same again." I thought how no one who lives in this forest is ever the same again. At best, it simply changes you; at worst, it kills you. I remembered being told by Irma, the woman in the timber camp who had first cooked for me, to leave this place before it killed me, because it surely would if I stayed.

Since the plane crash, I realized that this state called "life" is held together by threads that are easily broken. Security and well-being are illusions we take great pains to maintain. The scars on my face and those in my mind were a constant reminder that we're never in total control of our fate and that our hold on life is tenuous at best. So why did I stay? It was a question that I was asking myself more and more.

I realized that my desire to remain in Cockscomb was motivated by more than my concern for the jaguars. I had good data. I could leave and still fight the cause away from here. What held me? I knew that part of it was that I had never felt so alive as when I had had to fight to stay alive. It was a feeling similar to the one I'd had growing up in New York. The fear, the fistfights on Mott Avenue and McBride, the uncertainty—I had hated it all. Yet, with the hate, there had been an excitement and feeling of physical power at overcoming the odds. It had stimulated me. I had a similar feeling in Cockscomb.

Despite the hardships, I was at home in Cockscomb. I liked living with the Indians. They accepted me without always understanding or even agreeing with my goals. That was more than most people had done in my life. And I treasured what little time I still had with Maggie. Though it would all end soon,

I wanted to stretch it out. There wasn't anything in the United States I really wanted to return to.

Ek Chuah started spending more time in Cockscomb, particularly around Guam Bank. We had his movements well documented by now. Feces and scrapes clearly showed that he and Chac were delineating boundaries around camp in the same manner as Chac and Ah Puch had done earlier. Ek Chuah would usually enter the basin a mile west of Maya Center, hunt along the entrance road, then circle the camp and continue west about a mile farther before moving north toward the forest corridor from where he had first come. Whenever Ek Chuah was located near cattle, we'd track him continuously, as we had done Chac. His movements never took him near the pastures, and the ranchers in the area were having no depredation problems at that time.

Looking back at my data, I noticed a behavioral pattern common to Ek Chuah, Chac, and Ah Puch when they were located in the vicinity of Guam Bank and Maya Center. These jaguars readily killed pigs placed in the forest and didn't hesitate to walk into traps after pigs. They had also killed some of the Indians' dogs that had wandered off into the forest. Yet these same jaguars never came into camp or Maya Center after dogs or pigs. When near these areas, they circled or stayed on the perimeter, seemingly reluctant to cross the man-made edge between forest and village.

I had finally arrived at some clear conclusions about jaguar predation on domestic animals. It was clear that healthy jaguars can range close to livestock without preying upon them. Chac and Ek Chuah traveled near cattle, dogs, and pigs in pastures and villages without touching them. Both cats shifted farther into adjacent forest when a neighboring resident adult male jaguar died or left. At least part of the reason behind this behavior seemed to be that healthy adult jaguars were reluctant to cross open areas, such as pastures or villages, even when potential prey was present.

When these same potential prey animals are left untended or

allowed to roam in the jaguar's habitat, they are quickly killed. This happened to the pigs I had placed out for the jaguars and to untended dogs and pigs in the Maya villages. Such killing could be carried out by healthy jaguars simply hunting in their areas for food. In some circumstances, where livestock are left untended, as on some ranches, they are easy and reliable prey and can become a jaguar's major source of food.

Many reports of livestock deaths caused by jaguars could not be substantiated when investigated. It's likely that jaguars don't cause as much damage as is attributed to them. When a jaguar does cause problems and is killed, the problem is usually alleviated even if other jaguars are in the area.

Some of the most interesting data came from the examination of the carcasses of cattle-killing jaguars. Nearly 80 percent of these showed previous head or body wounds, mostly in the skull. All had been shot. Examination of nonproblem, or wild, jaguars showed no such previous injuries.

Shotguns are the only legal weapon in Belize, and birdshot (No. 7 1/2 or 8 shot) is the most available ammunition. It would be difficult to kill a large animal with such ammunition except at close range, and it was not uncommon for hunters to tell me stories of shooting but not killing jaguars. It seemed likely that the jaguars that were shot were animals living in the border areas between man and forest, like Chac and Ek Chuah. Their injuries might have been a contributing factor in their livestock depredation behavior.

Part of the problem is that an existing market for skins and a lack of police enforcement encourage illegal hunting. Even many ranchers feel that to avoid potential problems, they should kill all jaguars in the vicinity of their ranch. This practice could be creating problem jaguars out of animals that had caused no problems at all before they were shot.

Of the nonproblem jaguars I'd seen killed by hunters, a little under half were females. Yet, most of the problem jaguars killed were males. It is possible that certain behavioral characteristics of male jaguars, such as traveling over larger areas and taking more risks than females, put them in situations more conducive to livestock predation. Such factors as habitat destruction and hunting would affect males more than females.

Female jaguars do become livestock killers occasionally. If the female has kittens, she is likely to bring them to kills. Learning to feed on livestock as a cub may account for predation by healthy, subadult jaguars, such as Kukulcan.

It was more obvious now than before that better management of livestock would reduce jaguar predation where livestock is allowed to range freely in the jaguar habitat. If a problem jaguar appears, ranchers may have to be allowed to kill the cat. Capturing and moving the cat doesn't appear to be a feasible solution; if the cat moves and encounters livestock, it may resume its killing, as Ixchel did. However, most important, the data indicates that the indiscriminate shooting and wounding of healthy jaguars may create problems where none existed before.

These data could be powerful tools for the government to use. They supported previous theories I had offered and showed that much of the responsibility of management rests with the ranchers themselves. I knew the government would like that.

On my next trip into Dangriga I had a new surprise. A telegram from Chuck Carr informed me that Jane Alexander, the well-known stage and screen actress, was interested in developing a movie about a woman zoologist studying jaguars. She wanted to see what I was doing and work with me for a short while to get material for the script. Since there was no easy way to reach me, Ms. Alexander had gone ahead with plans to fly to Belize and then try to find me in Cockscomb. She was due in Belize in four days. I decided to drive up to Belize City to meet her, though I was at a complete loss as to what she looked like. This sounded like another interesting encounter.

Maggie drove with me to Belize. She was going to return to her family for a while and rethink her future plans. After working with us in Cockscomb, she realized her own need to get on with her life. Though we had both known there was no future for us beyond the project, her emotions were in turmoil knowing our relationship would soon end. When I dropped her off, neither of us suspected that she was never again to return to Cockscomb. Shortly after, she made a decision that would take her to the United States. I would see Maggie again before she left, but by then we were back in our own worlds.

24 THE JAGUAR'S WORLD

Several weeks before Ben left Cockscomb for a trip to the United States, he and Julian had a chance encounter neither would ever forget. Driving back into the basin they came upon two uncollared jaguars. It looked like Ah Kin and one of the females, whose tracks we'd been following. He described the encounter that night in his journal:

Where I stopped the truck we could view the pair about two hundred yards away. They didn't seem startled by the truck. The male was standing in the middle of the road, with the female lying by the side of the road. For the next three minutes, they stayed like that. Then the male moved behind the female. Soon afterward the female stood up and moved a short distance toward the truck and lay down again. The male stood over the female and lay his left paw on her abdomen. He followed this with a caressing stroke and a lick on the head and neck. Soon the female stood up and came again toward the truck. After walking about fifty yards toward us, the female crouched to the ground. The male came up behind her, started to mount her, but the female immediately got to her feet and came again toward the truck, the male following closely behind. As the jaguars came within three yards of the front of the truck, I began to slowly roll up my window. Julian seemed unconcerned and remained motionless and quiet. When they were at their closest point to the truck, the female crouched in the middle of the road, the male right behind her. Then she got up and walked off into the forest, the male following closely. Both cats gave us broadside views and I estimated their weights to be approximately a hundred and thirty pounds for the male and eighty pounds for the female. We had watched them for ten minutes. After moving into the bush, we heard the rustling of branches and low growls for ten to fifteen more minutes. Nothing was seen or heard after that.

This was only the second time during the project that two jaguars had been seen together in Cockscomb. Porfilio and I had seen two on returning from our hike to Victoria Peak in late May of the previous year, and now this sighting was in mid-July. Excited by these new developments, I worked that night on compiling all my data on jaguar reproduction.

Singling out the most reliable sightings, I used twenty-one instances when at least two adult jaguars were seen together, when females were seen with their young, or when lactating or pregnant females were killed. Studies of captive jaguars have shown that they have a gestation period of approximately three months and that kittens can accompany their mother at six to eight weeks of age. I could use these figures with my data to estimate the times of birth.

In the United States, parturition reportedly occurred from

April–May, while in Paraguay, Rennger's observations put most births from November–December. It's commonly believed that jaguars can breed any time of the year in the tropics. But there is no rationale for this in the wild, particularly in areas with distinct seasonality. Reproduction should coincide with the months of maximum food and water availability.

The data from my study showed such a pattern. It appeared that female jaguars in Belize could give birth from May through January. However, 85 percent of the births fell between May and September, specifically between June and August. The dry season lasted from February through May, so the young were always born in the rainy season.

The restricted behavioral flexibility of a female, just before and after parturition, would be least stressful during the rainy season, when food and water are more uniformly distributed. Chac's unusual movements along the Sittee River during the dry season indicated that jaguars may have to travel large distances this time of year. A June through August birth, at the onset of the rainy season, would assure that the young are at least several months old and thus more independent before the next dry season. Three sightings of pumas with their young showed that August was their time of parturition, probably for similar reasons. Of twenty-three sightings of jaguars with their young, 52 percent had two cubs, 35 percent had one cub, and 13 percent had three cubs.

Ben left Cockscomb for two weeks and I went to Belize City to meet Jane Alexander. I had no idea what she would be like, but I was worried about bringing a well-known actress, accustomed to a life of luxury, back into Cockscomb. Life here was hard enough once you were adjusted to it, but it was a difficult transition if you were unprepared. Shortly after I met her, I realized there had been no reason to worry.

Anyone who stays in Cockscomb for more than a couple of days forms a love-hate relationship with the hardships and the beauty of the place. If you stay long enough, the hardships take second place to the magic. Jane skipped the initial fears and discomforts and moved right into loving and feeling the magic of the area. The Indians, particularly the women, sensed her sincerity and immediately took to her. After the first day, I never even thought of Jane as an actress again, but merely as a friend come to visit.

I hadn't been able to talk to anyone since Sue the way I could talk with Jane. Maggie was very dear to me, but we were from different worlds. I felt refreshed and stimulated by Jane's company.

In the evenings we'd read poetry by kerosene lantern. I recited my favorite poem, Robert Frost's *The Road Not Taken,* and we talked of the roads we had chosen in our lives. She read me Coleridge's *Kubla Khan,* her voice changing with the lines, and I drifted off to Xanadu. During the day we walked in the forest or sat talking in the house as the heavy rains obscured the outside world. I learned that she had starred in such movies as *The Great White Hope, Eleanor and Franklin, Kramer versus Kramer, Testament,* and *Calamity Jane.* She had won several Emmy and Tony awards and had been nominated for the Academy Award four times. Yet, she played down her own accomplishments in life, wanting only to talk of my work with the jaguars.

"You're a hero, you know that, don't you?" she said to me one afternoon. I had just told her about Ah Puch's death.

"No, I'm no hero," I said. "I'm running away. Away from the world of people, to a much saner world, the world of animals. I'm doing what I love doing and helping living things that have no control over their own destiny."

"You just described the hero figure."

"I think of a hero as someone who sacrifices his own well-being to help or save others. I may be taking risks, helping the animals, but it's for myself as well. My motives are selfish. I'm not the savior of jaguars, but simply someone who feels more comfortable in their world than my own."

"You really don't see it, do you?" She smiled. "Whether it's a role you've chosen, or even want, makes little difference.

You're the archetypal great white hunter, but you're saving the animals instead of killing them."

I smiled at Jane's analogy.

"Alan," she continued, "you're a role model in a world where role models are hard to come by. People in my field only act the roles. You're living it."

I had never even considered the things Jane was saying. She could see her words were making me uncomfortable.

"Would you tell me more about the circumstances leading up to Ah Puch's death?" she asked, changing the subject.

I talked about Ah Puch with difficulty. It was a subject I hadn't let myself think about for quite a while. I told her how I hadn't been able to cry since his death, and she showed me how actors can make themselves cry when they needed the tears.

Then the sun would show its face, and we would jog along the timber road or Jane would go to the creek, strip, and do laundry alongside the bare-breasted Maya women.

Ten days passed quickly, and the day soon arrived when Jane had to leave. Real tears fell from her face, and when she was gone, Cockscomb felt emptier than ever. She filled a dark void within me I hadn't known existed. I hadn't tried to let myself cry yet, though I thought now would be a good time. But I was afraid once the tears came, they'd never stop.

After Jane left, the Maya women started saying again how I was evil for having so many different women stay with me. The facts, as they saw them, were that I was thirty years old, unmarried, and kept on bringing women into Cockscomb who would go away looking sad. Bad things would keep on happening if I kept on making people sad, they said.

The plane crash was used by some of the Indians as additional evidence that "something," maybe the "master jaguar," maybe an evil spirit, was trying to do me harm. Whatever it was, they felt, hadn't wished to kill me or it would have done so easily. It was just angry with me for doing things that shouldn't be done. The Indians had never fully accepted what I was doing with the jaguars, and I felt this was their way of helping rationalize their feelings. Yet the truth was, whenever I returned to the crash site and looked at the wreckage, I couldn't believe that I had lived.

Ben was glad to get back to Cockscomb. It was in his blood now too. Within a week of his return, Ben turned thirty years old, and Nari came back from the hospital and from visiting family in Guatemala. We held a barbecue to celebrate two such auspicious events. Nari proudly showed us how nicely his stumps were sewn up. In typical take-life-as-it-comes fashion, he now made lewd jokes about how he'd use that hand with women, instead of bemoaning what was lost. There was no other way to exist here.

As my headaches became less severe, I spent more time in the field but stayed away from the more strenuous work of fixing roads and bridges. The truck started leaking oil, and the spline on the drive shaft was coming off, but we had to keep the truck in the field for the time being.

I noticed suddenly that several Indians had been gone from the village for several weeks. I asked Cirillo about this, and he told me they were looking for new land to settle on outside Cockscomb. This was the first I'd heard of such thinking. After being put off from getting land in Cockscomb, and then experiencing the flooding that destroyed several of their milpas, their spirits were low. Prudencio, Martin, and Margarito had gone out to look at other areas. When they returned, the consensus was that there were few places still as rich and isolated as Cockscomb.

Their way of life in Cockscomb had disappeared from much of Belize. The wide-open untouched forest, free for the taking, was quickly becoming a thing of the past. Whether they realized it or not, living in Cockscomb kept them closer to the roots of their ancestry than any other place ever could. Despite the hardships, they would stay for a while longer. Again I wondered what would become of them if we achieved our goal of preserving this area.

After their return, Cirillo left for several weeks to visit with his family at a nearby village, Red Bank. In his absence, his brother Martin Chun decided to work for us. His plantation was one of those that had flooded and he needed money for food. Though Martin and I had never become very friendly, I realized after spending time with him now how much I had been missing. He was a warm, jovial person who could work well in short spurts.

Martin was the assistant preacher to Margarito, yet believed in ghosts and spirits more than anyone else in camp. He struck me as having more of the ancient Maya man in him than any of the Indians except old Emano Balong. I wasn't surprised when Martin eventually broke with the church and would not even attend special holiday services. One evening, after eating dinner with us, Martin sat at the table, his face hidden in the shadows and started talking of things that the Maya rarely speak of, especially to outsiders. For some reason, the mood felt right that night.

"Dere a man in de bush, he a man-ghost. He white, wear a big hat. If he look at you, it bad. He got de eye [evil eye]."

This was the first I had heard of this. We were all quiet. Martin wasn't finished. "Den dere special animals in de bush, dey ghost-animals. I see dem. One time I see a ghost sheep. A next time I see de ghost rooster."

"Can you always see them?" I asked him.

"No, we no can always see dem. Mostly you no see dem. But de dogs, dey see dem. Dat's why dey bark in de night at nutting. If you want for see dem, you take de water from de dog's eyes and put it in your eyes."

"What about the *duendes*, Martin? You ever see them in Cockscomb?" I could not forget what I had seen.

"Dere *duende* for sure back here. I never see dem, but dey here. I never see de big hairy man [Sismito], but he back dere too. I know."

He looked outside into the darkness as if he were seeing something. We all followed his eyes, but there was only the dark stillness of a Cockscomb night.

"You go in de bush plenty at night," he said to us. "I tell you dis. De bad time to be in de bush is near midnight, or two, tree in de morning. Dat when de spirits out. Bad tings happen den."

Ben changed the subject and started asking Martin about the Maya custom of marriage. I asked Ben if he had his eye on anyone in particular. Martin told us that if a Maya man wants a wife, he should go to a good "talker," usually an older, well-respected man of the community, who then goes to the family and talks for him. Sometimes you must pay the talker and give him food and drink.

It can take several visits from the talker, but when he arranges it, the family and groom-to-be must then meet the new in-laws. Pablo had told me that the future husband often must give the family of the bride presents, usually food, such as rice and flour, in large quantities to show he can provide for their daughter. Martin talked with us late into the night.

The next day one of Martin's sons, Telesporo, came running to the house. He had killed a large fer-de-lance while chopping in the bush. I had told the Indians several months earlier that I'd pay them Bze$5 for any intact fer-de-lance they brought me because I wanted to examine the stomach contents to see what they fed on. The idea didn't catch on very well despite the money. So far, I had examined only three stomachs. One of them contained a spiny rat.

This snake looked promising, however, as I watched Telesporo return with a six-foot-long snake draped over the end of a pole. Its stomach was extremely distended. As several Indians watched the procedure, I laid the snake down on my truck and made a single incision through the body wall.

Instead of its internal organs, thirty-four baby fer-de-lances came rolling out, each measuring six to eight inches long and still attached to their yolk sac. As they moved inside their sacs, the Indians ran as if the snakes would pursue them. I jumped back too. Then I stuck my hand in the mass of snakes and cut each of them free from the sac. I dropped them into a jar of alcohol I had prepared for the stomach contents. Fortunately,

Telesporo didn't think to ask me for $5 for each of these.

The Indians were frightened, believing that the young were more poisonous than the adults. After preserving all the snakes in alcohol, I closed the jar and passed it around among the Indians. Some of the Indians wouldn't even touch the jar. I put it on the shelf with the scorpions, tarantula, and fer-de-lance heads.

In the weeks that followed, my headaches diminished to a dull pain and I resumed much of the work of searching for the cats. Ben had his hands full with the prey density estimates. A second attempt I made at flying went well, despite the fact that I still broke into a cold sweat whenever we encountered turbulence.

Kukulcan was gone. Our last radio location on him had been several weeks earlier, when he was five miles north of Victoria Peak. He had still been moving north at the time, but I could no longer afford to search for him.

I was back to tracking two jaguars, the beautiful Ek Chuah, who traveled the entrance road, and angry Chac. Much had changed since the project began. During the first year of the study, the timber road was used by at least five adult male jaguars, two female jaguars, and a puma. I had collared four of the males and found out they moved over areas ranging from eleven to sixteen square miles. The two uncollared females were still moving in areas only a third as large, within the areas of the males.

Throughout the study we continued to see considerable overlap between adjacent male jaguars. It was most extensive with whichever jaguar occupied the central area, first Ah Puch and then Chac. The fact that this central area was the most closely monitored might have had something to do with it. Such roads are limited resources in jungle areas and are known to be a preferred route of travel and hunting for many large cats. We also lacked data on other jaguars, which might have been in the surrounding areas, far from the roads.

The early death of old Itzamna and the unfortunate death of Ah Puch resulted in shifts in the ranges of adjacent jaguars—Ah

Kin, Chac, and Ek Chuah—within four to eight weeks. This indicated that, despite the overlap of their movements, home areas were actively maintained among the resident adult male jaguars.

When we could follow the same male jaguars on consecutive days, we saw that, despite the size of their overall range, the jaguars would often stay within a square-mile area for about a week before shifting, in a single night, to another part of their range. The jaguars weren't just randomly moving looking for prey. While Roosevelt was in Brazil, he observed that jaguars may spend as much as a week in an area where game is plentiful. However, such small areas cannot sustain a jaguar long. Soon changes in prey density, or behavioral changes of the prey related to the jaguar's presence, make it inefficient to hunt an area of that size. Thus the jaguars in Cockscomb needed to move within overall areas thirty to forty times the size of these small transient feeding areas.

Based on the home-range sizes and the degree of overlap among the jaguars we had followed, I estimated a density of twenty-five to thirty jaguars in the one hundred and fifty-four square miles of the basin. This assumed an average of one female within the home range of each male. Observations of jaguars in other places indicate there can be large differences in their densities. Rarely are they considered common, as in many areas of Belize. Aldo Leopold thought that jaguars in their preferred habitat are highly sedentary. This is true only if the "preferred habitat" is an area dense with prey.

A. Almeida speculated that in the Pantanal, where food was abundant and easily available, jaguars moved over much smaller areas than in the Amazon, where they might have to travel many miles following prey. Areas of the Amazon, thought to be classic jaguar habitat, may actually have lower densities of jaguars because of lower densities of easily available prey.

In Cockscomb and other areas of Belize the "tumbled" forest created by both man and nature is a habitat hospitable to many small and medium-sized prey species. With the high densities of prey that Ben was finding in the basin, numerous jaguars could coexist in limited areas while retaining their solitary nature. By hunting in, and marking, small areas of their range, they could avoid encounters and minimize aggression.

I was attuned to Ek Chuah more than I had been to any other jaguar because I traveled through his area the most. As I jogged the entrance road every day, I always looked for his tracks and feces. As soon as he was around, I knew it. Sometimes I'd run across tracks only hours old. My adrenaline would flow and I'd pick up speed imagining him watching me from just inside the forest. When I returned to the shack, I'd plug in the radio receiver and often locate him right off the side of the road. He had been aware of me.

Life in Cockscomb returned to the normal pattern of agony and ecstasy. Julian was the only one of the Indians who had stuck with his weight-lifting training and continued to come over regularly, in the early morning or late afternoon, to pump iron. I began to see some definition in his muscles. He insisted on working out only to Kenny Rogers's *Greatest Hits* cassette, a favorite among the Indians.

Cirillo would come by after dinner or after working on his plantation and sit and talk with us. His endurance and stamina continually amazed me. On some days, he would work with us all day in the forest, then he'd go off on his bicycle for a twelve-mile round-trip ride to buy supplies in Kendall. Or he'd go right to his milpa and spend the rest of the day clearing weeds.

Yet sometimes, when he simply didn't want to work, Cirillo would lie in his hammock for days while Florencia continued her sunrise to sunset chores. There was no such thing as a Maya woman taking a day off because she felt like it or was tired. The men had periods of intense activity and periods of prolonged inactivity, and I no longer found this unusual for people who live in harmony with the earth. It was the pattern of their crops, from dormancy to bloom. Several times I tried falling into this cycle with them, just to see how it would feel, but I became too restless. My internal clock was not in harmony with the plants; it was more in harmony with a jaguar's activity pattern.

Every so often, when I started becoming too complacent in Cockscomb, reality would give me a lesson. An Indian brings me his dog, just bitten by a fer-de-lance. It is too late to help it and I watch it die in agonizing convulsions. Cirillo's one-year-old daughter nearly dies from dehydration brought on by an illness causing diarrhea and vomiting. She doesn't pass urine for two days before Cirillo tells me. Though she lives after I prepare a rehydration drink for Cirillo to give her, I wonder again, what if I were not here? She would be another accepted fatality in the jungle.

Toward the latter part of my second year on the project, it became increasingly difficult for me to feel a part of the flow of life in Cockscomb. I started to lose the connection and no longer felt the need to be in touch with the Indians. It was as if I was already beginning to consign Cockscomb to memory, and was now planning my future—after Cockscomb. After trying so hard to understand and at least partially be understood by the Indians, I now began to feel that I almost didn't care any longer.

One afternoon, Julian was talking with me by my motorcycle when a large yellow and black grasshopper landed on the seat. Without even a pause in the conversation, Julian reached over, picked up the grasshopper, and squeezed the life out of it, simply because it had come within his grasp. When I tried to stop him, telling him that he was at my house and must respect my wishes, he laughed and crushed it harder, then dropped it to the ground.

I grabbed Julian by the neck. I bore down with much of my strength and started to strangle him. I wanted him to feel the terror of losing his own life for no reason. He tried pulling away my hands but I was too strong for him. I continued to choke him until he got very pale and almost passed out.

I suddenly pulled away my hands, and he fell to the ground, gagging. I expected anger or at least indignation at such a violent, senseless act, but Julian said nothing. Instead he started laughing. He wasn't laughing at the fact that I had choked him, I learned, but at my anger over the life of a bug.

"You one crazy gringo," he said to me.

He was right. Cockscomb had made me crazy. I couldn't believe what I had almost done.

25 THE PRIME MINISTER

From my field notes, August 22, 1984, 0740 hours:

Survival, that's what biological and cultural evolution is all about. I've finally reached the point in my life that I've striven for, yet what price has been paid? Loss of innocence, of naïveté? Never again can I look upon new things or experiences with the awe of earlier days. Never again will I feel that tingling through my body telling me I know I'm where I should be. Never, never, again will I feel indestructible, physically or mentally. Never will I wonder if I can stomach blood and gore or if I'll panic in an emergency situation. My head hurts and I feel like a cripple, scared to do anything for fear of damage to my fragile body. Please, God, let my body be whole again, let me canoe more wild rivers, let me explore more wilderness, and let me feel strength permeate my entire being again.

In August, Chac walked back into the trap again. His anger was still there, but something else seemed wrong with him. Even after the capture of seven jaguars, Chac's violence frightened me. We sedated him and changed his radio collar.

He appeared in excellent condition, still his original weight of a hundred and ten pounds. Why, after passing the traps so often, had he decided to walk in again? Why was he so violent? His face was bloodied from banging the walls. What was in the mind of this animal I'd followed for thirteen months? If there's a master jaguar, I hope you're watching over Chac, I thought to myself.

The capture gave me a throbbing headache, just when my headaches seemed to be decreasing in intensity. For the first time, I really believed I might be harming myself by continuing this project. If I was going to stay in Cockscomb, I had to ease up on the fieldwork, I told myself for the tenth time.

Toward evening, just as the headache lessened to a dull throb, Adriana came over. Prudencia was very sick, she said. She was vomiting and unable to sleep at night and it was all Ben's fault. I looked over at Ben and his eyes were wide in surprise.

Several days before, Adriana explained, Ben had crept up behind Prudencia and grabbed her, lifting her high in the air. She had been badly frightened and now, Adriana said, was sick because of it. Adriana believed that her spirit had been jarred out of her, in a manner similar to *susto*, or fright sickness, in Mexican cultures.

She now wanted some of Ben's hair and, just to make sure, she wanted my hair. She had already gotten hair from several of the male animals in camp. We gave it to her. Then I followed her to her hut, where Ignacio confirmed the sickness, telling us it had happened to him once before. He agreed that the burning of hair was the best cure. Adriana built a fire and piled the hair onto the flames. When it started smoking, she made Prudencia lean over and inhale the smoke. The smell was unpleasant and Prudencia started coughing. She was well again by the next day.

When I congratulated Adriana on her curative powers, she looked at me very seriously and gave me some advice. Only my strong spirit had kept me from dying in Cockscomb, she said. My headaches would not go away while I stayed here. I must leave Cockscomb because the evil forces wouldn't follow me.

I had to acknowledge the feeling of strong forces in Cockscomb. I had felt them when I first arrived in March 1983, but I had thought it was just my fears of a new place. Now I believed it was something outside of me. Maybe nothing supernatural, just the intense energy flux in the jungle coming from the never-ending battles of life and death. Man can destroy but not easily control or live within this environment, I'd thought many times. One author on the subject, Richard Perry, described the "primeval and hostile environment" of the rain forest as over-whelming. I certainly found my physical well-being and my resolve weakening.

I spent less time in the field and wrote more letters to government officials and made periodic trips to Belmopan. My letters were rarely acknowledged. When I appeared at the government offices, my pleas for Cockscomb were greeted with compassion and concern, but nothing was done.

We were running out of time. I planned to end the project in three to four months, and I felt strongly that once I was out of the country, Cockscomb would never be protected. After the last dry season I could stand outside my house and, for the first time, actually see steep hillsides around Cockscomb denuded. When the first heavy rains came, the streams ran brown with what little topsoil there was from these clearings.

Some people took offense when they heard that the Indians might be forced to leave Cockscomb as a result of my efforts. Slash-and-burn agriculture has been going on for hundreds of years here, I was told over and over again. The forest and the jaguars have always survived. Shifting cultivation has been shown to be more efficient for tropical soils than permanent cultivation. How can I now say that what the Indians are doing is wrong?

These were popular arguments for preserving the modern Maya system, and they had to be addressed. It is true that shifting cultivation or rotation of fields is often more efficient than permanent cultivation where soils are poor, population density is low, and adequate land is available. However, Catherine Caufield, author of *In the Rainforest*, distinguishes shifting cultivation, involving balanced agricultural techniques, from slash-and-burn agriculture. The latter often involves a single crop—corn—and after the soil is depleted, the settlers may sell the land for more inefficient uses, such as cattle raising, or even abandon it permanently. The Maya in the vicinity of Cockscomb practiced slash-and-burn agriculture. They had simply lost their ancestors' knowledge of proper shifting cultivation.

Studies have shown that forest growth in Central America is relatively recent. However, even when the Maya and other cultures flourished in the area, all the forest was not cleared at the same time. Before the Spanish conquest, the Maya were relatively scattered and practiced proper shifting cultivation. The Maya empire was always heavily forested, except in the vicinity of the villages, where there was a patchwork of milpa clearings, just as there is today. When the Indians moved on, the surrounding forest provided the necessary raw materials, in the form of seeds and animals to disperse them, to regenerate the abandoned milpa.

The seeds of forest trees are less easily dispersed than the seeds of grasses and successional trees. Thus, for a cleared area to completely recover, primary forest must be close by. If clearings are large, the return to forest may take hundreds, even thousands, of years. When clearings become surrounded by more clearings, the forest may never recover.

Though the Maya in Cockscomb could not envision the demise of the forest and didn't concern themselves with the future, I had already seen the results of such thinking in other tropical countries. I knew without a doubt what the future would hold, and the Maya would lose. Unfortunately, much of the blame rested not with the Maya themselves, but with socioeconomic and political factors beyond their control, destroying mass acreages of land usually for the profit of a few. Meanwhile, the Maya were pushed into smaller and smaller pockets until their own way of life was helping to destroy even those pockets. Their agricultural system, though efficient in an extensive and balanced forest environment, cannot succeed over time in isolated pockets of forest.

With cattle ranches and citrus plantations impinging to the north and south, the Cockscomb Basin itself showed signs of becoming an isolated forest patch. Only the rugged, virtually impenetrable Maya Mountains to the west remained untouched. The jaguars might still have a future here, I thought, but not if everything around Cockscomb was eventually cut down. If we could first get Cockscomb protected, I hoped eventually to work on protecting corridors along waterways so that the jaguars within Cockscomb could move over wider areas. This would be crucial for such ecological processes as dispersal and genetic flow in order to maintain a viable jaguar population. That fight would come later, I told myself. First we needed a home ground.

Though the Indians represented our immediate threat to the Cockscomb forest, a far more important threat was coming from the wealthy element in Belize who wanted Cockscomb to cultivate citrus. They were hard to deal with. They cared nothing about either the Maya or the jaguars. I met with some of these people and found them to be friendly. They were willing to work out some kind of deal, I was told, maybe a little park on the edge of the plantation. Nothing I could say regarding the low agricultural potential of the area would dissuade them. I wasn't about to make deals regarding Cockscomb. It was time to pull out all the stops.

In October 1984 Chuck Carr flew down again to meet me in Belize. I had been working with Jim Waight of the Belize Audubon Society on arranging a meeting with the prime minister, the

Honorable George Price, and his cabinet. It had finally been granted. A luncheon was to be held in our honor, and we'd have an hour to present our case. After the meeting, I was to give a public lecture and slide show in Belize City, which would be announced on radio, on television, and in the newspapers. We'd finally get the opportunity to bring Cockscomb before the head of state, government officials, and the general public.

I flew to Belize City and checked into the Mopan Hotel to wait for Chuck. That night I sat at the bar drinking scotch and reminiscing with the owner, my friend Tom Shaw. He was delighted with the jar of pickled baby fer-de-lances I had brought him from Cockscomb. After numerous drinks, he decided he wanted to put them to good use. He hung a sign over an empty jar next to the snakes that read: "Guess the number of tommy-goff and win the money in the jar. $1.00/guess." It was an immediate success among the clientele he allowed at his bar, and the jar quickly filled with dollars. Tom, of course, had decided that there would be no winners; the money would go to the Belize Audubon Society.

Two days later I picked up Chuck Carr at the airport and that night at the hotel we discussed our strategy. The next day we arrived at a private luncheon with the leaders of the country. When I was introduced to Prime Minister Price, he smiled and had a surprising request. "Could you show me how a jaguar sounds?" he asked. "People talk about their calls in the night, but I have never heard them."

I looked around me. Several of the cabinet members had already arrived. "Would you like to hear a male or a female jaguar, sir?" I asked. He had never heard one, so I knew I was safe.

"Oh, either one."

I tried to act as dignified as possible standing in front of the prime minister and grunting like a jaguar. He laughed, throwing his head back. To start off a high-level government meeting it was quite an ice-breaker.

I showed slides while the prime minister and the cabinet members ate lunch. Starting with pictures of Cockscomb, I went on to the capturing of jaguars, tracking them in the forest, fer-de-lance stories, even the plane crash. I had their full attention.

Then I discussed how the rain forest was an economic asset to a country only when left intact or when properly managed. I said such forests have adapted to thrive on poor and shallow soils by capturing nearly all the nutrients that are available. The impression of fertile soil is deceiving. The richness is really locked up in the plants and animals above the ground. When the forest is cleared, decay can be swift as nutrients are rapidly leached out of the soil by heavy rains. Major problems can follow, such as erosion and siltation of waterways.

If only relatively small areas are cleared and adjacent forest is still intact, the land can be resettled. But this is not happening. Timbering, increasing slash-and-burn agriculture, and large-scale clear-cutting for citrus and cattle raising have resulted in massive deforestation. A few may benefit in the short term, but the populace will suffer in the years to come.

I talked about the impact of deforestation in places like Nepal and India. But Belize still had a chance with areas like Cockscomb. Cockscomb, already surrounded by numerous Indian villages and major cattle and citrus interests, was a crucial area for protection.

Yes, I wanted Cockscomb preserved for jaguars, I told them bluntly, but forgetting about the jaguars, if it was not protected, the consequences would be economically disastrous in the future. I showed them the results of the country's environmental profile funded by the United States Agency for International Development. The Cockscomb Basin consisted primarily of granite bedrock, two hundred to four hundred million years old, some of the oldest rocks of Central America. The siliceous soils were shallow, with low fertility, and probably highly erodible. There were exceptions of little pockets of alluvial soils, where the Indians cut milpa. The land use that the study recommended was as "protection forest."

I didn't let up on them. I showed how Cockscomb was a major

watershed, feeding three of the country's major waterways—South Stann Creek, Sittee River, and Swasey River. The government had recently approved the construction of new bridges across these rivers along the Southern Highway. All of them could be wiped out by flash flooding, I explained, if the forest was no longer there to regulate and slow the release of water into the rivers. Furthermore, the entrance into the basin was no more than ten miles from the ocean and thus from the barrier reef, the second largest in the world. Erosion and subsequent siltation of waterways would harm this marine ecosystem and consequently the fishing industry.

We presented our case in concise economic terms, but with the fervor of condemned men pleading for a stay of execution. At the end of our hour, they were still uncertain how to proceed, but no one called for an end to the meeting. I didn't want to give them a chance to, so I kept talking.

After two hours, everyone's meal long since finished except my own, I ended our presentation. The ball was in their court. The prime minister asked each cabinet member his opinion. The evidence was overwhelming, and these were intelligent men. They all realized the need to protect such a resource, but they didn't want to lose the economic benefits of the area either. Could they continue high-grade timbering while protecting the jaguars and watershed, they asked. I could sense we had them on the line but I couldn't proceed too quickly.

Yes, I answered, provided that there was absolutely no hunting or settlement allowed in the area. In fact, I explained, jaguars and other species used the roads and trails created by the timber operation. Though selective timbering actually affected much more forest than was generally believed, the results need not always be considered negative. Cockscomb was not a natural tall rain forest. The geology and topography of the area, combined with the periodic hurricanes, already created a dense, low canopy. I explained to them that, contrary to what their Forestry Department thought, large trees were relatively scarce back there.

The prime minister turned to the minister of natural resources and told him to move ahead with protecting Cockscomb.

The next evening, Dr. Carr and I gave a similar presentation, entitled "Jaguars of Belize," at the Bliss Institute. The audience numbered over four hundred people, the largest crowd ever attending one of these presentations, sponsored by the Belize Audubon Society. I had asked Ben to bring Cirillo up to Belize City to hear what I had to say. I didn't want the Indians to think I was doing anything behind their backs. I wanted Cirillo to know what was going on and the reasons behind our actions. Then he could form his own opinion and tell the others.

Cirillo was excited about this new adventure. I later learned he had gone out and spent some of his hard-earned money on a new shirt so that he might look presentable. After the lecture, I called Cirillo up on stage, where he was recognized instantly, having been in several of the slides. The audience gave him a warm welcome. He had never been in front of so many people in one place before.

I had brought a jaguar caller with me, hoping to play it for the audience. I put it into Cirillo's hands and asked him to play it. He wouldn't look at the audience but kept his eyes riveted on me, and when I nodded reassuringly to him, he played it.

The audience fell silent as the grunts reverberated through the hall. No one there could help but feel the primeval fear brought out by such a sound. Aldo Leopold described it well when he was writing about the wildlife of Mexico:

The chesty roar of jaguar in the night causes men to edge toward the blaze and draw serapes tighter. It silences the yapping dogs and starts the tethered horses milling. In announcing its mere presence in the blackness of night, the jaguar puts the animate world on edge.

Cirillo shared our room that night at the Mopan Hotel, and Jean and Tom Shaw treated him warmly. It was the first time Cirillo had ever slept in a bed or had a hot shower. He laughed when he felt how bouncy the mattress was. The next morning he returned to Cockscomb with Ben. He thanked me for the trip but never mentioned that night again. I knew he had understood the lecture plainly when I learned that he had told the other Indians our plans.

Public response to the lecture was overwhelming, and Chuck and I were gratified. I just hoped that the message wouldn't be too quickly forgotten in the light of more mundane matters. One well-respected member of the Belizean community came to my hotel the next day and told me how much he had learned from the talk. By the way, he had said, four beautiful jaguar skins were hanging on the wall in his house. Did I want to see them? I politely declined.

Later that day Ben called me from Cockscomb. His voice sounded strained and reminded me of the day I had spoken to Bader about Guermo. I sensed that death had come again. Still, when he said the words, I was unprepared.

"Ek Chuah's been killed, Alan."

26 RUNNING OUT OF TIME

When Ben called about Ek Chuah's death, I was getting ready to leave for Costa Rica with Chuck Carr. Chuck knew I needed to pull myself away from Cockscomb for a rest, so he had asked me to accompany him to Tortuguero beach on the Caribbean coast of Costa Rica. We were going to meet his father, Dr. Archie Carr, the guru of green-turtle research, and watch the annual pilgrimage of green sea turtles as they came during this one time of year to this single beach to lay their eggs. I had been wanting to see the phenomenon for some time. I was also curious about the status of the jaguar in the area.

Ben told me over the phone what little he knew about Ek Chuah's death. It had happened the night of the slide presentation. I knew that some hunters in the Kendall area watched my movements, but I hadn't counted on their efficiency. One of the neighbor's ranch hands, a Guatemalan named Osman, who lived along the highway, knew we had left and hadn't returned. He heard Ek Chuah's grunts behind the ranch and had dragged into the forest a dead calf that he'd been told to burn. He tied it to a tree and waited in the branches above. Ek Chuah was nearby and came in, possibly out of curiosity. A shotgun blast to the skull dropped him immediately. I wondered which slide I was showing when Ek Chuah died.

I wanted to cancel the Costa Rica trip and rush back to Cockscomb.

"What can you do about it now?" Chuck asked.

"Nothing really," I said. "I just feel that if I'd been there, it wouldn't have happened. I should be there now."

"Are you planning to stay in Cockscomb forever, Alan?" Chuck asked.

We both knew the answer to that question. There was nothing I could do, and going back to Cockscomb now would only create more problems.

On our way to Costa Rica I just couldn't shake the feeling that there was no point to anything we were doing. We work, we risk our lives, we dream of how things can change, but in the end —maybe it was already written. The only way I could keep going was to continually ask myself who I was doing it for. Was it for mankind? The answer was emphatically no! It was for the jaguars and it was for myself. That's what I had tried to explain to Jane Alexander.

The jaguar is one of the world's most powerful living carnivores, but it has absolutely no control over its own future. Mankind, unsatisfied with his own place in the world, wishes to absorb the place of all other living things. Our fragile ego drives us to possess the beauty and the strength of the jaguar, so we kill it, then hang it on the wall, walk on it on the floor, or wear it like an ancient Maya king. Or we lock it up, calling it a pet, rationalizing with some warped sense of logic that we have saved the animal from a difficult life in the wild. Our insatiable greed then drives us to possess its home, and the jaguar, despite its strength, is no match for the jungle-eating machinery of man. When we have fully succeeded in our endeavors, and they are finally gone from the wild, we admire them in captivity, outwardly sad that such a majestic creature no longer roams the earth and inwardly smug that we were powerful enough to bring such a creature under our domination.

There seems no end to the pointless slaughter, the endless cruelty of man toward beast. Just before I left for Costa Rica, people came to the Mopan Hotel and offered me a baby margay they had locked up in a small filthy cage. They had killed its mother just so that they could get this kitten and sell it, a common practice in the bush. They knew someone would buy it, never questioning how it was obtained. It would be taken home to show off to friends, or it would be turned into a submissive, obedient form of a wild tabby. Then when the owners got tired of it, or the cat wouldn't do the tricks or play the games they wanted it to play, it would be taken somewhere and released back into the wild, so that it could be "free" again. The owner would go home satisfied, never thinking of the animal slowly starving to death because it had never learned to hunt, or being shot by someone it approached for food or kindness.

Since coming to Belize for the survey, I'd been documenting illegal cat kills from reliable sources in Belize. During a twenty-one-month period, I documented the deaths of ninety jaguars, fifteen pumas, seventeen ocelots, and six margays. The data were not at all complete, especially for the smaller cats. I was sure that the true numbers of animals dying were much higher. It almost seemed like a no-win situation. But what if it was? I still had to try. It was still the only good fight in town.

The week in Costa Rica was idyllic. Dr. Archie Carr and his wife, Marjorie Carr, had devoted their lives to fighting for conservation, sometimes winning, often losing. But it was the few wins that had made it all worthwhile and had helped to save places and animals that might not be around otherwise. I'd been fighting for the jaguars a mere two years. It had taken Dr. Carr nearly ten years to obtain legal protection for these green sea turtles, and he'd been fighting for conservation for a lifetime. I had no right to even begin to get frustrated.

It was interesting to note how the ecology of the jaguar was affected by these ancient three-hundred-pound reptiles in areas where they occurred within the jaguar's habitat. Jaguars were known to scout the beaches when these giants left the water, their unwieldy bodies maladapted for land travel, but following instincts over which they had no control. We heard of one turtle being killed by a jaguar far down the beach while we were at Tortuguero, a rare event, as there were so few jaguars in the area now. Far easier prey were the eggs that the females buried on the beach, and Dr. Carr had reported seeing jaguars digging up turtle eggs, "their gold-flowered sides glowing under the low moon." Humboldt described watching jaguars kill turtles along the Amazon, explaining that "by placing one paw on top of the turtle and skillfully biting out a round hole along the line of the junction between the back and front shields, the jaguar then scoops out the flesh with his paw and cleans out the shell without breaking it."

We found evidence on two occasions of the jaguars in Cockscomb eating the smaller river turtles. Pieces of shell found in the feces showed that, with these turtles, it was probably easiest for the jaguars just to crush them between their powerful jaws. It was another indication that jaguars are opportunistic feeders, taking whatever prey species is easily available.

Jaguars have evolved the ability to kill prey much larger than themselves, which has allowed them to feed on a wide range of animal species. The taking of small prey is probably not so much a matter of choice as of necessity. In the southern areas of their range, where record-weight jaguars have been killed, jaguars are able to feast on relatively abundant large prey, such as capybaras and caimans. In Central America, the largest prey species, tapirs and peccaries, are not as readily available and easy to kill.

When Ben and I started to put together the data that we had collected on the densities of the different prey species in Cockscomb, I found what I'd been expecting. The armadillo, a dominant prey species for jaguars, showed the highest density of any species in the data. For a jaguar this is probably the easiest of all prey, with its limited mobility, lack of defenses, and muffled grunting as it forages. If small animals are abundant and uniformly distributed, it makes sense for jaguars to stay within small areas for as long as possible before moving on to new parts of their range. Thus, their true feeding areas are often small pockets, though their overall range appears large.

Male jaguars in captivity are often fed two to three pounds of meat daily. A wild jaguar would probably have to eat a minimum of one small animal each day just to maintain an energy balance. Though small prey may be more available in limited areas, feeding on them would also necessitate more frequent and more efficient foraging by the jaguars. In other areas, jaguars have been shown to select particular body parts when feeding on larger prey, or to simply abandon much of the kill. In Cockscomb they often consumed hooves, claws, and everything.

When I returned from Costa Rica, I felt relaxed and inspired. Though Costa Rica had numerous areas set aside as parks and reserves, there seemed to be only a few places there where jaguars might still roam in their natural state. Most of the land outside the parks was under cultivation, often impinging on park boundries. And the situation was often worse in other countries. I felt more strongly than ever that there was still a chance in Belize for conservation and wildlife management to be properly incorporated into the economic growth of the country. It was one of the jaguar's last stands.

Though no progress had been made on the status of Cockscomb as a reserve, the Indians were told by the government that no one else could move into the basin. They were also told that although they would not be granted land within the basin, they could have title to land in certain areas outside the Cockscomb.

The Indians knew that there was little available land as good as they had in Cockscomb, and there was no place they could move and stay together as a village. Yet they finally realized the need to own their land so that they could do what they wanted and no longer be manipulated. In the white man's eyes, the Indians were simply squatters. In their own eyes, the land belonged to everybody. My cause was justified—of that I had no doubt. I was just very sorry that I had to work against my friends to accomplish my goals.

I flew from Belize City to Dangriga and learned that the bridges were flooded in the south and no buses were able to travel that way. I met with a neighboring rancher and learned more details about the killing of Ek Chuah. His death was discovered when Osman, the man who shot him, tried selling the radio collar back to Ben. When Ben tried to confiscate Ek Chuah's skin and skull, Osman was ready to fight him with his machete. He wanted to know why we were so angry when the woman who had worked with me before (meaning Sue) had helped Pablo kill one of my collared jaguars and I still hired him to work with me. He didn't see the situations as being different. He then tried to pass Ek Chuah off as a cattle killer, having dragged his body from the forest into the pasture, in order to claim a reward from the rancher. That was exactly what I was fighting against.

I spoke with Jim Waight of the Belize Audubon Society, and we tried to initiate legal proceedings against Osman. We knew he'd never be locked up for killing a jaguar, but we wanted people to understand the importance of wildlife laws. When the Forestry Department procrastinated, we asked that they at least send a forestry officer to frighten Osman and officially inform people in the area that they could not shoot jaguars. They agreed to do that at the first available opportunity. They never did.

When the water went down and I finally made it back into Cockscomb, the situation looked bleak. Only Chac was left with a radio collar, though we still followed the tracks of two females, Ah Kin, and the puma. After Ek Chuah's death, I no longer saw feces along the entrance road.

There was no longer any doubt that most of the feces collected were within overlap areas of adjacent adult male jaguars, especially when a male jaguar started moving into a new area. Some feces were also collected within the areas of the puma and the female jaguars. Marking in the form of feces and scrapes probably had numerous meanings. In addition to boundary delineation of a home range it was possibly used for spatial and temporal orientation between sexes and species.

Scrapes by large cats were not found as frequently as fecal deposits. They were usually observed when more than one large cat, either adult male jaguars or a jaguar and a puma, were known to be in the same area at the same time. Scrapes by jaguars averaged fifteen inches long and four inches wide, while those by pumas were eight inches long and five inches wide. Fecal deposits were found in or along jaguar scrapes most of the time, while urine but no feces were detected in half of the six puma scrapes observed.

I was told that Juana was sick again, so I went to Adriana's hut to see if I could help. Adriana said that Juana had been lazy for several weeks and one day she caught her eating dirt. I looked at Juana's waxen complexion and knew she had a bad case of hookworm. To make her stop eating dirt, Adriana had forced her to eat some of Cleo's feces. I couldn't believe what Adriana told me and I started berating her. Didn't she know that eating Cleo's feces just made it worse? She looked at me innocently. I stopped lecturing her. How would she know? I gave Adriana some of the worm pills I used on myself and explained how feeding dog shit to people only made them sicker.

Later that day, when I told Julian what had happened, he said that it was a common practice. If children are caught eating dirt, they are often made to eat dog or chicken shit. If they wouldn't eat it, it was often forced into their mouths.

Ben had been keeping one trap still open, hoping to catch one of the female jaguars, despite heavy rains and flooding. We both thought that eventually one might walk in. When Cirillo couldn't work, Pedro helped Ben in the field, and so one morning, it was Pedro who burst into the house.

"Come quick, Ben catch tiger, he say bring de camera!" Pedro blurted out.

He must have finally caught the female, I thought. I gathered my equipment together and rushed off with Pedro.

What should have been an easy two-and-a-half-mile drive was now, because of the rains, a trek. The first bridge was under three yards of water, and the river was a miniature lake. We crossed it in a little one-man dory. Transporting two men and equipment in this little boat was extremely precarious. Then we ran half a mile, my rubber boots filled with water, to the next flooded bridge. Here we waded through waist-deep water, trying to stay on the running boards of the hidden bridge at our feet. After that, we ran again, crossing one more bridge in knee-deep water. This would have made a great stee-plechase race, I thought. Finally, we came upon Ben, standing quietly to one side of the trap. He had already drugged the jaguar. It was Chac.

The wooden planks lining the inside of the trap were shred-ded. He had chipped off about half an inch of his right canine. It was a serious injury under the circumstances, and though it was not as severe as Ah Puch's injury, again the greatest danger was infection.

We sat and watched him recover before slowly walking into the forest. "You're a different cat from the one I captured over a year ago," I said to myself. "Why the hell did you come back into a trap again? Why are you so violent?" I'd never know.

I tried to think of what I could have done differently. I could have used snares, but Chac would have done far worse damage to himself in a snare. I could have padded or built the traps differently. That might have helped. But it was much easier now to speculate on the what-ifs than to have known what was right at the time.

As time passed and still nothing happened with the legal redes-ignation of Cockscomb despite the mandate from the prime minister, I became worried. I felt that if too much time elapsed, we might lose any ground we'd gained with the cabinet.

I soon found out we were also running out of time. It had just been announced that the prime minister was calling for elections in December, two months away, and the odds were against his reelection. The House of Representatives could be disbanded at any time now, after which no major business could be acted upon. We had to get Cockscomb signed into a forest reserve immediately.

I gave Ben instructions to watch Chac closely while I went to Belmopan and Belize City for three weeks of lobbying. Jim Hyde, one of our few champions among the officials in the Ministry of Natural Resources, understood the urgency of the situation and tried pushing it through the bureaucracy. However, we soon learned there was a new obstacle in our path. A finance corporation held the note on a loan that was given to a previous timber concession in Cockscomb. The concessionaires had used a parcel of land in the basin as collateral. This had been an illegal act since the land was owned by the government, but unless the finance corporation acknowledged this and released the land from any legal arbitration, it could remain tied up for a long time. Fortunately, the corporation readily agreed on an exchange with the government.

More worrisome was the Indian problem. The government would not physically move the Indians from Cockscomb, nor could they allow legal designation of the area as a forest reserve while there were still residents there. There were several alternatives. One was to simply wait until the Indians left Cockscomb; another was to grant them several thousand acres within the basin and create the reserve around them. The latter might be the only quick alternative and would satisfy everyone. If the number of families in Cockscomb was not allowed to increase and enough land was provided to make shifting cultivation feasible, the situation would be no different from that of their ancestors. I thought that might work and was willing to agree to it, especially if it was the only quick solution. Suddenly, however, the government wouldn't even consider it, though it had been their idea in the first place. It was an interesting turnabout for which no reason was given.

With the help of Jim Waight and Jim Hyde, the designation process moved ahead, though the Indians' residency was still in question. Jim Hyde made sure the Cockscomb issue was put on the agenda for the final meeting of the legislature. Though the Forestry Department was hesitant to act without the Indian question resolved, the Ministry of Natural Resources decided to proceed, regardless.

Strangely enough, the Indian problem resolved itself while I was in Belmopan. I learned that their desire to obtain schooling for their children and to have a church on land that they owned overcame all else. They decided to all leave Cockscomb before Christmas. Most of them were going to Maya Center, just outside Cockscomb. Cirillo's and Martin's families would move to Red Bank, while Tyul's family planned to resettle near their relatives in nearby Maya Mopan. I immediately informed the government of their decision, knowing it would speed matters up.

That night I thought I would sleep well, but I didn't. I lay thinking about the jaguars and people whose lives this project had affected. Ah Puch, my first jaguar, was dead because of my actions. Ek Chuah, thinking he had found a new safe home in Cockscomb, dead. Itzamna, the old king, dead. Ixchel, the young cattle killer, killed in front of Sue. Wild, curious Xaman Ek, with those incredible eyes, fate unknown. Kukulcan, the young male cattle killer who had nearly jumped on me in the back of the truck, fate unknown. Even Chac, my most reliable animal, the jaguar I had followed and studied longer than any of the others, was injured.

Little Sylvino was living because of me. But Guermo had died in agony because he had hunted with me. I had driven off Sue, one of the most important people in my life. And now all the Maya in Cockscomb, my friends, were having to leave their homes forever because of me.

Was my project really successful?

27 DEATH AND DEPARTURE

Cockscomb seemed deserted when I returned from Belmopan. Only Cleo came to greet me, her head still noticeably bent toward the side. The quietness of the camp made me realize what it would be like when the Indians were gone. I went into the shack and found Ben's field notes lying on the table, so I caught up on the events of the last three weeks. He was off in the field as always.

I skimmed quickly through each day's events but suddenly stopped at the entry for October 8, nearly a week ago. The date was followed by only two words: "Chac dead." I jumped up from the table and ran into the bedroom to get the location file. I looked at the last entry for Chac, still not wanting to believe it. There it was: "97413—Death Site," the coordinates where Ben must have found the body.

"Damn!" I yelled and threw down the file. "It's over, it's all over." Chac, my last jaguar, tracked more than a year, surviving all the rest—dead.

I changed into running shorts and took off in the midday heat, knowing it was the worst thing for my headaches. I wanted to cry, I wanted to scream, but nothing would come. I could feel the expression of grim resignation on my face. I was dead inside, emotionally sapped. I ran harder and harder, and my head started pounding. I wanted to feel the pain. I wanted to make the pain block out all else. It was the only release I had for the guilt and sadness I felt inside.

Ben and I talked long into the night. He'd followed Chac closely, and when he was located in the same place for two days, Ben had walked in on the signal. He had just died, since the carcass was intact. A quick field necropsy showed an empty stomach filled with long white wormlike parasites, later identified as roundworms. Common in cats and sometimes in people, these worms can cause indigestion, weakness, and swollen bellies. In some cases, pneumonia may result, accompanied by coughing up of blood or blockage of the gut.

The most surprising bit of news Ben had to tell me was that both of Chac's canines were broken, though only one had been broken in the trap. Though the second break must have happened in the jungle, I felt it was related to the first injury. Ben had seen no obvious sign of infection. Though that chipped tooth shouldn't have been severe enough to kill Chac, it was another stress to overcome for an animal whose life was already filled with hardship.

I noticed during the study the scarcity of old jaguars among those killed. Though known to live up to twenty-three years in captivity, it seemed that jaguars didn't usually make it to half that age in the wild. Examination of the skeletal remains of thirty jaguars—thirteen problem and seventeen nonproblem jaguars—revealed only two over eleven years of age. Rengger speculated that "in inhabited areas, there will not be much of a chance for a jaguar to die a natural death." He was referring to excessive hunting practices. However, I now believed that the life-span of jaguars in the wild may never approach that of jaguars in captivity, whether hunters were present or not. Parasites are one of several factors that contribute to the stressful nature of their environment and a shortened life-span.

I'd never know why Chac really died. I'd never know if he suffered, or if, within his own framework of thinking, he wondered why it was all happening to him. What kind of thoughts and images passed through his mind before death? What role did my presence for over a year play in Chac's consciousness?

I was in the field with Cirillo the next day and asked him why the jaguars died when they broke their teeth. Now that I understood the basis of the Indians' thinking better, I respected many of their feelings about the behavior of wildlife. I knew they understood the balance of nature better than I or any scientist. Cirillo looked at me knowingly and I suddenly missed the many hours we used to spend alone together before Ben or Mike had come.

"Dey punish in bush. You hurt dem, dey punish bad, get weak, maybe die," he said to me.

"How do they punish, Cirillo? Why do they die when they can still hunt, still kill armadillo?"

"Tiger walk day and night, look for food. Sometime he eat, plenty time he no eat. If you make he punish more, maybe go long time and no eat. Den tiger die." It was as simple as that to him. I knew he was right.

Ben planned to leave the project in one month. As I watched him each night writing his notes by the kerosene lantern, I knew it was time he left Cockscomb. He was showing signs of the emotional and physical fatigue that I knew so well. The short break he had taken in the United States hadn't helped much. When I had returned from Belmopan this last time, he was raising a young fer-de-lance in a bucket behind our shack. He had finally encountered one and thought it would make an interesting pet.

Ben had learned to deal with the Indians on their own level of thought much better than I ever had. He had the patience and tolerance that one needed. I listened to Ben and Cirillo in the field during one of their last days together as Ben tried to pry some information from Cirillo.

"Cirillo, see this track?" Ben asked, trying to identify an animal that had walked across their track pad.

"What track?" Cirillo asked, looking right at the track.

"This track Cirillo. Do you see it?"

"Yeeees."

"What is it, Cirillo?"

"What?"

"This track, Cirillo. What animal is it?"

(Long pause.)

"Well, Cirillo, what animal this track from?"

"What?"

"Is it *gibnut* [paca], Cirillo?"

"Yeeees."

I had to keep from laughing. I remembered the day Cirillo had me stick my hand in the fire ant's nest. In this encounter on the track pad, I would have given up on the second go around. I never would have found out what the track was.

Ben's final quadrate was the most difficult. We decided it should be cut far back in Cockscomb, where the timber operation had not yet reached. After looking over various areas, beyond where we had trapped, we found a beautiful site surrounded by a few tall hardwoods, such as barba jolote, emory, Santa Maria, and ironwood. It seemed so tranquil, so nonthreatening. Only someone who had lived here for a while would know otherwise.

We set up a temporary camp, where Ben, Julian, and Cirillo could live for at least a week without having to return to Guam Bank. I planned to stay at Guam Bank, monitoring the roads for jaguar sign and making periodic trips with supplies to Ben's camp. Tracks and feces had been sparse along the entire timber road after Chac's death. It would be interesting to see what would happen now that the central area was once again up for grabs.

During one of my return trips from Ben's camp, I was on a part of the old timber road that I had walked over dozens of times. It was one of those hot, humid afternoons. I was watching the ground looking for jaguar sign but my mind was on that girl who had called me starry-eyed at Miami Airport. Suddenly I heard a rustling in the trees and looked up to see a large male coati running out onto a branch.

Called *quash* by the locals, this furry member of the raccoon family, with a pointed snout and long, slightly ringed tail, is an omnivorous, diurnal animal. Females and young males are social and wander in groups, while adult males, such as this one, are solitary. This distinction confused early naturalists, who classified them as separate species. Many natives today still consider them separate animals. I watched this innocuous-looking creature as it foraged in the treetop for a while, poking its snout here, clawing a piece of bark there.

I remembered my encounter with a male coati who had escaped from its cage at the Belize Zoo. I had just arrived in Belize for my first survey, and I came upon a single coati roaming in Richard Foster's yard. No one was around, so I assumed it was one of their tame animals. As I reached down to pet it, the animal snarled and leaped for my face. Fortunately, I threw up my hands in time and it only bit me on the arms and clawed my shoulder before I threw it off.

I heard more rustling and looked up as the coati jumped to another tree and disappeared from view. I looked around me to see how far I was from the truck. I had no idea where I was.

The forest was unfamiliar, the road was unfamiliar, and for all I knew, this wasn't even Cockscomb. I walked on farther, but it all looked new and different. It seemed crazy. This was the only road in the area, so I couldn't have gotten sidetracked. I should know this damn road like the back of my hand, I thought. I had trapped and followed jaguars and the puma along here and walked it day and night. Yet this was a different place.

I walked faster, realizing that I was getting more frightened for no logical reason. I was in Cockscomb! I had to be in Cockscomb! I was on the old timber road and I was fully awake and coherent. I suppressed an urge to run. Finally, after no more than a quarter of a mile, I rounded a bend in the road that I recognized. Everything was familiar again. I stopped and turned, looking back down the road I had just come on. It was all familiar to me now. But that was not what my mind had seen a few minutes before.

I started walking toward the truck again and with a jolt realized something. The portion of road I had just walked was the site of Kuchil Balum, the unexcavated Maya site I had found. For whatever reason, just this once, it seemed like I had been somewhere else, spatially or temporally, while I walked the road that traversed the central plaza of that site.

Four weeks after Chac's death, we found tracks from a new adult male jaguar on the entrance road. It was the cycle of death and rebirth coming full swing again. I knew that soon Cockscomb might be filled with new jaguars. There were few areas throughout the jaguar's range where this could still happen, where there were enough animals and forest to fill the empty niches, maintain the balance, the equilibrium. Many pockets of rain forest were already small islands, where the space left by the death of a jaguar would never be filled again.

The mysterious Ah Kin, who had eluded me for so long, was still out there, the crooked toe of his track easily recognizable. It was his turn now to take over the central range. Should I still go after him, I asked myself, and get a month or two of additional data on another male? Was it ethical? I didn't think so. The jaguars had paid their price. As a scientist, I would have liked the additional data, but the patterns were already clear. It was time to let the cycle of rebirth in Cockscomb occur without my interference. I would soon be gone.

The Indians and Ben were already packing up their belongings. Ben would be the first to leave. It seemed appropriate that the end of the jaguar project was coinciding with the end of the Cockscomb Maya community. We were a microcosm of a greater reality. The futures of the Maya and of the jaguars were being controlled and determined by factors beyond their understanding or control. Though both kept on shifting and readjusting their territories, soon there would be no more places to go. For the Maya, I saw no real hope of preserving their simple way of life in a society that regarded them as primitive and pagan. For the jaguars, their only hope was in the preservation of Cockscomb and areas like it, which might short-circuit the rapid process of habitat destruction.

As the project wound down, Julian started spending more time at my house working out with weights. I felt it was his way of saying good-bye before we went our separate ways. He had used some of the money he had earned working with us to buy bright yellow gym shorts and sneakers. As I watched this young Maya man pumping iron in his yellow shorts to the tunes of Kenny Rogers, I wanted to hug him. He would be the first and last graduate of the Cockscomb Health Club.

I had stopped thinking of Cockscomb as my home and started thinking of it as the place I was about to leave forever. I started to feel like an outsider looking in, finding fault with things I'd long since adjusted to. Finding faults made the leaving easier. Just as I'd resign myself to the fact that I'd be much better off when I was gone from this strange place, Agapita, Prudencia, Formenta, and Juana would come by my house to sit and play with me. Sometimes I felt I wanted to take them with me, back to the United States. But I knew that even if I could, I never would. What I loved best about them came from the jungle, from this way of life.

We held a large feast before Ben's departure and introduced the Indians, after much coercing, to hamburgers and barbecued ribs. Despite their love of meat, the Indians would not easily eat what they were not accustomed to. I thought of the variety of wild game I'd eaten with the Indians since my arrival in Cockscomb, all stewed in a hot, red, spicy sauce. There had been crested guan, tinamou, brocket deer, peccary, armadillo, agouti, paca, turtle, iguana, and iguana eggs. All of it had been delicious, though I cared for some animals more than others. Now it was their turn to eat our food.

As usual, the men and boys came over first and started eating, followed soon by the women and young children. Ben and I watched with pleasure as they ate with their usual fiesta gluttony. Nothing went to waste. Bones were broken, sucked out, chewed up, and sometimes eaten. Any scraps of food or pieces of bone left uneaten were often discarded on our floor alongside the various puddles of urine from the babies. Everyone loved the hamburgers, and I couldn't prepare them fast enough. For an instant I thought of the possible consequences of losing Cockscomb. I pictured a new fast-food chain selling Cockscomb jaguarburgers at the entrance to the basin. I shuddered at the thought.

The next morning, as we were finishing loading Ben's belongings into the back of the truck for the drive to Belize City, Adriana and the children came rushing over. She had tried to stay away but couldn't. As she came within three yards of the truck, she stopped and stood there. She could not hold back the tears, the first I'd seen from any Indian in Cockscomb. It was like watching her son leave her, she said, and I realized there was more to the Indians' emotions than met the eye.

In the nearly two years I spent with them, I never saw any display of affection among family members, nor did I see anyone dwell on feelings of sadness, anger, or happiness. I might have had the same impression as Mitchell-Hedges, who, after observing the Kekchi Maya in southern Belize, wrote: "In no way are the Maya Kekchi capable of deep feeling. I have yet to see an Indian shed tears. . . . They never kill; have no love or passion, and in their cohabitation they simply obey the primitive call."

It wasn't true. I came to realize that they were capable of deep emotion, operating within a framework of humility, of a timelessness in which there is only the ongoing cycle of birth and death.

Ben couldn't leave the project without a proper farewell from our truck as well. On the way to Belize City we lost half of the exhaust system and broke the left front strut arm where it joined the wheel.

28 GOOD-BYE

Driving back to Cockscomb after seeing Ben off felt strangely similar to the first day I arrived there twenty months before. Everything seemed the same, even the same Indians in front of their huts waving to me. Yet so much had happened.

The previous night I had woken at 4 A.M. in a cold sweat, dreaming of Chac's death. He had suffered. I sat in the darkness of my room at the Hotel Mopan until daybreak, feeling very alone and thinking of old friends living full and happy lives with wives and families. I felt a sharp pang inside me, thinking of the direction my life had taken and what I had sacrificed. Was it regret? Some. Would I change anything? No. Yet, I realized then and there what I was becoming and where my destiny was taking me. In the early-morning hours, before the light of day made the world sane again, I pictured myself a wizened, scarred adventurer, fiercely independent, no one to lean on, waking up alone in some other hotel room in some other strange part of the world. I was frightened.

This was what I had always wanted as a youth growing up in New York. One day, I always told myself, I'd search for truths apart from the world of man. I've lost some of my idealism since then and learned to deal more with people, yet I still search for those truths. Every now and then I think, What if . . . But I've gone too far to look back. I'm hooked on my way of life. In India some say, "He who rides a tiger cannot dismount." What terrified me most in those early-morning hours was that someday I might fall from the tiger's back and be brutally crushed. And that will be all there is.

The plane crash forced me to face the reality of death. It was not like the adventure stories I used to read and dream about as a boy. I couldn't close the book and walk away. It had no glamour, no follow-up, and I was terribly alone at that final moment. I'd been lucky, maybe luckier than I deserved when it turned out to not be final after all. But when the moment does come, I hope I'm taken to where the wild animals on the earth have gone.

Tracks from the new jaguar continued along the entrance road, yet no feces were evident in the areas where they had once been so common. Ah Kin was still back there, as were the two female jaguars, but the density of adult males at this point was low, so marking was not needed. Schaller had found this same situation in Brazil. Where there appeared to be low jaguar densities, marking was rarely observed.

Cirillo and Martin prepared to leave Cockscomb with their families the next week. It was an awkward time for Cirillo and me because neither of us knew how to express the maelstrom of emotions welling up inside. He had little time to spend with me during these last days, and I didn't really need him in the field with me anymore.

The day before he was to leave, he came into the jungle with me. I drove on the road as far as we could, then we continued on foot, ostensibly looking for jaguar sign. We ended up at the Maya ruin, and I smiled to myself thinking how appropriate a place this was for our good-bye. We took each other's picture at the altar stone, acting as if it was just another day in the field for us.

"So you all packed and ready for go?" I finally asked him.

"I ready for go, but I no want to go. Alan . . ." he started.

"What'd you say, Cirillo?" I asked.

He walked on, disappearing among the vegetation. We talked no more of his leaving and returned to camp soon after.

The next day a truck the Indians rented came to carry their belongings to Red Bank. No one left for the bush that day, and all the Indians gathered to help them pack the truck and see them off. I sat watching from my porch. Cirillo's and Martin's wives, Florencia and Juana, were in the front seat of the truck and Juana was crying. It was the second time in two years I watched an Indian cry.

In a few minutes, there'd be no more Cirillo, no more Martin. I was glad I was leaving soon. Then suddenly Cirillo broke away from the others and walked over to my house. It was a Cirillo I'd never seen before, with a downtrodden, sad look. He walked up to my screen door and looked down at the ground.

"You ever coming back here?" I asked, searching for the first words.

"Not for long time. Maybe never."

"I gone next Sunday from here too, you know," I said, my voice breaking.

His head turned to the side, and as he looked toward the forest, he spoke in a barely audible voice. "I ever see you again?"

I looked at the floor and I could barely get the words out. "I see you sometime again, Cirillo."

I looked up, and he was looking at me. Our eyes locked. No more needed to be said. Then the truck pulled up in front of the house and beeped its horn. Cirillo ran over and leaped in the back.

That night I lay on my bed looking out the window. A full moon was suspended just above one of the hills, and the fog was rising over the grass. As the insects made their usual chatterings, bats fluttered by the window, occasionally one of them coming too close, its wing brushing the screen inches from my face. I pressed my lips and nose against the screen, deforming my face as I used to do when I was a child.

"Good-bye, Cirillo," I whispered into the darkness.

I started giving away all the belongings in my house—my clothes, dishes, food, anything that didn't need to get back to the United States. Adriana, of course, made sure to send Agapita, knowing I couldn't resist her, to tell me exactly what in my house she wanted. Even when I had given her sheets, clothes, Tupperware, kitchen utensils, and a frying pan, Agapita would say, "My mother says you must give her de big pot too."

I laughed and added the big pot to the pile.

Three days before I left, Adriana told me that someone had killed three big red parrots. I knew immediately she was talking about scarlet macaws. I thought back to the day I had seen these birds for the first time when Cirillo and I were returning to camp after finding Itzamna's skeleton. Cirillo had told me then that the Indians would kill them if they came across them. I dropped everything and stormed over to Gregorio's house, where Adriana had seen them using the feathers for a duster. Gregorio and his wife, Liberata, were both frightened by my anger and told me immediately that it was Prudencio Bolong who had killed them.

Flocks of scarlet macaws, one of the most magnificent birds on earth, had been sighted in Cockscomb only four times while I had been there, and all of them far back in the basin. This was the first time they'd been seen near camp, and they were killed immediately. Some of my feelings of guilt at seeing the Indians leave Cockscomb vanished. I once again realized the impact they could have on wildlife in areas where they live. At least one place in Belize, like the Cockscomb Basin, deserved protection.

My last day. Saturday morning, in early December, a beautiful clear warm day in Cockscomb. Shortly after sunrise I packed a lunch and got on the motorcycle to drive back into the basin. I wanted to look for jaguars and say my good-byes to the forest. As I drove along the road, I slowed the motorcycle, pausing at each area where memorable events had taken place. Here was where I first caught angry Chac and realized my traps would work. Here was where we had come out of the forest the day Guermo was bitten. This was where we went in when the fer-de-lance head chased us. Up along this bend the jaguar broke out of my wooden trap. There's the knoll where I thought I saw a *duende*. I wanted to see a jaguar my last time back here—it would be a good omen. But it was not to happen. Instead, an agouti hopped across my path.

I parked the bike and started walking a skidder trail. No more than half a mile into the bush, a feeling of unease nearly overwhelmed me. I'm truly frightened of this forest now, I realized. It feels almost evil, a force working against me. It was definitely time to leave and, despite the sadness, I was ready to go. I returned to camp early, troubled by feelings of insecurity and fear. I just didn't have it in me to challenge this jungle anymore.

As I pulled up in front of my house, I found Cirillo waiting for me on the steps. Knowing I was leaving the next morning, he had ridden thirty miles on his bicycle to see me off. I was deeply touched. We stood in front of the house for an hour talking of his new house, the jaguars in Red Bank, and the new milpa he was planning to cut. Finally, the conversation died and we just stood there.

"I go back now," he said suddenly.

"What you mean go back, Cirillo, you only get here an hour ago. Stay for dinner, sleep in my house tonight, and I take you to the road tomorrow."

"I no can stay."

"Why, Cirillo? It's a long ride back. Stay with me tonight."

"I no can stay. I no want you see me bawl [cry]. I come say good-bye, but I must go now." He got on the bicycle.

"I won't forget you, Cirillo," I said quietly. "I never forget you, I promise," I said to his back.

He kept his back toward me. Then, just in the instant before he pushed off and with his face still turned away from me, he said something that I could tell had been on his mind a long time. "Alan, I tell dem no shoot tiger in Red Bank."

I watched him ride off down the road. I realized then that Cirillo had come back just to tell me that, and at that moment it meant more than anything anyone else could have given me.

After Ben's going-away bash, I had decided that I wanted to leave Cockscomb quietly and unobtrusively. I explained this to the Indians, telling them that I would just be gone one day. They understood this. In the week before I was to leave they came by one by one, simply to sit with me and talk. I packed up all my belongings and tied the motorcycle into the back of the truck.

From my field notes, Sunday, 0530 A.M.:

> Sitting at my desk. The house is empty and all my belongings are packed in the back of the truck around the motorcycle. It's cool and I have a blanket wrapped around me as I huddle over a kerosene lantern writing these last notes. The morning light is breaking, birds are starting their songs, and the roosters crow. Good-bye Cockscomb. Whatever comes after, I shall remember you.

I waited until 7 A.M., when all the Indians were in church and Mike was out in the back of camp checking his traps. As I got in the truck and looked around camp, there was absolute stillness. It was exactly as I wanted it to be. Yet I couldn't help but look around hoping that at the last minute Agapita, Prudencia, Juana, and Formenta would come running up the road, with

Adriana slowly waddling behind, a big grin on her face, a stack of corn torillas in her hands. Or Cleo would come wagging that tail of hers so hard she'd nearly knock herself over.

The morning was cold and foggy, and I was leaving the same way I came in—alone. I started the truck down the road but looked in my rearview mirror at the house, for a final glimpse. Adriana's face was peeking out from behind a tree toward the rear of the house, with Agapita's face at her waist. They had come to see me off after all. I smiled and turned on the windshield wipers to clear the early morning mist from the windows. It wouldn't clear. I realized that the mist wasn't on the windows.

29 THE CIRCLE CLOSES

On December 2, 1984, the Cockscomb Basin was declared a National Forest Reserve, with a no-hunting provision for protection of the jaguar. This made Belize the first country in the world to protect an area specifically for jaguars. It was officially called the Cockscomb Forest Reserve/Jaguar Preserve.

Countrywide elections were held on December 14, 1984. The long-standing administration under Prime Minister George Price's People's United Party (PUP) fell in a landslide election to the United Democratic Party (UDP), led by Manuel Esquivel. The new government gave its full support to the Cockscomb jaguar preserve.

By the end of December, every Indian family had left Cockscomb. The children were now attending school, and the Indians fell back into their normal patterns of life in their new homes. The forest quickly started taking over Guam Bank, and jaguar tracks were observed in the camp area for the first time.

In January 1985 a proposal to the World Wildlife Fund—US led to a tentative five-year agreement to support the establishment, protection, and maintenance of the Cockscomb Basin as a jaguar preserve.

In February 1985, Adriana's husband and son, Ignacio and Pedro, were hired as the first watchmen for the jaguar preserve in Cockscomb. Soon after, they became its first wardens.

BIBLIOGRAPHY

Books

Almeida, A. *Jaguar Hunting in the Mato Grosso*. England: Stanwill Press, 1976.

Ashmore, Wendy, ed. *Lowland Maya Settlement Patterns*. Albuquerque: University of New Mexico Press, 1981.

Bates, Henry Walter. *The Naturalist on the River Amazon*. London: John Murray, 1876.

Brinton, Daniel, ed. *The Maya Chronicles*. New York: AMS Press, 1969.

Caiger, Stephen L. *British Honduras*. London: George Allen Unwin, 1951.

Carr, Archie. *High Jungles and Low*. Gainesville: University of Florida Press, 1953.

Caufield, Catherine. *In the Rainforest*. New York: Knopf, 1985.

Coe, Michael. *The Maya*. New York: Thames and Hudson, 1984.

Darwin, Charles. *Journal of the Researches into the Natural History and Geology of the Countries Visited During the Voyage of H.M.S. "Beagle" Round the World.* London: Ward, Lock, & Co., 1889.

Davis, Richard H. *Three Gringos in Venezuela and Central America.* New York: Harper and Brothers, 1896.

Díaz del Castillo, Bernal. *Histoire véridique de la conquête de la Nouvelle-Espagne.* Paris: A. Lemerre, 1877.

Dobson, Narda. *A History of Belize.* Port of Spain: Longman Caribbean Ltd., 1973.

Forsyth, Adrian, and Kenneth Miyata. *Tropical Nature.* New York: Charles Scribner's Sons, 1984.

Gallenkamp, Charles. *Maya: The Riddle and Rediscovery of a Lost Civilization.* New York: Penguin Books, 1981.

Guggisberg, C. A. *Wild Cats of the World.* New York: Taplinger Press, 1975.

Hartshorn, Gary. *Belize, Country Environmental Profile.* Belize City: Robert Nicolait & Associates, 1984.

Hay, Clarence L. *et al.,* eds. *The Maya and Their Neighbors.* New York: Dover Publications, 1977.

Helms, Mary W., and Franklin O. Loveland, eds. *Frontier Adaptations in Lower Central America.* Philadelphia: Institute for the Study of Human Issues, 1976.

Humboldt, Alexander von. *Personal Narrative of Travels to the Equinoctial Regions of America During 1799–1804.* London: H. G. Bohn, 1852–1853; New York: Blom, 1971.

Janzen, Daniel, ed. *Costa Rican Natural History.* Chicago: University of Chicago Press, 1983.

Jones, Grant D. *Anthropology and History in Yucatan.* Austin: University of Texas Press, 1977.

Lamb, F. Bruce. *Wizard of the Upper Amazon: The Story of Manuel Cordova Rios.* Boston: Houghton Mifflin, 1974.

Leopold, Aldo S. *A Sand County Almanac.* New York: Oxford University Press, 1949.

——. *Wildlife of Mexico.* Berkeley: University of California Press, 1959.

Mitchell-Hedges, Frederick A. *Land of Wonder and Fear.* New York: The Century Co., 1931.

Morley, Sylvanus. *The Ancient Maya,* 3rd ed. Stanford: Stanford University Press, 1956.

Nelson, Edward W. *Wild Animals of North America: Intimate Studies of Big and Little Creatures of the Mammal Kingdom.* Washington, D.C.: National Geographic Society, 1918.

Olrog, Claes. "Die Jagd der gegenwart in Sued-Amerika." In *Jaeger, Jagd und Wild in aller Welt,* vol. 2. Munich-Hamburg: 1955.

Perry, Richard. *The World of the Jaguar.* New York: Newton-Abbot, 1970.

——. *Life in Forest and Jungle.* New York: Taplinger, 1976.

Rengger, Johann R. *Naturgeschichte der Saeugethiere von Paraguay.* Basel: Schweighausersche, 1830.

Roosevelt, Theodore. *Through the Brazilian Wilderness.* New York: Scribner's, 1914.

Sanderson, Ivan. *Living Treasure.* New York: Viking Press, 1941.

——. *Book of Great Jungles.* New York: Pocket Books, 1965.

Setzekorn, William D. *Formerly British Honduras: A Profile of the New Nation of Belize.* Athens: Ohio University Press, 1981.

Thompson, J. Eric S. *Ethnology of the Mayas of Southern and Central British Honduras.* Field Museum of Natural History, Publication No. 274, Anthropological Series, Chicago, vol. 17, no. 2, 1930.

——. *Maya Archaeologist.* Norman: University of Oklahoma Press, 1963.

——. *The Maya of Belize: Historical Chapters since Columbus.* Belize City: Benex Press, 1972.

Up de Graff, Fritz W. *Head-hunters of the Amazon.* New York: Duffield & Co., 1923.

Von Hagen, Victor W. *Maya Explorer: John Lloyd Stephens and the Lost Cities of Central America and Yucatan.* Norman: University of Oklahoma Press, 1947.

——. *World of the Maya.* New York: New American Library, 1960.

Wallace, Alfred R. *A Narrative of Travels on the Amazon and Rio Negro.* New York: Wand, Lock & Co., 1889.

Werner, David. *Where There Is No Doctor.* Palo Alto, Calif.: Hesperian Foundation, 1977.

Articles

Bellamy, J. "Expedition to the Cockscomb Mountains, British Honduras." *Proceedings of the Royal Geographical Society,* vol. 11, 1889, pp. 542–552.

De la Haba, Louis. "Belize, the Awakening Land." *National Geographic,* January, 1972, pp. 124–146.

Ewel, John, ed. "Tropical Succession." *Biotropica,* vol. 12, no. 2, 1980.

Gann, Thomas. "The Mayan Indians of S. Yucatan and N. British Honduras." *Bureau of American Ethnology,* Bulletin 64, Washington, D.C., 1918.

Grant, Herbert T. "Cockscomb Mountains, British Honduras, Revisited." *Geographical Journal,* vol. 70, no. 6, 1927, pp. 564–572.

——. "A Second Cockscomb Expedition in 1928." *Geographical Journal,* 1928.

Howard, Michael. "Ethnicity in Southern Belize." *Museum Brief No. 21,* University of Missouri, Columbia, 1975.

Johnson, R. P. "Scent Marking in Mammals." *Animal Behavior,* vol. 21, 1973, pp. 521–535.

Kidder, Alfred V., and Gordon F. Ekholm. "Some Archaeological Specimens From Pomona, British Honduras." *Carnegie Institution of Washington, Notes on Middle American Archaeology and Ethnology,* no. 102, 1951.

Kirkpatrick, R. D., and A. M. Cartwright. "List of Mammals Known to Occur in Belize." *Biotropica,* vol. 7, no. 2, 1975, pp. 136–140.

Mondolfi, Edgardo, and R. Hoogesteijn. "Biology and Status of the Jaguar in Venezuela." *International Cat Symposium Proceedings,* 1982.

Oliphant, J. N., and D. Stevenson. "Expedition to the Cockscomb Mountains, British Honduras in March 1928." *Geographical Journal,* vol. 73, no. 2, 1929, pp. 123–137.

Price, H. W. "Excavations on Sittee River, British Honduras." *Proceedings of the Society of Antiquaries,* London, vol. 17, 1899, pp. 399–444.

Rabinowitz, Alan. "In the Realm of the Master Jaguar." *Animal Kingdom,* March/April 1986, pp. 10–21.

——. "Jaguar Predation on Domestic Livestock." *Wildlife Society Bulletin,* vol. 14, no. 2, 1986.

——. "Ecology and Behavior of the Jaguar *(Panthera onca)* in Belize." *Journal of Zoology,* London, vol. 210, part I, 1986.

Schaller, G. "Epitaph for a Jaguar." *Animal Kingdom,* April/May, 1980, pp. 4–11.

——. "Mammals and Their Biomass on a Brazilian Ranch." *Arquivos de Zool.,* São Paulo, vol. 31, 1983, pp. 1–36.

Schaller, G., and P. G. Crawshaw. "Movement Patterns of Jaguar." *Biotropica*, vol. 12, 1980, pp. 161–168.

Schaller, G., and J. M. C. Vasconcelos. "Jaguar Predation on Capybara." *Zeitung Saugetierk*, vol. 43, 1978, pp. 296–301.

Seidensticker, J. "On the Ecological Separation Between Tigers and Leopards." *Biotropica*, vol. 8, 1976, pp. 225–234.

Smuts, G. L., J. L. Anderson, and J. C. Austin. "Age Determination of the African Lion *(Panthera leo)*." *Journal of Zoology*, London, vol. 185, 1978, pp. 115–146.

Steggerda, M. "Maya Indians of Yucatan." *Carnegie Institution of Washington, Publication No. 531*, 1941.

Sunquist, M. E. "The Social Organization of Tigers *(Panthera tigris)* in Royal Chitawan National Park, Nepal." *Smith. Contr. to Zool. No. 336*, 1981.

———. "Recognaissance and Excavation in British Honduras." *Carnegie Institution of Washington, Year Book No. 37*, 1938, pp. 16–17.

———. "Sixteenth and Seventeenth Century Reports on the Chol Mayas." *American Anthropologist*, vol. 40, 1938, pp. 584–603.

ACKNOWLEDGMENTS

The jaguar project described in this book was financed by Wildlife Conservation International (WCI) of the New York Zoological Society (NYZS). It would never had gotten under way had it not been for the concern and dedication of several special individuals. I would like to acknowledge Dora Weyer, founder of the Belize Audubon Society and the first to see the need for jaguar research in Belize; Dr. Archie Carr III, assistant director of WCI, who recognized the potential for such research and provided constant support in my battle to obtain protective status for the area; Dr. George Schaller, director of WCI, whose confidence enabled me to persevere under the most adverse circumstances; and Dr. William Conway, general director of NYZS, whose encouragement and avid concern for conservation helped carry the project to its successful conclusion.

I am indebted for permission to reproduce material that appeared in *Animal Kingdom* magazine and *The Wildlife Society Bulletin*.

My deepest gratitude goes to two very special friends who spent time down in the jungle with me, and shared some of the tribulations. Susan Walker, a truly remarkable woman, helped get me through some of the most difficult times of the project. She read the early draft of this book, cried in the right places, and reminded me of incidents I'd forgotten. In spite of what happened in this book, we have stayed the best of friends. Ben Nottingham saw to it that the project was able to reach completion, despite my injuries.

If not for the hard work and unrewarded time put in by many dedicated people in Belize, the Cockscomb Jaguar Preserve/Forest Reserve would never have become a reality. I would like to thank the entire Belize Audubon Society, particularly the president, Mr. James Waight, for their work in helping protect Cockscomb. I would also like to thank Mr. Jim Hyde, former permanent secretary to the Ministry of Natural Resources, who foresaw the long-term benefits of conservation in Belize. Sharon Matola, a good friend, helped lead the battle after I was gone. Richard Foster, a truly talented wildlife photographer, helped get initial protection and funding for Cockscomb, and continues to help us fight for the cause. Some of his photographs appear in this book.

I wish to acknowledge Bader Hassan, whose interest, knowledge, and skill helped make this project a success and whose friendship and camaraderie I will always remember.

Nancy Hammond of World Wildlife Fund–US was instrumental in realizing the potential of the jaguar preserve and helped us set up initial and long-term funding for its protection and maintenance.

How can I thank the Maya Indians from Cockscomb who will probably never see this book? Let me acknowledge their kindness to me when I needed it, and their tolerance of me when I was at my most difficult. I hope that they felt my love for them before we parted.

To James Raimes, my editor at Arbor House, I wish to express sincere thanks for having worked so closely and diligently with me and for having unwavering faith in the outcome. Many thanks, too, to Tanya Ivanow for her superb work on my manuscript.

The support and encouragement from my parents are difficult to acknowledge in words. Everything I am and everything I have accomplished in life I owe to them.

INDEX